THE BLOGFATHER

THE BLOGFATHER:
THE BEST OF IAIN DALE'S DIARY

IAIN DALE

Biteback Publishing

First published in Great Britain in 2012 by
Biteback Publishing Ltd
Westminster Tower
3 Albert Embankment
London SE1 7SP

ISBN 978-1-84954-461-0

10 9 8 7 6 5 4 3 2 1

A CIP catalogue record for this book is available from the British Library.

Set in Sabon and Franchise

Printed and bound in Great Britain by
CPI Group (UK) Ltd, Croydon CR0 4YY

In memory of my darling mother, Jane Elizabeth Dale

27 March 1931 – 9 June 2012

CONTENTS

FOREWORD

So there I was, visiting a friend in Washington DC in the spring of 2002, and he asked me if I had a blog. 'Er, no,' I said, 'I haven't,' adding, 'What's a blog?' His answer proved to be a revelation and it was one which in time was to change my life. Within ten minutes he had created a blog for me and off I went.

Up until then, unless you were a technical geek, it was quite cumbersome to update a website. Usually someone else had to do it for you. But blogs meant that you could update your own website in seconds, and tell the world what you were thinking in real time. But so what? I instantly understood what a blog could do, not just for me, but more generally. Different people use blogs in different ways, but essentially they are a hugely democratising force: blogging gives everyone the chance to have their say.

Up until the advent of blogging, Mrs Miggins from 32 Acacia Avenue, Scunthorpe would have had precious little chance to make her views known. She might get a letter published in the local paper, possibly even a national one on the odd occasion. She could phone in to a radio show, but that was about it. With a blog, Mrs Miggins can have her say when she wants. Now, she might not attract the hugest of audiences but, in a sense, that doesn't matter. No one sets out to blog with the aim of competing with the mainstream media. But the truth is that blogging over the last decade has indeed started to eat a wedge into mainstream media influence. So much so that, having once viewed it as a pastime for sad geeks who tapped away at their keyboards in their bedrooms while wearing stripy pyjamas, mainstream media journalists have now embraced it – not just in politics, but across the gamut of journalism. Indeed, some believe that mainstream media blogs have now eaten up the blogosphere and diminished the influence of independents.

I decided early on that I wanted to make mine a very human blog. I wanted to write about my life, my experiences and my emotions, as well as providing political commentary and the odd dose of humour. It was a mix people seemed to like, and I always got a massive reaction whenever I wrote about anything in my personal life. So when reading this book, don't expect it just to centre around political shenanigans. I write about my dog dying. I write about delivering a eulogy at a funeral for the first time. I share my feelings on my football team reaching the FA Cup Final, only for their hopes to be dashed in the last minute. I write about my family and my civil partnership.

Writing a blog inevitably means that you become a bit of a hate figure, and writing about politics doubles your chances. I managed to make a lot of enemies along the way, but also a lot of friends and fans. Even now, people come up to me and tell me how much they miss my blog.

The blog started as a personal diary, with little political content. Unfortunately, the original blog got deleted. In October 2003, I was selected as a Conservative candidate to fight the North Norfolk seat at the next general election. I decided to use my blog as an innovative way to have a dialogue with the electorate. Judging by the landslide result against me, it wasn't a success! I then took a break from blogging for six months while I worked as Chief of Staff to David Davis during his leadership campaign. So my story really starts at the end of 2005 when I restarted the blog. It instantly attracted a sizeable readership due to a number of political news stories I broke on the blog. And it was the John Prescott affair which really catapulted it into the favourites of the Westminster Village.

At its peak, the blog was attracting 20,000 readers a day, and more than 150,000 unique users a month. If I tell you that the circulation of the *New Statesman* is 20,000 and *The Spectator* 70,000, you will understand that writing the blog became a bit of a responsibility. People expected me to write at least five or six new blog posts every day. Fifty per cent of the people who read the blog returned three or more times every day. Their appetite needed more. I loved the interaction but, in the end, maintaining my prolific output proved too much. In September 2010, I achieved a lifetime's ambition and was hired by LBC Radio to present their weeknight evening show. But I also had the day job running Biteback Publishing and *Total Politics* magazine. Effectively I was doing two full-time jobs, five days a week, and then also trying to write five stories a day on the blog. Something had to give. I knew that my writing was suffering and I wasn't providing the readers with what they had been used to. So I took the decision to close down the blog. When I announced it in December 2010, it was the nearest thing I can think of to witnessing my own death. It even made the *Today* programme. I never actually quite said I would never blog again, though. I always intended to find some way of finding an outlet for my views and, in July 2011, I launched Dale & Co, a group blog with dozens of contributors.

But if I am honest, I miss the interaction provided by my own personal blog – so watch this space. I might be back sooner than you think. And if I am, it will be at www.iaindale.com!

Iain Dale
Tunbridge Wells
November 2012

2004

DEVASTATING NEWS
MONDAY 15 MARCH

Maybe this isn't the appropriate place to write about this, but I'm sitting here with tears streaming down my face having learnt that one of my former employees has been killed in a sky-diving accident in Australia. Clare Barnes was the daughter of my friend Denis MacShane (Labour MP and Minister for Europe) and the former ITN newsreader Carol Barnes.

About four years ago Denis MacShane asked me if I would give some work experience to his daughter, Clare. He felt she was drifting in her life. What was meant to be a three-week stint working in our bookshop† turned into a year. She worked as a publicist for our publishing company‡ and was really learning the job well when she decided that she wanted to go travelling again. She was a girl with a tremendous wanderlust. Clare had a terrifically bubbly personality and everyone liked her. Even when she had done something wrong it was impossible to tell her off without feeling guilty yourself. I am devastated for Denis and Carol and can hardly imagine the pain they must be feeling. The world has lost a smiling face and at Politico's we all grieve for her.

RONALD REAGAN RIP
SATURDAY 5 JUNE

Ronald Reagan died tonight after a ten-year fight against Alzheimer's. He, more than anyone, was responsible for the West

---

† Politico's Bookshop in Artillery Row, Victoria.
‡ Politico's Publishing.

winning the Cold War and the fact that the countries of Eastern Europe are now free. He, Mikhail Gorbachev and Margaret Thatcher were the political giants of the latter quarter of the twentieth century. Reagan was a truly great American President and I cherish his memory. I remember his inspirational speech at Pointe du Hoc in France on the fortieth anniversary of the D-Day landings. I remember his words of comfort to the relatives of those who died on the ill-fated space shuttle in 1986 and I remember his speech in Berlin where he said: 'Mr Gorbachev, tear down this wall.' A truly great man.

I just received an email from one of my best friends, who lives in Washington. I met Daniel[†] in 1992 when he was over here working for Patrick Thompson MP in Norwich North. We hit it off instantly and even though he is 3,000 miles away he remains the friend who understands me best of all.

In 1994, Daniel and I took our fathers to the Normandy beaches just before the fiftieth anniversary events. It was one of the most moving few days of my life. Daniel's father died four years ago yesterday. In the subject line of his email Daniel wrote, 'You've got to win North Norfolk for the Gipper, Iain!'

UKIP AND THE BNP
TUESDAY 8 JUNE

This week has been spent mainly on the doorsteps of North Norfolk.[‡] Yesterday evening I went to Happisburgh Parish Council. The Deputy Leader of the local council, Clive Stockton (a Lib Dem), is the chairman of the council. He owns the Hill House pub in Happisburgh and is a political opponent who also happens to be a genuinely nice guy.

Today I have been in Southrepps, Northrepps, Sheringham and Holt. It's been very interesting how the political climate has changed. Up until last week I had barely come across a UKIP supporter. Sadly I cannot say the same today. Bizarrely, several Lib Dem voters say they are voting UKIP. I even had a UKIP voter who quite liked the

---

† Daniel Forrester.
‡ In October 2003 Iain was chosen to fight North Norfolk for the Conservatives at the 2005 general election.

idea of the euro! How I managed to keep a straight face I just do not know. But this evening I experienced a first. I've been doorstep canvassing for twenty years but I have never – never – had anyone actually look me straight in the eye and say they are considering voting for the BNP. It happened tonight. Twice. In Sheringham of all places. And both people were well-to-do middle-aged ladies. Yesterday it happened once, in a very sleepy North Norfolk village. There is a real sense out there that the main parties are not address- ing people's concerns, so they therefore look elsewhere to lodge a protest. If our national leaders do not start addressing this soon there could be terrible consequences. I actually think I persuaded the two potential BNP voters not to do it, but it makes me wonder how many others there are out there who I will never get to.

A DAY ON PLANET BORIS
FRIDAY 18 JUNE

I really ought to pay more attention to the advice Keith Simpson MP[†] gives me. I saw him at the Lord Lieutenant's bash in Norwich and told him Boris Johnson was coming to North Norfolk today. He chuckled and asked if I had a backup plan and suggested that Boris might not know which station to go to, to get to Norwich. Sure enough, at a quarter to nine this morning the phone rings. 'Boris here, now look here old boy, it is King's Cross isn't it?' As he was supposed to be on the 9 a.m. train from Liverpool Street this was not a promising start to my day. I remained as calm as I could while inwardly cursing and suggested he got a train from King's Cross to King's Lynn. 'OK, no probs,' he said. Five minutes later the phone rings again. 'No luck, old bean, no train till 9.45, gets in at 11.30'. At 11.30 we were due in Stody for North Norfolk Radio. More cursing. Silently, naturellement. Thinking quickly I dialled up the trains website and found a 9 a.m. train to Peterborough. 'Excellent,' trills Boris. Three minutes later the phone goes again. 'Damn and blast,' says Boris, 'we missed it'. Luckily there was another one five minutes later. Which left me with the small problem of how to get

---

† Conservative MP for Mid Norfolk 1997–2010; Conservative MP for Broadland 2010–.

to Peterborough from Swanton Abbott[†] in fifteen minutes. I might be a fast driver but I'm not that fast. In the end Boris got a taxi from Peterborough and I picked him up on a rather nasty industrial estate in Wisbech. We arrived at North Norfolk Radio fifteen minutes late. Then on to Langham Glass where Boris made a pig. Next stop Pinewoods Leisure Centre for Boris to speak at a Conservative fundraiser. A mere ninety minutes late. If it had been anyone else but Boris they'd have lynched us. We auctioned a glass pig signed (or rather etched) by Boris. Some farmers gave him an excellent briefing on sugar beet and everyone seemed happy. Except for me. I was supposed to have him safely delivered in Great Yarmouth where he was speaking for their PPC[‡] Mark Fox by 4 p.m. At 3.20 we still hadn't left. Then came the journey from hell. We got stuck behind every lorry and tractor in Norfolk and eventually got there at about 4.30. So having travelled about 150 miles and been driven to the verge of a nervous breakdown I made my way home to Swanton Abbott looking forward to a trip to Sainsbury's. Back to reality after a day on Planet Boris. What a superstar he is!

SURVEY
SUNDAY 21 NOVEMBER

Just finished going through my surveys – must have looked at about 2,000 today. Especially liked the person who answered 'Communism' to the question: 'What single thing would you suggest to improve the quality of life in your area?' Turned out to be a UKIP voter. Hmmm. I particularly liked the person (anonymous of course) who replied, 'For you to **** off back to London where you belong. You are not wanted here.' Charming! Seeing as I haven't lived in London for seven years and don't even work there I'm not quite sure where he got that idea from. Another suggestion was 'Making the national lottery easier to win'. I liked that one. But the winner of best answer to that question goes to Mr B from Hoveton who suggested, 'Let down the tyres on Margaret Beckett's caravan and give Labour a reality check.' I like his way of thinking.

---

† Iain's Norfolk cottage was in the small village of Swanton Abbott, a few miles north of Norwich.
‡ Prospective Parliamentary Candidate.

WELL, WHAT DID YOU THINK?
MONDAY 29 NOVEMBER

I have just got back from appearing on *Newsnight* to talk about the David Blunkett situation.† I was on with Labour MP Clive Betts,‡ with whom I had done a *News 24* interview earlier this evening. Clive is a nice guy but does rant a bit. So in contrast I seemed to be the voice of sweet reason (for once!). I will happily admit that I was quite nervous about appearing on this programme and was a little suspicious as to why I had been asked. But when I was sitting there waiting for the opening titles to roll I felt remarkably calm. Jeremy Paxman, who had obviously seen the earlier *News 24* piece, had settled me down by greeting me with the words, 'Hello, you attack dog!' I replied that I thought that was normally his role. He then said, 'Oh, you're not going to have a go at me about the Michael Howard interview are you?' Luckily I hadn't seen it. Anyway, everyone tells me I did OK. Roll on *Question Time*!

BYE BYE BLUNKETT?
WEDNESDAY 1 DECEMBER

Well it's not looking good for Mr Blunkett is it? I have to say that on a personal level I feel very sorry for him, but it is looking increasingly obvious that his personal circumstances have, at the very least, coloured his judgement. If you examine all eight of the allegations it really does not look very good. I'm tempted to rehearse them all here, but I'll spare you that. I was in the House of Commons yesterday and the general feeling was that he would survive. I don't think he will. And remember, this prediction comes from the man who bet £20 at 80–1 on a Conservative majority of twenty-one in 1992. Just a shame my friend (an esteemed solicitor in Hoveton) forgot to put the bet on for me ... I've nearly forgiven him. Almost. Sort of. OK, all right then, I'm still seething. I may forgive, but I *never* forget.

---

† Blunkett was under pressure to resign over his relationship with the publisher of *The Spectator*.
‡ Labour MP for Sheffield Attercliffe 1992–2010; Labour MP for Sheffield South East 2010–.

TODAY, TOMORROW
SATURDAY 18 DECEMBER

It's 1 a.m. and I am about to go to bed. Very frenetic day. Iain Duncan Smith arrived over an hour late due to traffic. What is it with me and visiting speakers? Boris Johnson went to Peterborough instead of Norwich, Cecil Parkinson ended up driving down the M11 the wrong way, and now this! IDS did an hour on North Norfolk Radio and we then went to the Princess Diana Drug and Alcohol Rehabilitation Centre at Mundesley. It's a truly superb facility and we spent an engaging two hours there talking to the staff and patients. Then on to The Feathers in Holt for a dinner. IDS and I had a superb time in the bar talking to local people and having drinks bought for us! He scored a real hit with a group of about twenty raucous young ladies. I think they thought we were the strippograms!

PASS THE SICK BAG
SUNDAY 19 DECEMBER

I've done it again. On Boxing Day, I'm going to brave freezing temperatures to take part in the annual Boxing Day dip at Cromer. I'll be joining the intrepid North Norfolk Beach Runners for the festive swim to raise funds for BREAK. The money will be used to provide seaside holidays for children and adults with disabilities at BREAK centres in Norfolk. I hope the good people of Cromer will have lined their stomachs after the Christmas Day festivities, because the sight of me in my trunks might be a little too much for some. I only hesitated for a few, er, weeks before agreeing to take part in the Boxing Day plunge. It was either that or do a sponsored walk over red-hot coals. I'm used to having my fingers burnt but I drew the line at my toes.

TSUNAMI
WEDNESDAY 31 DECEMBER

I don't think any of us fully appreciated the horror of what happened in south-east Asia when we heard the news on Boxing Day. We do now. The pictures are truly horrific – none more graphic than the front page of today's *Sun* newspaper. I'm watching Sky News as I type this and can only imagine the grief of those who have lost loved ones. My sister has spent quite some time in Thailand, but I have never been there apart from a two-hour stopover on the way to Australia.

I was in Lloyds Bank in Cromer this morning and in front of me a man brought in a bag of money which had been collected on the streets of Cromer during the morning. There must have been a couple of thousand pounds in it at least. The lady behind me donated £100 to the appeal. It's not just governments who are duty-bound to help on occasions like this and it is magnificent that individuals are doing their bit too.

It makes party politics look all rather petty.

2005

A REAL ACHIEVEMENT
FRIDAY 14 JANUARY

Well, I achieved something of real value today – in more ways than one. I secured free transport for two container-loads of blankets and clothing collected by the people of Sheringham to the Banda Aceh region of Indonesia. The goods will be distributed to the hardest-hit areas by the Indonesian Ministry of Welfare.

Late last week I was contacted by one of the organisers of the Sheringham Tsunami Appeal Collection, Tabitha van der Does, to ask if I could cut through the barriers which had been put in their way. More than forty tonnes of clothing and blankets were collected at Sheringham Fire Station last Friday, which I helped dozens of Sheringham residents to load into lorries. Since then the goods have been stored in a barn at Stratton Strawless. Tabitha and Eroica Mildmay (the other organiser) were then left with the problem of what to do next.

I must admit I took a deep breath when Tabi phoned to tell me that she was having difficulty finding a way of getting the blankets and clothes to Indonesia. I used to work in the ports and shipping world, so I opened up an old contacts book and got on the phone. I managed to persuade Norman Global Logistics, the Yang Min Shipping Line and the Port of Felixstowe to waive all port dues and shipping charges. We had offered to get the goods to Felixstowe ourselves but instead the containers are coming to Stratton Strawless at the end of next week, where we will have a large team of volunteers to help fill them. Job done.

DRUGS REHAB
THURSDAY 3 FEBRUARY

Spent the morning at the Princess Diana Drugs Rehabilitation Centre in Mundesley yesterday. I took IDS there in December but thought I would go back on my own to learn a bit more about what they do. Met several of the patients, all of whom were fearful of the level of support they would get in the community when they had finished their treatment. This was exemplified by a guy I had met in December who had been there for eight months and had become completely free of drugs. He is now in a hostel in King's Lynn, sharing a room with a man who openly takes drugs. This is terrible. I've taken it upon myself to try to find him alternative accommodation but I can't say I'm hopeful. It seems from what I have found out about the area of drugs rehab that the whole system is a shambles. Mundesley has room for seventy people yet it has fewer than forty because of local authority and social services bureaucracy. If we actually managed our rehab policy properly, the crime rate would plummet.

REJOICE! REJOICE!
FRIDAY 11 FEBRUARY

Today is the thirtieth anniversary of Margaret Thatcher's election as leader of the Conservative Party. I was twelve at the time but remember it well. I remember running upstairs to tell my grandmother, who was ill in bed. She burst into tears. She couldn't believe that it was possible for a woman to lead a political party. My grandmother was a bit of a feminist at heart, but a deep-rooted Tory. She sparked my interest in politics. She would have been 109 today.

THE DUREX BUNNY
SATURDAY 12 FEBRUARY

Hilarious end to the day when I called on a lady who had had a large Lib Dem poster at the last election on a prime poster site. Apparently they just put it up without asking and she said she didn't like to cause trouble! She also asked us while we were there if we would mind changing the battery in her clock. I said I'd be delighted to. She then told me to fetch the Durex battery from the sideboard!

I'D DO ANYTHING FOR A VOTE, BUT I WON'T DO THAT!
FRIDAY 8 APRIL

Meat Loaf is becoming a theme of this campaign. I booked tickets the other day for his concert at Blickling on my birthday in July. Yesterday I said something to a voter and she replied, 'You took the words right out of my mouth', to which I replied, 'It must have been while you were kissing me!' She roared. Today I had my picture taken with a lady with a Meat Loaf tattoo.

SATURDAY CAMPAIGN
SATURDAY 9 APRIL

Started the day off with a group of supporters, wandering around Sheringham market and then down the high street. Said a quick hello to Norman Lamb[†] who was doing the same thing with a couple of his groupies. We then moved on to Cromer, North Walsham and finished up in Swanton Abbott. By far the best day so far, with many switchers, especially from the Lib Dems.

We've had a number of examples today of our posters being vandalised. Always happens. Funny how the Lib Dem posters always stay intact.

The EDP[‡] called to ask for my comments on a story they are running on Monday on Norman Lamb's decision to carry on canvassing during the Pope's funeral. They asked if I would call for him to apologise. I decided not to. In the end people can make up their own minds about how appropriate it was. It seems the Lib Dems had a national ban on campaigning but he broke it.

So, what issues are people raising on the doorstep? Today it was predominantly council tax and immigration.

---

† Liberal Democrat MP for North Norfolk 2001–.
‡ *Eastern Daily Press*, Norfolk's daily newspaper.

Someone saw a black hearse tonight covered with Lamb stickers. Nothing to do with me. Promise!

Strangest question of the day? 'So, Mr Dale, what are your views on the Suez Crisis?'

DEBATES
TUESDAY 26 APRIL

Yesterday was the first debate between the four candidates for North Norfolk, in Wells. Tonight was the second, in Fakenham. The third is in Sheringham on Thursday.

Last night it was all a little too cosy and gentlemanly. Lots of 'Well, I agree with you, Norman' and 'Iain is absolutely right.' There were about 100 people present in Wells, about thirty more than were at Fakenham tonight. I can hardly believe that the issue of Wells Hospital didn't come up at all, nor indeed did health-care of any description.

Tonight's debate was a little sparkier and all the better for it, I thought. It's difficult to know how many floating voters attend these events but I hope they got something out of them.

For the record, I think Wells was a score draw but I felt tonight I came out marginally on top. It has to be said the star of the show was the Reverend Adrian Bell,† who chaired the event brilliantly – and at times eccentrically! Highly entertaining. He obviously fancies a career change as a *Today* programme interviewer!

REJOICE
WEDNESDAY 4 MAY

I just heard *Channel 4 News* has tipped us to gain the seat. Also, I just had a fax from Margaret Thatcher wishing me well for tomorrow. Brought a tear to the eye. I had a nice letter from John Major the other day too.

Michael Howard came to Norwich this afternoon. He had to divert from Yarmouth because his helicopter could not land in the fog. It all went well. I have to say, he looks great. I think I look

---

† Rector of Fakenham Parish Church.

exhausted at the moment, but he looked fresh as a daisy. Got him to do a phone interview with North Norfolk Radio.

Off to my favourite restaurant now (Jacques) for a bite to eat. Feels like the Last Supper! I have to tell you, I feel very odd now. Strangely calm.

MORNING AFTER THE NIGHT BEFORE
FRIDAY 6 MAY[†]

This is obviously something I hoped I wouldn't have to post. Last night's result was devastating for me personally and for the local Conservative Party. I have put body and soul into my campaign over the last eighteen months, so to lose by such a margin was a bitter pill to have to swallow.[‡] But it wasn't just me. I have received the support of scores of local people who have campaigned with me, night and day, to win North Norfolk back for the Conservatives, and it is to them I owe everything. I have received very loyal support from the local Party and I'd like to thank each and every one of them for their encouragement and backing. I'd like also to thank all those who have phoned or emailed me about the result. I'm very touched by your comments and will reply to each one.

Obviously the day after such a defeat is not the best time to contemplate the future, but I wish to make one thing clear. I am not about to disappear from the North Norfolk scene. I live here and intend to continue to do so. I'm going to take some time out to think about my future and what I should do next. Answers on a postcard please...

HOW TO ATTEND A COUNT AND LOSE GRACEFULLY (I THINK)
SATURDAY 7 MAY[§]

If I am honest, polling day was a disaster. We had set up fifteen or so committee rooms across the constituency and had teams of people knocking up. Time and again I kept being asked the same

---

† The day after polling day at the 2005 general election.
‡ The Liberal Democrat majority increased from 483 to 10,606.
§ This was actually written in 2010, but it fits better here.

question: 'Are you sure these knocking-up slips are right? We seem to be knocking up Lib Dem voters.' Surely the agent hadn't printed off the wrong codes, I kept asking myself. She and I had been at daggers drawn since the day of my selection. Let's put it this way, she had gone out of her way to make clear that she favoured anyone but me. Half the local association wouldn't work with her, and I seemed to spend much of my time mending fences with people whose noses she had put out of joint. After a row on day one of the campaign, she walked out, only to repeat the exercise later in the campaign. But surely, I thought, she wouldn't have been so incompetent as to print out the wrong knocking-up cards, would she? It was only six months later, when I learnt that she had gone round telling people she hadn't even voted for me, that I began to wonder. Anyway, I digress.

I had known for some time that winning was highly unlikely. I remember a day in February canvassing in the coastal village of Overstrand. Every single house we went to seemed to deliver the same message: 'Well, we're really Conservatives but we're going to vote for that nice Mr Lamb.' I remember going back to my house in Swanton Abbott that night and saying to John,[†] 'That's it, I know now I can't win.' If people like that weren't going to vote for me, the game was up. But I knew that I couldn't tell that to my supporters who had sweated blood in helping my campaign. The problem was that Norman Lamb was (and is) essentially a Conservative. His and my views were almost indistinguishable on local issues. He was even vaguely Eurosceptic (for a Lib Dem). He had fought three elections and made it his business to be a good constituency MP.

My strategy had been to play him at his own game, and demonstrate that I too would be a good constituency representative – but one who could get things done by dint of being an MP for one of the two major parties. By the time the election campaign started I had undertaken a huge amount of constituency casework, and had got a very good reputation for taking up local campaigns and getting things done. I probably got more good local publicity in local press and radio than any other candidate in the country. We produced good literature and built up an excellent delivery network, but the fact remained – he was the MP and I was a candidate.

In retrospect I made too much of an effort at name recognition. It was a mistake to book a giant poster site (the only one in the

---

† John Simmons, Iain's partner since 1995.

constituency) for the few weeks before the election, and it was also a mistake to make a CD-ROM and deliver it to every house. The money spent on those two things would have been far better spent on more newsletters and constituency-wide newspapers.

Two other things worked against me. The fact that I was quite often on TV, I originally thought, would be a good thing – name recognition etc. But all it did was give people the impression I was in London all the time and not local. I could witter on about how I lived in the constituency – and I did – while Norman Lamb lived twenty miles away in Norwich, but a fat lot of good it did me.

So I expected to lose. It didn't help that nationally the party wasn't making any sort of breakthrough. Although Michael Howard had done his best, people were still in thrall to Tony Blair. Howard hadn't been able to attract back those soft Conservative voters who had turned North Norfolk Lib Dem back in 2001. Nor, it seemed, had I.

So as I criss-crossed the constituency on polling day, I had a fairly good idea of what was to happen later that night, although not even I could have guessed that the result would be quite so bad.

As the polls closed, I went back to my cottage to change and collect John. I felt strangely numb. I craved that feeling most other candidates in marginal seats would have been feeling at that moment – the feeling that they were hours away from their biggest ever achievement.

I've never understood candidates who turn up at their counts after most of the hard work has been done. I wanted to be there to support my counting agents, and to make sure that nothing went wrong. In such a massive constituency it was always going to take a long time to get the ballot boxes in. And so it proved. Just after midnight the other candidates started to arrive, and I made it my business to chat to them all and their aides, many of whom I had got to know over the previous eighteen months.

The first few boxes seemed OK from our point of view. For a fleeting moment I let myself wonder if I was being unduly pessimistic. But it was only when I sat down and did some counting myself that I realised that a defeat was definitely on the cards. The counting seemed to be going very slowly. I was keeping touch with outside events on a small hand-sized portable TV. I remember Justine Greening winning. I think I even let out a cheer. I was sitting on a bench cradling this small, CD-sized TV in my hands. One of the fringe candidates, who was dressed as a circus clown, came over and watched with me. He put his hand on my shoulder. The EDP picture next day was of this touching scene but was captioned: 'A tearful Iain Dale is comforted by a clown.' I wasn't tearful at all, I was watching David Dimbleby!

The moment came when the returning officer asked all the candidates and agents to gather round to go through the questionable votes. He then read out the figures. I could hardly believe what I was hearing. Norman Lamb understandably struggled to contain himself. His majority had increased from 500 to 10,600. My initial reaction was to laugh in disbelief. To this day I struggle to believe it. One or two of my people suggested we request a bundle check, just to make sure that some votes hadn't been put in the wrong piles. But before that could be requested the agent had accepted the result. I too was not in a mood to question anything after hearing such a devastating piece of news. To be honest, my only thought was how I was going to get through the concession speech. Some weeks after the count I kept being told by my party workers: 'There was something wrong at the count. We didn't like to say anything at the time.' To this day I don't know what they think happened.

As we waited for the formalities to begin, Norman Lamb apologised to me for some rather nasty, homophobic comments made about me by one of his councillors. I thanked him and said I appreciated that he hadn't run that sort of campaign.

Norman was then asked to the platform and he gave a gracious speech in which he made clear he had at some points over the previous eighteen months feared the worst. It was then my turn. I have inherited my mother's tendency to have a good cry at the worst possible moment. Even an episode of *Emmerdale* has been known to set me off, so as I climbed up on to the stage I made sure I breathed very deeply and made sure that I didn't catch the eye of Deborah Slattery, my campaign manager and loyal friend. I knew she would be howling her eyes out.

It remains a speech I am proud of. I got through it intact, thanked everyone who needed to be thanked and paid tribute to Norman Lamb. I was told afterwards by several Lib Dem and Labour supporters that they were quite moved by it. As I left the stage I have a vague recollection of Norman Lamb putting his arm around me!

As John and I left Cromer High School to make the short drive to a party worker's house for some food and drink, it all came out.

I broke down completely in the car. John said nothing, but just drove. There was nothing he could say. By the time we had arrived, I had pulled myself together. It was meant to be a party but the atmosphere was simply awful and I couldn't wait to go home. I made another short speech thanking everyone, but it seemed like going through the motions. It was about 6.30 a.m. before we got home. I got about two hours' sleep.

The next morning was the count for the county council elections. I was determined to go to it. No one was going to accuse me of not being able to show my face. As I walked into the school hall, many people (including Lib Dems and Labour supporters) spontaneously applauded. At that moment my sister Sheena (the punk rocker) phoned. I had to tell her I couldn't speak to her as I would break down again.

And that was that. I cleared out my office and started to think about what on earth I would do in the future. If the result had been anywhere near three figures I would have stayed, but this was just one of those occasions when there was little I could have done to change things.

Did my sexuality play a role? I didn't lose because North Norfolk rejected a gay candidate. I lost because the Lib Dems ran a relentless campaign to persuade Labour supporters to vote tactically. I lost because our national campaign, though highly professional and slick, did not ignite the fires of optimism among an electorate sick of personal insults and negativity. It may not be racist to talk about immigration, but it is perhaps not clever to put the words 'racist' and 'Conservative' on the same poster. And I lost because the Lib Dem MP had a huge personal vote, far beyond anything I've encountered anywhere else.

A candidate is perhaps not the ideal person to understand fully the reasons for a shattering defeat. Others can judge that, and many have offered their two-pennyworth over the last four years. All I know is that I can look myself in the mirror and know that I could not have done more. I almost bankrupted myself, put in far more hours than most other candidates I know and in many ways ran a textbook campaign. Of course I made mistakes, and I have alluded to some of them here, but my biggest mistake was to ignore those who advised me not to go for this particular seat in the first place! Lib Dem chief executive Chris Rennard, who knows a thing or two about these things, was one of them. He told me before I was selected that he expected Norman Lamb to get a five-figure majority. I thought I knew better. I won't make that particular mistake again!

Other than perhaps the initial decision, I have few regrets. I thoroughly enjoyed the eighteen months up to the election, even if I hated the campaign itself. I met some wonderful people and would like to think that even as a candidate I made a bit of a difference to some people's lives.

The most important thing is to learn from what life – and the electorate – throws at you.

In the twenty-four hours after polling day I received more than 250 emails, as well as dozens of phone calls from friends, colleagues and many people I have never met, expressing their sympathy. I have to say, it was a bit like being present at your own funeral, but they certainly kept my spirits up. Having gone through a very difficult few hours and had a bit of sleep, my mind turned towards the future – as one door closes, another opens.

Here are a few of the emails I received:

I was devastated to hear this news. Of all our candidates throughout the country, you especially deserved to win. It must seem indescribably hard after your amazing efforts and first-class media campaign, which I constantly pointed out to other friends as an example of what a candidate should do. C. K. E.

I am stunned. We have just arrived back from Stansted after a business visit to Spain. This was fixed long before the date of the election so we voted by post. All your friends and colleagues will be devastated. The feeling I got from everyone I spoke to was that your campaign was hitting all the right notes. You certainly showed a powerful level of commitment, with thoughtful and valid perspectives on both local and national issues of importance. Please do not lose heart; I know you will not. R. H.

You know we all feel for you. Nobody could have worked harder than you've done over the last two years and it's a dreadful shame the way things have worked out. B. C.

My wife and I are so very sorry about this disastrous election result. After all your magnificent efforts for North Norfolk, putting your opponent in the shade, I might add, you did deserve to win. R. D.

I want you to know that there are more than a few people who noted your support for the hospital; not just your support but your intelligent, incisive, challenging words and ensuing action i.e. getting national commitment to reopen the hospital. Secondly I want you to know that several of these people commented on your evident talents: he is a man for the future; he is ministerial material; could he be a PM in this century? It must be very discouraging to work so hard: foot slogging door to door, day after day, rain after rain – and then face overwhelming defeat. I do hope you will not allow yourself to be crushed and that we will hear that your most evident talents and clarity of intellectual energy have found a way into an MP position, somewhere, before long. I wish you well, so well. S. T.

When we appointed you, you told us you would not let us down and you didn't. No one could have worked harder or more effectively than you. Take your time and you will have our support whatever you decide. C. T.

SHAME ON YOU, SIMON HEFFER
SATURDAY 7 MAY

Simon Heffer has written a poisonous piece in the *Daily Mail* today about the fact that Nick Boles and I lost both our seats – he blames it on the fact that we are gay and that people outside London don't like 'that sort of thing'. Strange how he doesn't mention the fact that Nick Herbert, who won Arundel, is gay too and has a huge majority. I thought we had got beyond this, but it is clear that the media will sink to any level to be homophobic. I understand the *Mail on Sunday* will be writing a similar article tomorrow. In twenty months here I can count on the fingers of two hands the number of people who have had an issue with my sexuality. The very same people would have had a problem if I had been black, a single mother or anything other than a white Volvo-driving husband with 2.4 children. Frankly, if they didn't vote for me I'm rather glad. The Conservative Party can do without bigots.

LUNCHTIME IN ROUGHTON
SUNDAY 22 MAY

This lunchtime I held a thank-you lunch for sixty of my campaign team who did so much for my election campaign. It was held in Roughton at the home of two people who have become very close friends, Bert and Sylvia. The weather held off and I think everyone enjoyed it. I said a few words and to be honest was very worried I might not hold it together as it was inevitably a little emotional. Anyway, I got through it and said what I wanted to say. There were some very special people involved in the campaign and I will never be able to thank them enough for all they did.

NEW BEGINNINGS
WEDNESDAY 25 MAY

I have a new job. On Tuesday, I start work as Chief of Staff to David Davis. I have therefore regretfully decided that I have to close down the blog. I am sure you will all understand the reasons. It's my decision and my decision alone. Basically I am bound to say something which either I or David will live to regret!

The six months working for David Davis were not happy ones. I'm not blaming him at all, but I was a round peg in a square hole. I was used to making decisions and standing by them. Contrary to popular rumour, I was not running his leadership campaign. That was Andrew Mitchell MP's job. He and I didn't really agree on strategy or approach, but this was a campaign where if you didn't have the letters MP after your name, you weren't taken entirely seriously. My mistake was in not clamping down on that from the very beginning. David Davis was and is one of my closest friends in politics. We didn't serve him well. Any of us. That campaign should have been won, and won easily. True, he could have played it differently too but, looking back, we all let each other down. Badly. By the end of November the campaign was entering its last few days and my mind started to turn to the future. What on earth would I do now? I had been expecting to be running David's office as Leader of the Opposition. Well, the first thing to do was to restart the blog...

AND THE WINNER IS...
TUESDAY 6 DECEMBER

In a few hours' time the new leader of the Conservative Party will be preparing for PMQs. Last night the Davis diehards held an end-of-campaign party to thank all those who had worked on the leadership election. We held it at our office in Victoria Street. Quite a number of MPs were there as well as the staffers and volunteers. Bearing in mind the press are acting as if they already know the result, the mood was rather cheerful! Among those present were Andrew Mitchell, Damian Green, Nick Herbert, Paul Goodman, Shailesh Vara, James Brokenshire, the Wintertons, David Davies, Patrick Mercer, Dominic Grieve, John Baron, David Willetts, David Ruffley, Richard Spring and a host of others. Andrew Mitchell made an extremely witty speech and then it was my turn to introduce the campaign awards. No doubt several of them will find their way into diary columns anyway, so Andrew Mitchell agreed I should post some of them here for your delectation! Anyone without a fully developed sense of humour had better stop reading NOW!

Most irritating campaign slogans
This is the end of the era of spin. (DD)
We're all in this together. (DC)
Championing the victims of state failure. (DD)
The Broken Society. (LF)
And the winner is... 'Sharing the proceeds of growth'. (DC)

Most feared words of the campaign
Anyone: Have you seen what's in the *Daily Mail* today?
DD: So what's the latest on the speech?
Andrew Mitchell: Let's have a leak inquiry!
Derek Conway: I think Nadine's fully signed up.
DD: Get me a helicopter.
Juliet, DD's secretary: I've got David on the line for you.
Gloria, DD's secretary: I've had a 'pink pussy'.

Top seven things least likely to be said on the DD campaign
DD: I want to share the proceeds of growth.
DD: Isn't the *Daily Mail* a great newspaper?

Derek Conway: I think I want Greg Barker as my deputy.
David Willetts: I agree entirely that we need a £38 billion tax cut.
Campaign receptionist: David? No one here by that name...
DD: Don't worry about a helicopter, a 2CV will do me.

Best quote of the campaign
On hearing DD say on *Woman's Hour* that DD preferred briefs to
boxers, Ashley Crossley (Head of Research) was heard to comment:
'Well he's lost the gay vote, then!'

Andrew Mitchell: So why exactly does Cameron have more
supporters on his website than we have on ours?
William Norton (campaign team): Because he's got more supporters, Andrew.

At the London hustings:
   William Norton: Would you like a Davis leaflet, sir?
   Tobias Ellwood MP: Er, no, I'm an MP and I'm a declared
Cameron supporter.
   William Norton: Don't worry, there aren't any long words in it.

David Davis: I'll have to go, my helicopter's at the door!

Beat that!
   The one thing you can safely say about the DD campaign is that
we never lost our sense of humour. Whoever wins this afternoon is
going to need to keep theirs for the next four years!

THINGS I WISH I'D SAID: NO. 94
WEDNESDAY 7 DECEMBER

At lunchtime I ran into my opponent from the election in North
Norfolk, Lib Dem MP Norman Lamb. He asked me what I was
going to do now that the leadership election is over. Instead of telling him the truth, what I should have said was, 'I've been offered
the job of Head of Programming at North Norfolk Radio!'
   Actually, Norman and I get on quite well. I was walking through
Portcullis House chatting to him a couple of weeks ago and encountered the *Mail on Sunday*'s Simon Walters: 'Ah,' he said, 'The dream

team reunited!' Norman went a very odd shade of pale ... although I gather he has been relating the tale too.

AN EYEFUL FOR HER MAJ
SUNDAY 11 DECEMBER

All-round good egg Gyles Brandreth[†] was in top form at the Parliamentary Press Gallery Christmas bash this week, modestly informing the assembled hacks he was there in his role as prophet. The head hasn't got any smaller then, Gyles! Brandreth, it seems, is laying claim to have spotted David Cameron's potential as early as 1993, when the 27-year-old Tory golden boy was serving as Norman Lamont's Special Adviser at the Treasury. In his capacity as best friend of the royals, he went on to describe the Royal Variety Performance as a 'kind of Eurovision Song Contest endurance test with the added shame that all the acts are British', before regaling journalists with an anecdote about how the Queen got more than she bargained for at a recent Royal Variety Performance. At the climax of a performance of the stripping scene from *The Full Monty*, she copped a full eyeful of British manhood – in both senses of the phrase. Brandreth was horrified until Prince Philip leaned over and whispered to him: 'I wouldn't worry, she's been to Papua New Guinea, you know. She's seen it all before.'

Anyone but Davis?
Having fought eleven general elections you might be forgiven for thinking that Michael Howard would be familiar with putting a cross in a box on a ballot paper. But my spies in the 1922 Committee tell me that he almost managed to spoil his ballot paper in the Tory leadership election ballot among MPs. Apparently he ticked a box rather than putting a cross in it. Realising his mistake, he asked if that was OK and was reassured his vote would still count. I'm told that when the ballot boxes were emptied only one of the 198 ballot papers had a tick on it. All the money in the world couldn't drag from me whose box he had ticked – it is after all a secret ballot! – but suffice to say it wasn't against the box marked Davis.

---

† Conservative MP for Chester 1992–7.

Now here's to you, Mrs Hamilton

Gay icon Christine Hamilton tells me she has been invited to three civil partnership ceremonies next week. 'The stiffies came in the post this morning,' she shrills. The mind boggles...

THE STRANGE CASE OF MENZIES CAMPBELL
TUESDAY 13 DECEMBER

A few days ago Andrew Neil announced to the nation that he had it on very good authority that Charles Kennedy would resign in March next year. Strange that this happened the night after Menzies Campbell was reportedly the only Lib Dem present at Andrew Neil's Christmas party. Very strange. And no doubt purely coincidental.

EXCLUSIVE: Lib Dems Plan Vote of No Confidence in Kennedy

Sources in the Lib Dems tell me that a Vote of No Confidence in Charles Kennedy could be launched as early as tomorrow's meeting of the Lib Dem Parliamentary Party. I understand two national newspapers might run the story tomorrow, but Lib Dem officials are frantically trying to head them off and kill it. Let's see if they're successful. If they're not, I suspect it will be all-out war between the Orange Bookers and the Sandal Wearers. Expect an Oaten v. Hughes runoff. Although if they had any sense they'd go for Nick Clegg or David Laws ... or, dare I say it, Norman Lamb!

Update: 22.05: Just spoken to another contact who confirms that there was a heated discussion in Lib Dem shadow Cabinet today about the Andrew Neil comment and that Kennedy issued a 'back me or sack me' threat. I'm told there were many raised voices. The level of unhappiness with Kennedy is, to quote my source, 'the worst I have ever known it'.

EXCLUSIVE: CHARLES KENNEDY'S WESTMINSTER NO SHOW
WEDNESDAY 14 DECEMBER

Rumours were sweeping Westminster tonight that Charles Kennedy's appearance before the Lib Dem Parliamentary Party this afternoon had taken more out of him than first thought. He was

due to read the lesson at the Westminster Carol Service this evening
but didn't show up. I daren't even print some of the speculation
that was going round the building about the reason for his shyness.
He was due to read from Luke. One of the lines I am told he was
due to read was 'For he shall be great in the sight of the Lord,
and shall drink neither wine nor strong drink.' Indeed, indeed. Wise
advice for any leader in trouble. Hic.

Tomorrow I'm off to the Isle of Man to host *An Evening with
Ann Widdecombe* for a local charity. I'm ashamed at how little I
know about the Isle of Man and its history and relationship with
the rest of the UK. Widders and I have been invited to lunch with the
Governor, who apparently knew her father. It's commonly thought
that homosexuality is still illegal among Manx-kind, but that's a
misunderstanding. It was decriminalised a decade ago. But they
do still have a law similar to our old Section 28 – in their case
it's Section 38. It forbids the public promotion of homosexuality.
Perhaps I should warn the Governor that by inviting me to lunch
he might be breaking his own law. But I suppose if he doesn't tell
anyone it won't matter. So that's all right then.

THANK YOU, MR WIDDECOMBE
THURSDAY 15 DECEMBER

Just arrived with Ann Widdecombe on the Isle of Man. Great
hotel (The Sefton, in Douglas) which has wireless internet access.
Just about to go to lunch with the Governor. Hilarious moment
at Gatwick when I gave my boarding card to the lady at check
in. 'Thank you, Mr Widdecombe,' she said. I'd better not describe
the various thoughts going round in my head... Ann's face was a
picture. Best thing of all, they don't have the Human Rights Act in
the Isle of Man. Not quite sure what I can do to take advantage of
that, so any ideas, please feel free to post a comment.

EXCLUSIVE: KOFI OR BLACK COFFEE?

Now if I were a member of Her Majesty's Press digging around
the Charles Kennedy story, I might well be trying to find out what
happened when Kofi Annan visited Charles Kennedy at Cowley

Street. It has been suggested that the UN Secretary General found the Lib Dem leader in an, ahem, er, 'unprepared' state. His aides were mortified.

PICKING THE LIB DEM LEADERSHIP?
SATURDAY 17 DECEMBER

Nick Clegg seems a bit too good to be true. But if the Lib Dems have any sense, he is the one they'll pick to take over from the beleaguered Charles Kennedy. I suspect that they'll actually go for Ming Campbell, but this would be an error.

The Lib Dems need their own Cameron, and Nick Clegg is the one that fits the bill. He looks the part, he's got the experience (despite only being elected in 2005 he has gained good experience as an MEP – if that's not an oxymoron) and he's got the charisma and sense of humour. Hughes would be the choice of every Conservative I know. Oaten doesn't frighten us and Ming Campbell would just be a stop-gap. People say he gives the Lib Dems much-needed gravitas, and to an extent that's true, but he is totally uninterested in domestic politics and the economy, and that would become clear very quickly. Nick Clegg is the only one who, as a Conservative, I would not look forward to fighting.

Update 1: Just seen Ming Campbell and Nick Clegg in deep conversation over a coffee in Portcullis House. Can't imagine what they are discussing.

Update 2: Ran into Mark Oaten at lunchtime, who was yawning his head off. Question: why is he so tired? Is it a) because he was up all night preparing for today's police debate, or is it b) because he was putting together his leadership campaign team?

GIGGLE THE GUINEA PIG, RIP
THURSDAY 22 DECEMBER

RIP Giggle, editor of the Sheringham *Guineapendent*. Just received word from my friend Tabitha Van der Does that my biggest fan in North Norfolk, her guinea pig, has died. Giggle interviewed me for Tabi's *Sheringham Independent* magazine once. A unique experience. As a tribute to Giggle, here's the interview from 2 June 2004. Enjoy...

Giggle: You have very nice teeth, Mr Dale. How do you keep them clean?

Iain: Contrary to popular rumour, I do not bite my opponents. I am on a strict diet and eat lots of fruit so that keeps my teeth nice and healthy. My new campaign slogan is DOWN WITH MARS BARS!

G: How many carrots do you eat a day?

I: Not as many as you.

G: What is a Conservative and do they have any policies on guinea pigs?

I: A Conservative was once described as a man who sits and thinks – mostly sits. We believe in freedom for guinea pigs everywhere. We totally reject the Lib Dem policy of taxing every squeak a guinea pig makes.

G: Have you ever lived with a rabbit?

I: No, but my friend Jenny lives with one. She lets it roam around the house. I think she believes it is a dog.

G: Do you think I'm on Freddie Starr's hit list?

I: I think he has a mild preference for your cousin the hamster. I would be more afraid of a visit from John Prescott if I were you.

G: I have heard you bred guinea pigs? For what purpose?

I: As a good Conservative I bred them to make money. I was only ten years old and we had about fifty at one stage. We used to sell them for 5p each. That was in the days before the rampant inflation in the late 1970s. It would be about £1 in today's money.

G: My favourite Shakespearean quote is 'Over hill, over dale'. What's yours?

I: I am not very conversant with Shakespeare, I prefer Goethe. My favourite Goethe quote is *Man tue was man will* (Do what you want).

G: Do you agree with the philosophy of George Orwell's 'four legs good, two legs bad'?

I: *Animal Farm* is one of my favourite books, so yes, I do agree. My best friend has four legs. His name is Gio and he is my Jack Russell. I wouldn't get too near him if I were you. It might be the last thing you ever do!

G: Thank you, Mr Dale.

I: You are welcome, Miss Giggle.

As you can imagine, this was one of my more memorable interviews...

KNOCK, KNOCK
THURSDAY 29 DECEMBER

Wife: There's trouble with the car. It has water in the carburettor.
Husband: Water in the carburettor? That's ridiculous.
Wife: I tell you it's true.
Husband: You don't even know what a carburettor is. Where's the car?
Wife: In the swimming pool.

2006

CHARLES KENNEDY RESIGNS
SATURDAY 7 JANUARY

I have just watched Charles Kennedy's dignified statement on Sky News announcing his resignation as leader of the Liberal Democrats. This is a political assassination almost on a par with that of Margaret Thatcher in 1990. Few realised the Lib Dem Parliamentary Party could be so ruthless. The Tory Party has taken fifteen years to recover from that. I wonder if it will take Lib Dems as long. I feel particularly for Sarah, Kennedy's wife. I interviewed her for a job more than ten years ago and she's a wonderful woman. She'll be a critical support for him over the next few weeks, which are bound to be very lonely ones for him. I wonder who will be first out of the traps...

TONY BANKS HAS DIED
MONDAY 9 JANUARY

Just heard that Tony Banks has died. Such a shame. One memory of him is that he seemed to be a permanent fixture in the Pugin Room in the House of Commons. Whenever I went in there he was sat with a bevy of blondes and a bottle of champagne. He was very helpful to me when Politico's started and we'd exchange notes about various items of political memorabilia. I remember asking him to be one of the speakers when we opened Politico's, but there were so many people there he couldn't get in. Instead, he stuck his tongue out at the window. Class. We'll miss him.

MICHAEL HESELTINE – MY PART IN HIS DOWNFALL
THURSDAY 12 JANUARY

Michael Heseltine has today called for a fresh inquiry into the Westland Affair and the release of paperwork relating to the crisis under the Freedom of Information Act. He also alleged there was an illegal 'concert party' – an arrangement between various investors to secretly manipulate share price – to buy the company, including the late financier Sir James Goldsmith. And in evidence, he cites a book I published nearly four years ago called *Here Today, Gone Tomorrow* by Sir John Nott, the former Defence Secretary who was Chairman of Lazard, Westland's bankers. Heseltine said today:

> What I said at the time was true, and every time there is a revelation it confirms what I said. John Nott's autobiography was another very interesting step in that direction and he names people involved. He was forced to take the names out, but if you look at the index to his memoirs you will see that the name Jimmy Goldsmith features there but if you look up the biography text it's gone.

I remember the day well. The book was about to be sent out to bookshops and we were told by the *Daily Telegraph*'s libel lawyers that a page had to be removed – they were serialising the book the next day. It ended up being a page one news story and we had to send all the books down to a warehouse in Cornwall for them to replace the offending page. Not part of the game plan at all. I can't confirm what Heseltine says about James Goldsmith, but he is probably right about the index. One other thing I remember is being at a small private dinner in October 1985 at which one of Michael Heseltine's senior civil servants was present. He was adamant that Heseltine was looking for an issue to resign over. We all pooh-poohed the very thought, yet three months later he was gone. Coincidence? You decide.

OLDER CANDIDATES – DON'T FORGET THE WRINKLIES!
THURSDAY 19 JANUARY

Having reached the ripe old age of forty-three I find that the leader of my Party is four years younger than me. What hope is there?!

Will the Conservative Party come to mirror society's obsession with youth and decide to pick its Parliamentary candidates who are broadly speaking on the right side of forty? If it does, it will be making a profound mistake, and ignoring a huge well of talent that is just waiting to be tapped. In many ways the mistake has already been made, in that we already tend to ignore anyone over fifty, let alone, God forbid, anyone approaching sixty. That's got to change if we are to reflect the society in which we live and use all the talent available to us. At the last election there were very few candidates in target seats over the age of sixty – Stanley Johnson and Brian Binley are the obvious ones. There were very few over fifty. At the 2001 election Angela Watkinson was the only new MP over the age of sixty. None of these politicians decided to go into Parliament expecting to be Prime Minister, or even a minister. It's not a prerequisite for the job. Instead of the Party's current obsession with meeting every minority target going, it should be focusing on a forgotten group of people – those who have 'made it' and want to give something back. We should be identifying successful businessmen in their fifties, retired chief constables, retired service personnel, charity chief executives, social entrepreneurs who've been there, done that. What about the likes of retired sportspeople and Conservative supporters like Trevor Brooking, Graham Gooch or Ian Botham? Imagine Graham Gooch standing in a marginal seat like Thurrock or Basildon, or Ian Botham standing in Batley & Spen. Wouldn't they do better than a 26-year-old ex-CCO apparatchik? You bet they would. Most of these groups of people have the time and money to commit to the task – and believe me, having been a (albeit unsuccessful) candidate in a marginal seat I know just what time pressures there are, and the amount of money it costs. Until you've done it you just have no idea. I reckon it cost me the best part of £30,000.

What we really need in the Parliamentary Conservative Party is a mix of talents, backgrounds, experience and idealism. I suspect I am not alone in wondering if that balance is right at the moment. A growing number, and indeed proportion, of MPs in each of the political parties go into Parliament only ever having worked in politics, cocooned in a surreal existence without having been sullied by the extremities of the outside world. We may all be in this together, but without the right skill mix we may not be quite as successful as we'd like to be. We need to get it right next time, because if we don't we'll be a poorer government for it. Of course we need young idealists, but we also need people with a wide range of experience and these may tend to be people over the age of fifty. It is perfectly possible that MPs elected at the next election could be appointed as junior ministers in their first week. So it's up to constituencies, especially in 'safe' seats or the top target seats, to choose candidates who could be expected to run the country from week one. These people need to have experience of the world, of running things, of leading teams, of inspiring their colleagues. So how do we go about attracting a range of older applicants to apply to go on the Candidates List now?[†]

Nobody quite knows how the so-called 'A' List will work. People are naturally suspicious about it but until we see the detail no one can know. However it is constructed and operated a key priority has to be not to lose the talents of those not on it. But it must also not be seen as a barrier over which the over-fifties cannot jump. Let me use Stanley Johnson as an example. If the 'A' List had been operating at the last election, would he have even bothered to become a candidate? We'll never know, but whatever happens in the future, the Stanley Johnsons of this world must not feel that the Conservative Party is seeking to exclude them. I would like to see Francis Maude set up an Older Candidates Task Force whose remit would be to identify people whose shoulder could be tapped. These may be people who would never have considered becoming an MP in a million years but just by putting the thought into their heads we might ignite a spark. The hit rate may not be huge, but just think of the benefits we could all experience if we tried it. Some years ago Peta Buscombe was appointed a vice-chairman of the Party to identify leading professional women to stand for Parliament. Francis Maude could do worse than make a similar appointment in this area – a sort of Third Age Ambassador with a remit stretching more widely than just attracting candidates. So yes, let's have more women candidates, let's have more ethnic minority and gay candidates. But let's have people with a few wrinkles too.

---

† This is a list of centrally approved candidates which Conservative Central Office gives to local associations to select from.

THE DAVID DAVIS CAMPAIGN LAST SUPPER
FRIDAY 20 JANUARY

A couple of nights ago Andrew Mitchell (DD's Campaign Manager) organised an excellent dinner to say thanks to all those of us who worked on the David Davis campaign. It was held at Gran Paradiso in Victoria and attended by thirty or so MPs and staffers. It can fairly be said that a riotous time was had by all, although perhaps not on the scale of a night out at Annabel's.

Moving swiftly on, the evening started with a drinks sesh which was dominated by discussions about why Derek Conway was the only person present without a tie. There were also musings about the absence of stalwart supporter David Ruffley, until some unkind wag pointed out there must be a Cameron Campaign dinner on at the same time.[†] The meal itself was regularly interrupted by paper darts flying across the table from the direction of Eric Forth.[‡] I speculated that this was a particularly untimely occasion to be securing thirty names.[§] Much tutting all round.

Andrew Mitchell made a hilarious speech laced with gallows humour. He showed us a Christmas card he had received with the message 'A Christmas & New Year Message to All Conservatives from Bob Geldof'. Inside were the words 'FUCK OFF!'

Andrew was followed by DD, who took the Geldof story on a stage further. He too had received the card and thought it a little odd, to say the least, so he called Bob Geldof on his mobile and Bob denied all knowledge. Indeed, he wasn't best pleased that someone should impersonate him. So they collectively decided to report the matter to Inspector Knacker of the Yard. Only later did it transpire that one of DD's chief MP supporters, and a particularly gifted user of Photoshop, was to blame. Quite how true the bit about reporting it to the police was, I'm not sure – or, quite frankly, any of the rest of it – but it gave everyone a good laugh.

DD issued a rallying call to everyone to ensure that David Cameron received their full support and this received a genuine cheer. He ended up proposing a toast. Everyone raised their glasses. 'To the end of Blairism,' said DD. 'To the end of Blairism,' bellowed

---

† Ruffley was rumoured to have offered his support to the Cameron campaign while publicly supporting Davis.

‡ Conservative MP for Bromley & Chislehurst 1997–2006, Forth died in 2006.

§ Thirty signatures would have been needed to trigger a new leadership election.

everyone else. 'Especially in the Conservative Party,' shrilled Eric Forth! You just can't keep a good man down! I left at around 11.30, but I'm told a dozen of them were still to be found guzzling at 2.30 in the morning. Good job Andrew Neil wasn't there or Christ knows where they would have ended up...

RONALD REAGAN REMEMBERED
SATURDAY 21 JANUARY

Today is a very special day. Twenty-five years ago today Ronald Reagan was sworn in as President of the United States. A great man, a great visionary, a great leader of a great country. If you're ever visiting Los Angeles make sure you visit the Reagan Library in Simi Valley. I spent a fantastic day there about ten years ago. However, the best Presidential Library is the Nixon Library and Birthplace in Yorba Linda, also just outside L.A. I expected to spend a morning there and ended up spending the whole day, and going back for a few hours the next. Call me sad, if you like. In contrast, the Kennedy Library in Boston is deeply disappointing. Little to see, little content and all in all rather tedious. A few years ago I thought about organising a trip to the US for a group of a dozen political anoraks to visit about a dozen of the Presidential Libraries. I worked out an itinerary but the whole thing would have cost about £4,000 each.

MARK OATEN – WHO'S NEXT TO FALL IN THE LIB DEM SCANDAL STAKES?
SUNDAY 22 JANUARY

Before you rush to judge him too quickly, imagine how Mark Oaten must have felt when he opened his eyes this morning.[†] More importantly, imagine how his wife felt. Yes, this is a political scandal of the first order, but more immediately it's a human tragedy. The TV pundits have already been hard at it, some saying they can't understand what all the fuss is about and others asking how on earth he felt he could stand for the leadership of the Party when he

---

† The *News of the World* reported on a relationship between Oaten and a rent boy.

must have known this might emerge. Ann Leslie on Sky speculated about the thirst for danger and she's probably nearest the mark. I just don't buy Helena Kennedy's argument on *Sunday AM* that this has nothing to do with anyone but Oaten and his family. But nor do I think he deserves to be ripped to shreds.

Following on from Kennedy's alcoholism, yesterday's revelations about Lord McNally[†] and now Mark Oaten, there is undoubtedly an appetite in the media for more Lib Dem scandals. So if I were someone in a prominent position in the Party and I knew I had some skeletons, I'd certainly be feeling a little nervous this morning. Guido[‡] speculates that on this basis the betting markets are shifting from Simon Hughes to Chris Huhne (who, incidentally, put in another good performance on *Sunday AM*). I'm not sure about this. But remember what the media were like in the 1990s in the infamous Back to Basics episode when they exposed one supposed scandal after another. It culminated in the rather ridiculous resignation of Tory MP Hartley Booth who had written a poem to his researcher. He hadn't even touched her, yet he was forced to resign as a lowly PPS. I know of one prominent Lib Dem (not a leadership contender) who may well have cause to be more nervous than others.

SIMON HUGHES DESERVES BOTH OUR CONDEMNATION AND UNDERSTANDING
THURSDAY 26 JANUARY

And then there were two. Only Chris Huhne and Ming Campbell remain as serious contenders in the Lib Dem leadership race following Simon Hughes's outing in today's *Sun*. It's not the fact that he's gay that's the problem. It's the fact that, like Mark Oaten and Charles Kennedy, he has lied. Although you wouldn't know it from his comments on the media today. Let's be clear, when questioned by *The Independent* he didn't hedge around the question, he said quite categorically he was not gay, not once but twice. He repeated the answer in another newspaper. That, in my book, is a lie. I was on Radio 5 Live this morning talking about this with gay Lib Dem MP Stephen Williams. He seemed outraged that Simon Hughes could

---

† McNally revealed he had been dependent on alcohol in the 1980s.
‡ Guido Fawkes, blogger.

be accused of lying. Indeed, he said that Charles Kennedy hadn't lied over his drinking. He must be living on a parallel planet. To people out in the real world, the fact that politicians don't tell the truth is far more serious than what they get up to in the bedroom. As I said on 5 Live this morning, the most damaging aspect of the Oaten and Hughes sagas is that young men all round the country who are firmly in the closet will probably remain there for that bit longer because Simon Hughes's behaviour indicates a feeling of shame. The other aspect to this is Simon Hughes's behaviour during his by-election campaign against Peter Tatchell in 1983. I heard Tatchell on 5 Live Drive this evening and he was quietly impressive in his protection of Simon Hughes. He accepted his apology and praised him for his voting record on gay rights and human rights issues. Hughes was a young man at that time and probably didn't control the direction of his campaign, which included the infamous 'Simon Hughes – the straight candidate' poster.

There's no question that Hughes is a man of courage. At great personal risk to himself he appeared in court to give evidence against a gang of thugs and contributed to them being put away for a long time. He received threats of physical violence and I am told death threats. Despite this he persevered and justice prevailed.

We must also remember that he is fifty-four years old and for him to come out now will have been psychologically trying to say the least. I know myself the traumas one goes through when one 'comes out', particularly with regard to the reaction of one's family and friends. When I decided to go into politics, I came out before being selected as a candidate. I remember having to tell friends of twenty years' standing something they may have suspected but we had never talked about. Without exception their reaction was amazing and it made me think I should have done it years earlier. But I had regarded it as no one's business but my own. But if you go into politics you know what can happen. You know that journalists are always looking out for a saucy story, and being gay still provides them with the salacious headlines they love. I made up my mind that the only way to avoid the 7 p.m. phone call on a Saturday night from the *News of the World* was to be open. If people couldn't cope with it, well that was their problem. But Simon Hughes couldn't have done that in 1983. Since then he has been circumspect and avoided the issue. Many people in Parliament suspected he was gay and he had been seen in gay bars and nightclubs. Apparently in his constituency it was an open secret. And that's how he would have preferred it to stay. He didn't want to worry his ageing mother with it and his Christian activities mitigated against making any form of public statement. I totally understand that. Where he went wrong was to give interviews to two newspapers where he told an untruth. Or perhaps where he went wrong was to stand for the Lib Dem leadership in the first place, if he wasn't willing to be open. But we also have to face the fact that if Mark Oaten hadn't been outed on Sunday, Simon Hughes probably wouldn't have been today. My great fear now is that the media smell blood. I wouldn't be at all surprised if there were further revelations between now and Sunday. If I were an MP with a personal secret I don't think I'd look forward to answering my phone on Saturday.

So is Simon Hughes finished as a leadership candidate? I think it's difficult to tell, but if I had to fall off the fence, I'd say yes. I am not familiar enough with the grassroots Lib Dem members who have the vote to make a judgement on whether being gay will lose him any votes. I suspect it may cost him a few in rural areas, but the issue of having told a lie will cost him more. Alternatively, depending on how he copes with the next few weeks he may get quite a decent sympathy vote. Time will tell.

But just spare a thought for two other men tonight – firstly, Charles Kennedy. He can be forgiven if he has a slight feeling of 'serves 'em all right'. And finally, Mark Oaten, who has reportedly been told by his wife that their marriage is over. No one can derive any pleasure from seeing a man's life fall apart in the space of five days, no matter what he has done. I just hope he has some good friends to count on.

TOP TEN THINGS WHICH WOULD BE DIFFERENT IF MY JACK RUSSELL, GIO, WAS PRIME MINISTER
FRIDAY 27 JANUARY

---

1. Lib Dem HQ replaced by giant fire hydrant
2. Abolition of Pets Means Prizes
3. Capital punishment restored for Dale Winton
4. Doggy door at the front of No. 10
5. Dog biscuits on the NHS
6. Compulsory sterilisation for cats

7.   Life sentences for tail dockers
8.   Battersea Dogs' Home to replace Chequers as PM's country residence (Gio was born there!)
9.   First Lady to be renamed First Bitch
10. PM to have mandatory right to shag the legs of all fellow Cabinet ministers

MEETING THE 7/7 CHALLENGE†
FRIDAY 7 JULY

Oh well, here goes...

7 things to do before I die
1.   Get elected
2.   Write a proper book
3.   Persuade my partner to take more holidays
4.   Have enough money so I don't continually worry about it
5.   Learn to play the piano
6.   Finish the Robert Caro books on LBJ
7.   Learn to speak Dutch

7 things I cannot do
1.   Anything slowly
2.   Tie my shoelaces properly. Really
3.   Whistle
4.   Resist reality TV programmes
5.   Make my mobile phone receive email
6.   Keep anything tidy for very long
7.   Keep a gadget twelve months without replacing it with a newer version

7 things that attract me to London
1.   The Houses of Parliament
2.   The Dickensian feel of the streets around Shad Thames
3.   West Ham United
4.   The buzz of Soho
5.   Gotham City aka Docklands

---

†   This is what is known as a blog meme. You are nominated to answer questions from a fellow blogger and then you nominate five others.

6. Nightlife, not that I often partake in it
7. TV and radio studios

7 things I often say
1. You have to be kidding me
2. Das gibt's doch nicht
3. I'm forever blowing bubbles, pretty bubbles in the air
4. The cheque's in the post
5. Big Mac and large fries, please
6. Gio, be a good boy and give it back
7. Jesus wept

7 books that I love
1. *Animal Farm* by George Orwell
2. *Watership Down* by Richard Adams
3. *In the Arena* by Richard Nixon
4. *The Insider* by Piers Morgan
5. *The Rats* by James Herbert
6. *Breaking the Code* by Gyles Brandreth
7. *Diaries* by Alan Clark

7 movies I watch over and over again
1. *Airplane*
2. *Independence Day*
3. *Strictly Ballroom*
4. *Muriel's Wedding*
5. *Back to the Future*
6. *Thief of Hearts*
7. *Four Weddings and a Funeral*

THE DELUSIONS OF A WEST HAM FAN
SUNDAY 29 JANUARY

Having witnessed West Ham's 4–2 drubbing of Blackburn yesterday (what a shame Jack Straw was in Davos...), I dreamt last night that the Hammers reached the FA Cup Final and became the first team to win at the new Wembley. It would be fitting for them to do so as they were also the first team to win at the Old Wembley in 1923 when they played Bolton Wanderers in the famous White Horse final. And we all know that the god of football likes coincidences. Imagine the paroxysms it would send John Motson into. 'Well yes indeed Gary, the omens are good for West Ham, in 1923 they had a white horse, in 2006 they've got a manager with white hair. The Hamas won an election in Palestine this year, will the Hammers be lucky in the Cup? Gary, they'll be cheering on the streets of Teddy Sheringham on a Christian Dailly basis if the Hammers triumph today. Back to the studio.' Sorry, I got a bit carried away there...

But there are other omens...

1. When the Hammers won the Cup in 1975, Alan Taylor scored six goals. West Ham's current manager is called Alan.

2. When West Ham won the Cup in 1980 they beat Ipswich along the way. This year they've beaten their East Anglian rivals Norwich.

Desperate? Moi? I'm sure in the end reality will dawn in the line from 'I'm Forever Blowing Bubbles' which reads, 'just like my dreams, they fade and die'. As a West Ham fan, I'm used to it.

YOU'RE S**T AND YOU KNOW YOU ARE
WEDNESDAY 1 FEBRUARY

I type this as West Ham are about to kick off at Highbury, so excuse any foul language that might emanate from my fingertips. In case you're wondering I'm not at Highbury, I'm watching it on Sky! To take a break from politics for a moment I thought I'd share some particularly funny football chants that have come my way this afternoon from a mate.

Apparently this was the chant to the 'Lord of the Dance' tune at Man United the other day:

> Park, Park, Where-ever you may be
> You eat dogs in your home country
> But it could be worse –
> You could be a Scouse
> Eating rats in your council house

Newcastle fans towards Sunderland fans:

> Going down, going down, going down

Sunderland fans reply:

> So are we, so are we, so are we.

Charlton fans to Shaun Wright-Phillips:
Where's your real dad, where's your real dad!?

Toon fans to Jimmy Floyd Hasselbaink (he even laughed!):

> You're just a fat Eddie Murphy

To the tune of 'When the Saints', West Brom sang:

> The premier league (the premier league),
> Is upside down (is upside down),
> The premier league is upside down.
> We're up the top and Chelsea's at the bottom,
> The premier league is upside down

Then a few seconds later:

> Champions! ... Champions! ... Champions!

A song about Tim Howard's Tourette's syndrome in the style of 'Chim-Chiminey':

> Tim timminy, Tim timminy, Tim Tim Tirooo
> We've got Tim Howard and he says F*CK YOU!

Sung by Birmingham fans after Heskey started banging in the goals at St Andrew's:

> There's only one Emile Heskey,
> one Emile Heskey,
> he used to be shite,
> But now he's all right,
> Walking in a Heskey wonderland

To the tune of 'Rebel Rebel':

Neville Neville, you play in defence,
Neville Neville, your play is immense,
Neville Neville, like Jacko you're bad,
Neville Neville is the name of your dad

Celtic fans to Andy Goram after it's revealed the chubby keeper was diagnosed with schizophrenia.

Two Andy Gorams, there's only two Andy Gorams

THE SEVENTEEN-YEAR-LONG SILENCE OF SIR HARRY KERBY MP
THURSDAY 2 FEBRUARY

Yesterday I had a delightful lunch at the Reform Club with a journalist from the 'old school'. We were talking about Howard Flight's sacking in Arundel & South Downs and he told me a wonderful tale about how parliamentary selections were run in the 'good' old days. In 1954 the seat's Conservative MP, W. C. Cuthbert, announced he would not be standing at the next election so Arundel & Shoreham Conservative Association advertised for applicants. One of them was Sir Harry Kerby, but he didn't meet with much favour and the Association decided to go for a female applicant. However, Mr Cuthbert rather inconveniently died at this juncture which meant a by-election would have to be held. Unfortunately for the lady in question, she had chosen that particular moment to go on a lecture tour to the United States and, try as they might, the Association couldn't contact her. So in desperation they gave up and decided to go for what they saw as the solidity of Sir Harry Kerby. Sir Harry was duly elected and spent seventeen years in the House of Commons until his death in 1971. My journalist friend tells me he never actually made a speech. I wonder if his constituents noticed. I also wonder who the lady was who should have been the MP and what became of her.

INDY SPECULATES ON CAMERON'S GAY LIST
SUNDAY 5 FEBRUARY

Today's *Independent on Sunday* carries an article about a supposed gay list being drawn up by CCO. Marie Woolf, the paper's political editor, suggests that Nicholas Boles, Margot James, Ashley Crossley and, ahem, a certain Iain Dale will be given 'preferential treatment'. I normally shy away from 'pigeon-holing' articles such as this, but I wanted to make clear to her that the 'A' List system does not mean so-called 'preferential treatment' and I certainly wouldn't either expect or want any. I explained to her that 550 people had been sent the application form, not 'the chosen few'. I am quoted as saying 'I am going to apply to be on the "A" List. But everyone has to be on it on merit. We don't want any kind of tokenism ... I want to be selected because of who I am, and what I can do.'

WHY CONSERVATIVES SHOULD BOYCOTT THE CARLTON CLUB

Last night I broke the habit of a lifetime and attended an event at the Carlton Club. It was a fundraising dinner for a female Conservative marginal seat candidate, who's a friend of mine, with William Hague as guest speaker. Why do I say 'break the habit of a lifetime'? Because up to now I've refused to enter the hallowed portals because the Carlton still refuses to admit women as full members. In this day and age it's a disgrace. Their defence is that it's a private club and they can do what they like, and in any case women are allowed in the club as associate members. Big deal. They're right that they can do what they like, but the Carlton is seen as the ancestral home of the Conservative Party and, in my view, until it changes its policy Conservatives should have nothing to do with it. So why did I break my self-imposed rule? Simple. I said I would go to the dinner to support my friend before I knew where the dinner was taking place. Yes, I could have pulled out, but it gave me the opportunity to canvass opinion among my fellow diners about the Carlton, and every single person agreed with me its policy was fundamentally wrong and they felt profoundly uncomfortable being there. So come on, Carlton Club, the least you could do is enter the twentieth century, if not the twenty-first. You might well lose a few of the more fuddy-duddy people among your membership, but you might then attract a new breed of members who would breathe some life into the Club. I'm now battening down the hatches and preparing for the barrage...

A TRIBUTE TO NORWICH CONSERVATIVE ACTIVIST MARJORIE LLOYD
THURSDAY 23 FEBRUARY

I've just had a very sad phone call from a good friend in Norwich to tell me that a lady called Marjorie Lloyd has died. I doubt whether anyone reading this will have met her, but she was one of a kind. I first met her in the mid-1980s when I was working for Patrick Thompson, the then MP for Norwich North. She replied to an In Touch leaflet and offered to deliver a whole housing estate for us. As the 1987 election approached, she came to work in the party HQ and was an invaluable member of our team. Whenever I went back to Norwich I tried to visit her. She was always someone who knew how to look on the bright side of life. She loved her bowls and was the most active 84-year-old I have ever met. Even on Friday, she was playing tennis! She collapsed on Sunday on her way home from church with a massive stroke. I'll remember her with a great deal of affection.

A LESSON IN ENGLISH FOR SEÑOR BECKHAM
SUNDAY 26 FEBRUARY

Fantastic quote from David Beckham in the *News of the World* today, explaining that he can't do his six-year-old son's maths homework. 'Maths is totally done differently to what I was teached when I was at school.' English too, apparently.

ANNE DIAMOND AND MY NUDE INTERVIEW
MONDAY 6 MARCH

I've always had a bit of a soft spot for Anne Diamond. In fact I have just finished reading her autobiography. It's quite a traumatic read in places, as she details the terrible death of her son Sebastian, who she found dead in his cot one morning. She's obviously never completely got over it. Who would? She and Nick Owen were a superb duo and sparked off each other brilliantly and it's a shame she's no longer on our TV screens. I was interviewed by her on her breakfast show on BBC Oxford a few weeks ago. I had to laugh when she wrote in her book that she once interviewed Desmond Tutu live on the phone and in the end he had to ask to finish the interview as he had just got out of the shower and was dripping wet. She wrote: 'I think that's the only nude interview I have ever done.' Well, no, Anne, actually it isn't. I hate to tell her but when she interviewed me about why anyone would ever want to go into politics, I too was 'sans clothes'. It was ten past seven in the morning, after all!

STRANDED ON THE M25
WEDNESDAY 8 MARCH

I'm in Norwich at the moment, having just attended a funeral. Three and a half hours it took to get here ... I was stuck on the M25 in the slow lane when I noticed a woman in the fast lane who had steam coming out of the back of her MG. She got out to look at it, leaving her elderly mother looking rather fearful, but not a single person near her made any effort to go and help her. So I got out of my car, crossed two lanes of traffic and pushed her car onto the hard shoulder for her. Again, no one else bothered to get out to help. In fact, they appeared considerably angry that I had left my car and were trying to manoeuvre round it. What has happened to the British public? At least one mother brought her son up to know when to come to someone's rescue. I feel very angry about it!

THE MAN RESPONSIBLE FOR THE RISE OF EDWARD HEATH
WEDNESDAY 8 MARCH

Sir Walter Bromley-Davenport was the Tory MP for Knutsford, and an opposition whip shortly after the war. Once, seeing an unfamiliar figure leaving the building, he assumed this was a Tory MP trying to evade a three-line whip. When the man refused to stop, Sir Walter kicked him down the stairs. It turned out to be the Belgian ambassador. The consequent vacancy in the whips' office was filled by Lt Col. Edward Heath, in his first frontbench job. The Belgian ambassador has a lot to answer for.

MY TOP TEN POLITICAL HEROES
THURSDAY 9 MARCH

Some of my political heroes won't surprise you, but others will. This sort of thing is very personal and any such list will inevitably be dominated by contemporary figures from one's own political life, and also heroes in history. Mine is no different.

1. **Margaret Thatcher**
   That's surprised you hasn't it?! Mrs T inspired me to get involved in politics and she was the greatest peacetime PM of the last century. A giant among pygmies. Tony Blair would not have been possible without her. Her achievements are huge, but restoring Britain's self-belief was the greatest.
2. **Winston Churchill**
   His inspirational leadership saved the nation in its darkest hour. A flawed man in many ways, he rose to the occasion and knew what had to be done.
3. **Ronald Reagan**
   A man whose vision saved the world from nuclear catastrophe and, with Mikhail Gorbachev and Margaret Thatcher, ended the Cold War. Much underestimated by Europeans, he tapped into the American psyche in a way few other recent Presidents have been able to emulate.
4. **Konrad Adenauer**
   Achieved the impossible and transformed West Germany from a war-torn wreck to the economic powerhouse of Europe within twenty years. The true father of modern-day Germany.
5. **Mikhail Gorbachev**
   Had the foresight to realise the Soviet Union had to reform and that the arms race was heading to oblivion. Now reviled in his own country, he deserves the respect of those in others. He was by no means a convert to capitalism, but he knew the Soviet Union's command economy was a total failure.
6. **David Lloyd George**
   A politician whose failings were legion, but whose talents were

many. Imagine how he would have coped with the Committee on Standards in Public Life! A great war leader and an innovative Chancellor.

7. **Otto von Bismarck**

   He achieved the impossible and united the disparate German states. Showed a remarkable talent for diplomacy and had a great military brain.

8. **Richard Nixon**

   Yes, you read correctly. You can't take Watergate out of the equation, but Nixon's achievements in other spheres were huge. He is one of my favourite political authors and his book *In the Arena* is a must-read for any politico.

9. **Roger Douglas**

   Douglas was Finance Minister in one of the most revolutionary governments of the twentieth century – in New Zealand. He was a pioneer in deregulation and privatisation and his legacy will be felt for decades. One of the few people to understand the opportunities provided by the free market.

10. **Tony Benn**

    I never thought I could ever agree with much of what Tony Benn said, but his views on many aspects of the constitution, Europe and the supremacy of Parliament strike a chord with many on the right nowadays. He is one of the few politicians who can engage the interest of the public.

A FUNNY THING HAPPENED THIS MORNING
FRIDAY 10 MARCH

You know those weird coincidences that you just can't explain? Well, a funny thing happened to me this morning. I had just finished an interview with News 24 from the BBC Tunbridge Wells studios on the death of John Profumo and I was walking back to the car. I put my iPod on and, bearing in mind it has nearly 11,000 tracks on it, guess what the first song to appear was? Dusty Springfield singing the theme from *Scandal*, the movie about the Profumo affair. Spooky eh?

MY NIGHT WITH CLIFF RICHARD (AND LULU!)
SUNDAY 2 APRIL

Last night I attended what must surely be one of the parties of the year, if not the decade – Michael Ashcroft's sixtieth birthday bash. It was a total privilege to be there. However I describe it, I won't be able to do justice to the evening. If I live to be ninety I doubt whether I will attend another party that will ever come near it. The Grosvenor House Hotel ballroom area was done out as a tropical paradise, complete with palm trees. Almost the first person I saw was Cliff Richard. Those of you who know me well can imagine my reaction. I'm proud to say I am a total Cliff fan and have more than 100 Cliff CDs. But I was rendered untypically dumbstruck and didn't say anything to him! Go on, mock all you like – water off a duck's back! Cliff performed an impromptu rendition of 'Congratulations' for the birthday boy when the cake was wheeled out, and as he finished Denise van Outen jumped out of the cake and proceeded to perform a 'Marilynesque' version of 'Happy Birthday To You'. I imagine Michael's eyes were popping out of his head. Jasper Carrott compèred the whole evening, one highlight of which was a hilarious tour de force by William Hague. We were also treated to John Culshaw from *Dead Ringers*, Lulu (who I've never really liked, but she was superb!), the Band of the Scots Guards and, to round it off, Tom Jones, who performed seven or eight of his hits – not a dry seat in the house. I'm not really a Tom Jones fan, but it was quite something to witness, particularly when Christine Hamilton and half a dozen Tom Jones groupies got on stage with him! And on top of that, the evening raised more than £190,000 for Crimestoppers, a charity which Michael started in 1988. So, as I said at the beginning, a huge privilege to be there. If you were able to celebrate your sixtieth birthday by having four famous acts perform at your party, who would they be? I'd have Cliff, Sparks, Roxette and one of the girls from Abba. Well, two would be greedy, wouldn't it?!

LOST YOUR TICKET? DO I LOOK BOVVERED?
THURSDAY 20 APRIL

Alex Foster has a saga about his missed train today, so I thought I'd share my train ticket story with you too. Brace yourself. I arrived at Tonbridge station this morning in plenty of time to get the 8.02 to Charing Cross. Or so I thought. Only one of the ticket machines worked (better than the normal none) so I bought my ticket like the good little one-day-a-week commuter I am and proceeded to the barrier. I stuck my ticket into it and went to take it out ... only there was no ticket emerging from the slot. The two barrier staff were mystified. 'You can't have put a ticket in,' they chorused. 'Er, here's the return portion,' I protested. 'I don't think I've lost the outgoing ticket within the last eight feet.' They looked bemused. 'Well, we'll let you through. I'm sure it'll be OK at the other end,' one of them said. 'I think not. I want a replacement ticket, please,' I said, knowing what the Nazi guards are like at Charing X. 'We're not allowed to issue replacements,' said Jobsworth Number 1. 'No, we're not allowed to,' said his oppo, who reminded me of the thug on *Dick Emery* who was always saying: 'Dad, I fink we've got a problem.' In the end they agreed to give me a ticket receipt which said 'Machine mangled ticket' but I had got to the platform before I realised they'd stamped it with yesterday's date. Back up to the ticket office. I just managed to get the 8.12, making me ten minutes late for a meeting. All in a day's travel on South East Trains. Aren't you glad I shared that with you? Oh, and at Charing X? They never even looked at the bloody ticket...

NO WONDER SKY NEWSREADERS HAVE A PERMANENT SMILE ON THEIR FACES
MONDAY 24 APRIL

When I was on Sky on Saturday morning I had to be 'made up' – well, the wrinkles of forty-three years' hard living are beginning to show. But it's the first time I experienced Sky Make-Up's new gadget, which seems to blast your entire face with gunge. It sort of blows it on to you like an icy cold blow-torch. I read in *The Independent* media diary today that it is known among Sky news-readers as 'The Blow-Job Gun'. If only I'd known that at the time...

EXCLUSIVE: WHAT THE *MAIL ON SUNDAY* DIDN'T PRINT
MONDAY 1 MAY

Far from threatening to take the *Mail on Sunday* to the Press Complaints Commission, John Prescott should be sitting down tonight and writing a handwritten letter of thanks to their editor, Peter Wright. Because if the *Mail on Sunday* had printed the un-expurgated version of Tracey Temple's diary, Prescott would not only have been forced out of office by lunchtime yesterday, but his marriage would be over too. Why didn't they? Because it couldn't be printed in a mainstream Sunday newspaper. The journalists at Associated Newspapers are hopping mad at the way they're being painted – as if they're the guilty party. Yet it is their newspaper which has, admittedly in a weird sort of way, protected Prescott. I understand that the deleted pieces were 'beyond unflattering', 'very grim' and present an 'overall impression of ghastliness'. There are apparently references to the Deputy Prime Minister's use of Viagra (which didn't always work), the size of his, er, well, you can guess and his propensity to take his clothes off in his office. Mr Prescott should be very careful in issuing his threats about reporting the *Mail on Sunday* to the PCC. He wouldn't want to provoke even more unwelcome publicity, would he?

John Prescott Quote of the Day
Overheard in a Westminster bar: 'They say power is an aphrodisiac, but it ain't f***ing rohypnol!'

COMMENT ON JULIA GOLDSWORTHY
THURSDAY 4 MAY

While watching *Question Time*:
Me: Isn't that Julia Goldsworthy just appalling?
Partner: Yes, but she's got lovely hair.

I'VE GIVEN AWAY MY CUP FINAL TICKET!
SUNDAY 7 MAY

Next week's FA Cup Final will be an emotional occasion for the supporters of my own team, West Ham United, as it's the first time in twenty-six years they've played in it. But there are also some very unhappy Hammers due to the ridiculous allocation of 23,500 tickets each for both teams. Bearing in mind the stadium seats 74,500 one wonders where the other 26,500 tickets have gone

– no doubt to mates of the 'FA Suits'. Of the twelve people who hold season tickets in my block at Upton Park, I'm the only one to have managed to get a ticket. I spent an hour on the phone and on the internet to do so. My neighbour has had an Upton Park season ticket since 1958 and is distraught at not having got a ticket. So I've made the ultimate sacrifice and given him mine. What a fool. Anyone got a spare ticket?

THE 'A' LIST LETTER ARRIVES
WEDNESDAY 10 MAY

I heard this morning that I am not on the Conservative Party's 'A' List of candidates for the next election. I can't deny that I'm disappointed, but perhaps not wholly surprised. I'm afraid I shall be disappointing those who will be expecting me to get bitter and twisted about it. I am not going to say anything more, for the moment, because whatever I do say will be interpreted as 'sour grapes' and I really don't want that to happen. Obviously it has given me a lot to think about with regard to my own future in politics. I wish all those who have got onto the 'A' List the very best of luck.

Update: 6.13 p.m. Not all bad news today. I think I may have a ticket for the Cup Final after all. Which would I rather have had – a ticket for the Cup Final or being on the 'A' List? Hmmm. Difficult one, that.

Update: 6.20 p.m. I much enjoyed this post on Con-servativeHome from someone called Realist: 'Sure Iain Dale is a nice guy, but reading all the dedications on his blog about him not getting on, you would think Lady Thatcher had just died.' I said to a friend earlier today that having read the comments it feels like I am reading my own obituary! Very touched though.

Update: 7.30 p.m. Well, I never. *Channel 4 News* carried screen-shots of this blog and read out a couple of your comments about the fact I haven't made the 'A' List. What is the world coming to!

Update: 8.30 p.m. I've been asked to go on *Newsnight* tonight to talk about the 'A' List. I'll be on in a discussion with Sayeeda Warsi. I've thought long and hard about whether to do it. Don't expect toys to be thrown out of prams, but I have a few points I want to make. I don't normally get nervous about interviews ... but...

Update: 11.30 p.m. For those of you who missed *Newsnight*'s report on the 'A' List, featuring an interview with your humble servant. I admit to being extremely nervous about doing this interview because I feared accusations of 'sour grapes' and worse. It felt like walking a tightrope, but I felt I just had to speak up for the 400 or so colleagues who will have been feeling just as disappointed – if not worse – as me. As I say in the interview, I totally accept the referee's decision and I am genuinely not bitter about it, but I do think there are lessons to be learnt from this process.

MY FA CUP EMOTIONAL ROLLER COASTER
SATURDAY 13 MAY

I am in a bit of an emotional state as I type this. Firstly, let me say it was an absolute privilege to have attended one of the greatest FA Cup Finals in history. There were three winners in this game – Liverpool, West Ham and football itself. I spent most of the game on the verge of tears and could quite easily howl my eyes out now. I don't know how it appeared on TV but West Ham were superb for most of the game and were only outplayed by one player: Steven Gerrard. If he hadn't been in the Liverpool team the result today would have been very different. My team did its supporters proud and I salute every single one of them. It was a team performance and I can't think of a single player who had a bad game. Despite conceding three goals you can't fault either Shaka Hislop or the defence for the goals. Carl Fletcher and Nigel Reo-Coker were outstanding in midfield and Yossi Benayoun was a constant problem for the Liverpool defenders. And Lionel Scaloni had a great game, even if it was from his clearance that Gerrard equalised in the ninetieth minute. I think when Steven Gerrard scored that third goal we all knew the writing was on the wall. Somehow the crowd's mood changed. But even then we nearly won it in the last minute of extra time. We hit the post and if Marlon Harewood hadn't been crippled he would have undoubtedly scored the rebound. It's the same old story of having to take your chances when they present themselves. I cannot describe how I feel at the moment. I don't actually feel as if we lost the game. And, to be honest, if we had won the penalty shoot-out I am not sure I would have felt we had won it 'properly'. That's why everyone came out of that game on top. And next season we're in Europe. Who would have thought it back in August. I remember the first forty-five minutes of our opening home game against Blackburn and thinking we would be facing a relegation fight. Far from it. Top Ten finish. FA Cup finalists. Qualified for Europe. And Alan Pardew must surely be the Manager of the Year. And tonight? For someone who doesn't drink, I think I am going to get very, very drunk...

MY 'A' LIST ARTICLE IN THE *SUNDAY TIMES*
SUNDAY 14 MAY

The *Sunday Times* has published an article by me on the 'A' List today. Here's the unedited version:

It wasn't a political academic this week who told the Conservative Party the scale of the challenge facing it, it was its leader. David Cameron said: 'We need to win over 120 seats; wipe out a third of the Lib Dems; win back seats in Scotland. It's a big task.' He's right. But in little more than five months he has transformed the Party's electoral prospects and many of us believe that we can for the first time in ten years see an electoral victory on the horizon. That in itself is a major step forward. But to do that the Party has got to ensure that its cadre of Parliamentary Candidates is enthused, and then given the tools and support they will need to finish the job. There is little doubt that the 550 people on the Party's list of approved candidates – in effect, the Party's 'Shock Troops' – who worked so hard to ensure that the Party achieved its superb local election results on 5 May are enthused and relishing the battles ahead. Or at least, we ought to be. But on Wednesday those 500 people (of which I was one) received a letter which told us whether we had made it onto the 'A' List of 104 Candidates who are more or less guaranteed selection in a winnable seat. By applying to get onto that list we all accepted the rules and I make absolutely no complaint that I was not among the chosen few. I abide by the referee's decision and certainly won't be launching a Tottenham Hotspur-type appeal claiming I had eaten the wrong type of lasagne on the day of my interview. Having seen some of the outstanding names, including some high fliers close to David Cameron, who haven't made it onto the 'A' List, who am I to complain?

At the age of forty-three I now have a big decision to make, and my decision is one which more than 400 of my colleagues are also wrestling with. Do we read the writing on the wall and walk away from a political career, or do we stay on the Candidates' List and work even harder to ensure that the powers that be will see the merits of our case when they come to top up the 'A' List in July? Some made an instant decision and immediately resigned from the Approved List.

As well as huge disappointment there is undoubtedly an understandable feeling of betrayal and bitterness. On my blog I've had so many messages of commiseration that at times it has felt like I've attended my own political funeral. I've had candidates on the phone to me who have been in tears. They question why they worked their guts out, invested thousands of hours of their time and thousands of pounds of their money in a Party which appears to cast them aside. Such emotion is natural and I am sure that Bernard Jenkin, the Party's Vice Chairman in charge of candidates, will understand it.

The worrying thing for everyone is the number of younger, thirty-something candidates I know of who are considering walking away. There are some very bruised egos and I have lost count of the number of conversations I have had this week urging my younger colleagues not to give up. The fact is, they have several more electoral chances ahead of them, whereas people of my age and older have (or had) only one.

Those thinking of walking away should have a very close look at the first tranche of thirty seats which the 'A' List will be applying for. It is not quite what it seems. Many of the seats are ones which people on the 'A' List fought last time and quite rightly will be encouraged to fight again – George Freeman in Stevenage, Ali Miraj in Watford, Hannah Hall in Luton North, Mark Menzies in Selby, Mark Coote in Hastings and Nick Boles in Hove are all candidates who fall into this category. Many of the more attractive marginal seats will come in the second tranche.

What unites everyone in the Party is the desire to see more women candidates selected – and selected in winnable seats. But is the 'A' List the right way to achieve this laudable aim? In the short term maybe, but in some ways it's attacking the problem from the wrong end. We will only ever come close to achieve parity and equality between men and women when we encourage enough women to come forward as candidates to ensure equality of numbers of the wider Approved List of 600 people. David Cameron will really know he's achieved something when he has recruited 300 women onto the main list.

At the last election we had 1,150 people on the Approved List with only 150 women. It is a wonder, with that ratio, that as many as 17 per cent of our selected candidates were women. What we need now is a professional headhunting approach, and that's why Anne Jenkin's WomenToWin initiative is to be welcomed. If women don't come forward voluntarily we need people who will go around tapping them on the shoulder and encouraging them to think about a career in politics.

Let's face it, if you put 100 different people in a room and asked them to come up with an 'A' List of 100 star candidates, each of them would come up with a different list. But we should be open and transparent about who's on it and why they're on it. If the Party wants to reinforce its 'Change Agenda' it should publish the hundred names. Indeed, it should be shouting about them from the rooftops. The influential ConservativeHome.com website has already published fifty of them within forty-eight hours. Far better for the Party to do it themselves and demonstrate to the world the breadth and range of people on the list. But it's not all about getting more women candidates.

We need an 'A' List of northern candidates, of Scottish and Welsh candidates, who can help rejuvenate the Party in our cities. We want to see more people with public service and public sector backgrounds making it. By necessity this means that new people, who sometimes have no background at all in the Party – and may only have been members for a matter of months – edge aside those who have given much of their adult lives to serving a Party they love. It's easy to pick on actors and environmentalists but it's missing the point. Any Party that is seeking to renew itself needs an injection of fresh talent. My only worry is that the 'newbies' are not totally aware of what they are letting themselves in for. It takes a huge commitment to be a candidate three years out from an election – in terms of both time and money. It's a very hard slog, totally without glamour albeit with a huge reward for success at the end of it. To those who have been given the chance to reap that reward, I wish them all the best. To those who haven't, I say 'keep at it'. In the end we all want the same thing – to see David Cameron on the doorsteps of No. 10.

ERIC FORTH HAS DIED
THURSDAY 18 MAY

I don't mind admitting I'm in tears as I type this. I have just learnt that my friend Eric Forth died last night. I just cannot believe it.

Eric Forth: A Personal Obituary

Eric Forth, who died last night, was someone I am proud to call a friend. Indeed, if you were a friend of Eric's he was the most loyal friend you could wish for. And the mark of a loyal friend is that he will tell you the truth, even when it is uncomfortable. I am sure his career will be covered in many other obituaries so I will restrict myself to some personal observations. I first met Eric at a Bournemouth party conference in 2002. He, David Davis, Eric's wife, Carroll, and I went for dinner at a restaurant Eric knew in Poole. Up until then I only knew what I had heard about Eric. He was a wonderful dinner companion, a great raconteur and slightly to my surprise I found him to be a great political strategist with an acute political brain.

Eric had a nineteenth-century approach to constituency politics. He never, ever held a surgery, yet his majority increased at every election. He believed he was in politics to be a parliamentarian, not a quasi social worker. And even his most bitter opponents would admit he was a parliamentarian of the first order. He knew how to work the system and to hold the Executive to account. He and John Bercow did more to hold the 1997–2001 Blair administration to account than anyone. They proved to be a real thorn in the side of many a Labour minister.

The job Eric loved more than any was his tenure as shadow Leader of the House of Commons under IDS. He was a true House of Commons man and he made Business Questions a 'must attend' session for MPs of all parties. He knew the writing was on the wall when Michael Howard became leader and took his departure from the shadow Cabinet with good grace.

Eric loved America. He married Carroll, who hails from the US, and they had a holiday home in Florida, where they spent an increasing amount of time.

Eric was hardly what one would call a classic 'Cameroon', yet I know the two of them got on rather well. It is to Eric's credit that over the five months of David Cameron's leadership he largely kept his reservations to himself. David Cameron made a point of talking to Eric and explaining what he was doing and Eric respected it. His views on such things as the 'A' List were more or less unprintable, and it is deeply ironic that it is from the 'A' List that his successor will be chosen. Part of me thinks he would be chuckling at that – as well as throwing his garish ties out of the pram!

I haven't spoken to David Davis yet, but I know he will be utterly devastated. Eric was his most loyal friend in politics. That quality of friendship is rare in politics. Eric was one of the few MPs who would tell DD to his face exactly what he thought. He was very critical of DD's decision to stand aside in 2003 and allow a Michael Howard coronation, and to the end believed it was the wrong thing to do. Eric decided that he shouldn't play much of a role in the 2005 contest because he felt his divisive reputation would damage David. So he took a back seat. DD and his allies have lost a great friend today.

GREAT QUOTES OF OUR TIME: NO. 94
MONDAY 29 MAY

On my way to play golf – classic radio phone-in moment from an ex-teacher: 'I joined the police when I realised I would rather arrest children than teach them.'

THINGS THAT COME BACK TO HAUNT YOU
FRIDAY 16 JUNE

The revelation that Tony Blair wrote a pseudo-Marxist letter to Michael Foot should come as little surprise to anyone. Blair has always been what Tony Benn would describe as a weathercock rather than a signpost – a blank canvas on which to paint. I was trying to think of other examples of things people have written which later came back to haunt them, but it's obviously too early in the morning.

My personal example is a one-page essay I wrote in 1974 at the age of eleven. I decided to pen a piece for my parents advising them how to vote in the February election. Even at that age I had seen right through Ted Heath and I was none too enamoured with the EEC after my father was forced to sell his herd of beef cattle. So early one morning I wandered into my parents' bedroom and solemnly advised them to vote Labour. My bleary-eyed mother briefly awoke from her slumbers and told me not to be so stupid and to go back to bed, and that she would be voting for that rather 'dishy' Mr Thorpe. My career as a political pundit had not got off to a promising start.

MY SISTER, MY HEROINE
SATURDAY 17 JUNE

My sister Sheena is a sports instructor at a leisure centre in Saffron Walden. A few days ago someone rushed in and screamed for someone with first aid experience to come and help at a scene of an accident. It turned out this was no ordinary accident. A cyclist had been hit – and hit badly – by a lorry carrying a skip. The cyclist was to all intents and purposes gone. There was blood everywhere. Sheena had no mask but without a thought for her own safety carried out mouth-to-mouth resuscitation and tried to get the cyclist's heart restarted. After a while she felt a pulse and he started breathing again. In the meantime a rubber-necking crowd had gathered as people came out of their houses to see what was happening. Sheena asked someone for a handkerchief to wipe the blood away. No one offered. So she carried on regardless. Unbelievably parents brought their young children to watch this scene of utter carnage. A few minutes later the air ambulance arrived. Apparently the paramedics wanted the air ambulance to take the guy to Addenbrooke's Hospital in Cambridge as they were best suited to treat his injuries and it was only fourteen miles away. The air ambulance refused on the basis that Addenbrooke's didn't have a helipad and they insisted on taking him to Harlow, more than twenty miles away. Sadly he didn't make it. But I'm very proud of my sister. She did what we'd all like to think we'd do in the circumstances, but if we're honest with ourselves we're not sure we could. It's people like her who deserve to be in the Honours List.

MY MEMORY OF 7/7
FRIDAY 7 JULY

I don't know if you remember where you were on the morning of 7 July last year when you heard the news of the terrorist bombings in London. I was sitting at my desk in the House of Commons (for the uninitiated, I was working for David Davis, the shadow Home Secretary) and a colleague popped his head round the door to say there was something on the radio about a big bang in a tube station. Shortly afterwards Rachel Sylvester and Alice Thomson[†] arrived to do a feature interview with David. Gradually news started coming in that there were several attacks. I kept interrupting his interview with news. I rang home and rang my parents to reassure them I was OK. I began to get calls from friends.

My work colleague began to get hysterical about her son, who she feared might have been on one of the trains. She rang his school and he had not arrived. As the morning wore on, and she couldn't make contact with him, even I began to fear the worst. But I had to make a decision. I was trying to coordinate our response and ensure the office ran smoothly, yet my colleague (and very good friend) was frantic. Did I try to soothe her or did I do my job. I'm slightly ashamed to say I chose the latter and 'delegated' the former. Hard bastard, I thought to myself. Her son rang to say he was OK shortly afterwards.

None of us knew what it all meant. The thought ran through my mind that if this was a repeat of 9/11, our office wasn't exactly the best place to be. It was located almost directly under Big Ben. But you just get on with your job. David Davis was the coolest man in London. If ever I doubted his leadership qualities, they were on full display that day. Alice Thomson and Rachel Sylvester would confirm that.

David then had to respond to Charles Clarke's statement in the House of Commons. We were glued to the TV. He caught the mood of the House and gave a speech which even his enemies had to admit was striking.

The next day, I was walking to work along the Embankment with the sound of helicopters and police sirens ringing through the air. I remember thinking to myself: 'This is not the London I love.' I felt as if I was walking along a street in an alien city. I admit that a tear rolled down my face. Would life ever be the same?

A year on and life has returned to normal – until the next time. But what's normal any more? For some, life can never be normal again, because they either lost family or friends on 7/7 or they

---

† Journalists with the *Daily Telegraph*. Both have since moved to *The Times*.

themselves lost limbs. And it is them who I think of as I write this. And, in particular, I think of Rachel from North London – a blogger who has had more effect on people than she probably realises.

IAIN DALE AND RICK STEIN – A PERSONAL STATEMENT
WEDNESDAY 12 JULY

Following allegations on this blog and others that Rick Stein and I are one and the same person and share the same voice box I would like to make it clear that the fact that we have never been seen in the same radio studio together is entirely coincidental. And I hate fish.

Seriously, whenever I host one of the theatre evenings with Ann Widdecombe, someone usually comes up at the end and says, 'Do you realise your voice sounds identical to Rick Stein?' Several people have also emailed to say the same thing after listening to my podcasts. To be honest, I only vaguely knew who Rick Stein was. Well, a voice is all we have in common. I don't cook, don't eat fish, don't live in Cornwall and am not rich. Apart from the voice, you can't tell us apart!

Update: I'm informed that Rick Stein also has a Jack Russell called Chalky. My Jack Russell, Gio, is suitably unimpressed.

FLYIN' IS VIRGIN' ON A SIN (AND SO'S DRIVING AN AUDI)
SUNDAY 23 JULY

Sometimes I really do despair of the Church of England. Its rituals now include sacrificing creed to convenience and conviction to political correctness. I could scarcely believe what I was reading on the front page of the *Sunday Times* today. IT'S A SIN TO FLY, SAYS CHURCH. Now I think I've got a good grip on the definition of sinning (no comments please!), but I can't see where in the Bible it mentions air travel, or driving an Audi (as I do), being in need of repentance. The Bishop of London, the Right Reverend Richard Chartres, disagrees: 'Making selfish choices such as flying on holiday or buying a large car are a symptom of sin. Sin is not just a restricted list of moral mistakes. It is living a life turned in on itself where people ignore the consequences of their actions.'

Claire Foster, the church's environment policy director, said: 'Indiscriminate use of the earth's resources must be seen as profoundly wrong, just as we now see slavery as wrong.'

So all those Anglican bishops attending the next big Anglican jamboree had better find alternative means of getting there. All this does is remind me why I rarely go to church any more. And if I did, it would be to a Catholic one. At least I'd only be lectured on proper sins.

Update: A correspondent reminds me that Richard Chartres spent two months this year on a luxury cruise, lecturing on theology. He was heavily criticised for being on a cruise ship over Easter rather than attending services at St Paul's Cathedral. I am absolutely positive cruise ships give off no carbon emissions at all. Of course not.

A GOOD WALK SPOILED BY A 13 HANDICAP
THURSDAY 3 AUGUST

Yesterday was a very odd day. I got my 'A' List letter (I'm now on it – as a sort of 'B' class 'A' Lister) and learnt that I had a golf handicap of 13. Now for those who know nothing about golf and care even less, please look away now.

I'm not a bad golfer, but I'm certainly not a good one. And I'm definitely not a 13 handicapper. I handed in three cards with scores of 94, 98 and 102. The 102 card included a blowout 12 on one hole. Apparently they disregard blowout-holes when calculating your handicap and because I parred quite a few they calculated me at 13.

This is despite the fact that a friend of mine who plays with me has a handicap of 20 and beats me nine times out of ten. So being given this handicap probably means I'll never win a game of golf again. However, when I played nine holes yesterday I scored fifteen points in Stableford, which means I roughly played to my handicap. What a frustrating game golf can be. But that's why I love it.

When I was a candidate I didn't have time to play and only started up again in May this year. I had forgotten what a wonderful game it is and how much I enjoy it. Whatever I do in the future work-wise or politically, I do know one thing for sure. I'm going to make time for golf. So there!

TOP TEN LIST OF THINGS WHICH WOULD BE DIFFERENT IF DD HAD BECOME LEADER
SUNDAY 6 AUGUST

10. Iain Dale would have been on the 'A' List first time around (or perhaps not!)
9. The *Daily Telegraph* writes supportive articles
8. ConservativeHome shut down for insubordination
7. Mandatory blue stripy ties for all members of the shadow Cabinet
6. Leader travels to work in a Vulcan Bomber followed by Lear Jet carrying leaders' shoes and briefcase
5. Free broken nose jobs on the NHS
4. No more compulsory Eton education for Leader's Office staff
3. Shadow Home Secretary David Cameron instructed to introduce Mug-a-Hoodie policy
2. Jamie Oliver tasked with providing school meal recipes containing Chocolate Oranges
1. New shadow Secretary of State for Fashion appointed to introduce compulsory wearing of 'It's DD for Me' T-shirts at all Conservative Future events – for men

THE PERILS OF OWNING A JACK RUSSELL
THURSDAY 15 AUGUST

I am the proud owner of a wonderful Jack Russell, called Gio. I am pleased to say he has never behaved quite as badly as Bert, a Jack Russell owned by Tory MP Andrew Turner. Bert took it upon himself to embarrass his owner while visiting the Isle of Wight Show when he savaged a polecat to death. I wonder if it was 'semi-house trained' à la Michael Foot's description of Norman Tebbit. Her Majesty's Press certainly missed a trick today by failing to get a quote from Tebbit.

My worst public moment with Gio was when I was taking him for his evening constitutional and somehow he got hit by a car while still on his lead. Thankfully he was OK, but I think I was more traumatised by the experience than he was.

THE MEME OF 3
SUNDAY 20 AUGUST

Paul Burgin at the increasingly unmissable Mars Hill Blog has done his entry for the Meme of 3 which is buzzing round the blogosphere at the moment. Here's my effort...

1. **Things that scare me:**
   - Rats
   - When I'm on a flight, thinking just that little bit too much about how planes actually get off the ground
   - A full-blown Julian Dicks tackle

2. **People who make me laugh:**
   - Julie Walters
   - Sir Les Patterson
   - Frankie Howerd

3. **Things I hate the most:**
   - Avocado and prawns
   - White people who affect to speak like black people
   - Being overweight

4. **Things I don't understand:**
   - Rugby
   - HTML
   - How to get my new 10,000 station digital radio working with my wireless internet connection

5. **Things I'm doing right now:**
   - Watching the Test Match – Kevin Pietersen is out for 96
   - Listening to my dog, Gio, bark
   - Wondering what the week ahead is about to bring...

6. **Things I want to do before I die:**
   - Write a political biography
   - See West Ham in the Champions' League
   - Become Secretary of State for Culture, Media and Sport

7. **Things I can do:**
   - Speak near fluent German (well, I used to be able to!)
   - Not embarrass myself at golf
   - Unintentionally impersonate Rick Stein

8. **Ways to describe my personality:**
   - Loyal
   - Argumentative
   - Shy (but I manage to hide it!)

9. **Things I can't do:**
   - Tie things – including shoelaces
   - Whistle
   - Resist cheesecake

10. **Things I think you should listen to:**
    - The national anthem sung at Twickenham
    - Me, when I'm on the radio!
    - Churchill's wartime speeches

11. **Things you should never listen to:**
    - Magic FM
    - José Mourinho or Sir Alex Ferguson. Take your pick.
    - Patricia Hewitt

12. **Things I'd like to learn:**
    - Dutch
    - How to play the piano
    - HTML

13. **Favourite foods:**
    - Chicken fajitas
    - Yorkshire pudding
    - Baked raspberry cheesecake. OK, let's be honest. Any cheesecake.

14. **Beverages I drink regularly:**
    I'm teetotal and hate tea or coffee, so...
    - Any kind of fruit juice
    - Sparkling mineral water
    - Britvic 55

15. **Shows I watched as a kid:**
  - *Val Meets the VIPs* (Valerie Singleton)
  - *Timeslip*
  - *Skippy the Bush Kangaroo*

HAMMERS ENTER THE BIG TIME
THURSDAY 31 AUGUST

I have spent the whole day in a state of nervous exhaustion, constantly refreshing the West Ham website homepage to see if it really could be true that the two best footballers in South America had really signed for us. Other Hammers fans will know the meaning of the words 'just like my dreams, they fade and die'. We all expected it to be some massive hoax that Carlitos Tevez and Javier Mascherano had signed for us, but signed for us they have. This deal reminds me of the one that brought Ossie Ardiles and Ricky Villa to Tottenham in the late 1970s. It gave Spurs a huge boost and this really could propel the Hammers into the big time. But let's not get carried away. Oh sod it, let's.

Some useful phrases (courtesy of the West Ham mailing list) for our new Argie Argentinian players:

> *el pastel doble y tritura por favor amor* – double pie and mash please luv
> *así que usted ha hecho página tres?* – so you've done page 3?
> *mejor marca mina un shandy* – better make mine half a shandy
> *yo siempre he admirado a chicas inglesas* – I've always liked English birds
> *estoy aquí como la parte del trato de Carrick* – I'm here as part of the Carrick deal
> *he soñado de jugar delante del corral durante muchos años* – I have dreamt of playing in front of the Chicken Run for many years

THE BOOK MEME
FRIDAY 1 SEPTEMBER

---

1. **Name one book that changed your life.**
   I can't say that a book ever has. I guess *Animal Farm* had

an effect on me as a teenager when I read it at school, as it confirmed all my gut instincts about socialism. Latterly, *In the Arena* by Richard Nixon was an inspiration to me. Before anyone pokes fun at that, read the book.

2. **One book you've read more than once.**
   Watership Down by Richard Adams. As a child I used to read and re-read *The Magic Faraway Tree* by Enid Blyton over and over again.

3. **One book you'd want on a desert island.**
   The seven-volume biography of Churchill by Randolph Churchill and Martin Gilbert. It's the only situation when I would ever have the time to read it.

4. **One book that made you laugh.**
   Frank Skinner's autobiography and *I am an Oil Tanker* by Fi Glover. OK, that's two.

5. **One book that made you cry.**
   Being Gazza by Gazza. OK, you may laugh, but it is quite a harrowing read.

6. **One book you wish you'd written.**
   The Aachen Memorandum by Andrew Roberts. A brilliant Eurospectic novel.

7. **One book you wish had never been written.**
   Mein Kampf. It would have meant Hitler had never existed.

8. **One book you're currently reading.**
   There's Only One Neil Redfearn: The Ups and Downs of My Footballing Life by Neil Redfearn.

9. **One book you've been meaning to read.**
   Helmut Kohl's memoirs – in the original German!

THAT BLAIR STATEMENT IN FULL
THURSDAY 7 SEPTEMBER

Gulp.

Furrow brow.

Y'know.

Best interests.

Sigh.

No date.

Take onion out of pocket.

On and on and on.
F*** you, Gordon.
Determined look.
The Labour Party can go **** itself.
I just want to be the Prime Minister of People's hearts.

WHAT WERE YOU DOING ON SEPTEMBER 11, 2001?
MONDAY 11 SEPTEMBER

I was sitting at my desk on the balcony at Politico's talking to my bookkeeper when I suddenly noticed that Sky News had switched to Fox and were showing smoke coming from a tall tower. As the situation became clearer I remember seeing a spec on the skyline coming closer to the tower. I assumed a small light aircraft had hit it. In the corner of the screen I noticed a spec moving across the screen. 'Jesus, there's another plane', I remember saying. 'Oh my God, it's going to hit the other tower.' Crash. Fire. Carnage. But it wasn't until the first tower collapsed that the true horror hit me. People down below in the shop stood watching the bigger screen in silence. Someone rushed out the door saying her sister worked at the World Trade Center and she had to phone her.

At that moment I thought of my friend Daniel Forrester who I knew worked there from time to time. Indeed his father had a corner office in one of the towers. I tried to ring him. The number didn't work. I remember helping a customer ring her boyfriend in China to tell him what was happening. His father worked in one of the towers. I kept trying to call Daniel, becoming increasingly frantic. Eventually he called me. The emotion of the day caught up with me and I can remember speaking to him with tears running down my face, trying to keep my voice from breaking up completely.

It wasn't until much later in the day that I started to think about the political implications. I could not understand why President Bush hadn't sought to immediately reassure his weeping nation. It was not his finest hour.

September 11, 2001 was a day that changed the world. It robbed a generation of its innocence, and its consequences will be felt for decades to come.

THE TALE OF THE RAMPANT RABBIT
SUNDAY 24 SEPTEMBER

When I drive home from doing a newspaper review on *News 24*, I usually listen to Stephen Nolan's phone-in programme on Radio 5 Live. Last night I tuned in at a quarter past midnight to be 'entertained' by a discussion about the merits of a rampant rabbit. I have to admit that I had never heard of such an implement but soon came to understand that it is, how shall I put it, something which enables ladies to (as the tabloids would say) pleasure themselves.

It was a strangely compelling forty-five minutes in that I kept wanting to switch over to something else but didn't want to miss out on anything! There was a fantastic caller called Anne, who was obviously of fairly advanced years, who had me laughing out loud. She was obviously gagging to buy one but couldn't quite imagine herself walking into an Ann Summers shop. And then this morning, flicking through the *Indy on Sunday* I spotted an article on the same subject by Rowan Pelling.

The point I am coming to, in a Ronnie Corbett-esque manner, is this. Why is it now socially acceptable to discuss women's masturbatory aids in polite circles, when if one were to have the same conversation about blow-up dolls for men (and God alone knows what else) you would be hung, drawn and quartered by the feminist lobby, which no doubt believes blow-up dolls are demeaning to women. Well what about the poor bloody rabbits!

Imagine, you're a poor little fluffy bunny wandering around a nice country garden, and suddenly you look through the conservatory windows and spy the Mistress of the House... [end this NOW – Ed.]

I'll just get my coat...

MOLLY SCOTCHER 1931–2006
SATURDAY 21 OCTOBER

Yesterday I went to a funeral near Bury St Edmunds to bury my godmother, Molly Scotcher, who died last week. I'm not very good at funerals. No matter how much I tell myself I'm going to maintain a stiff upper lip, my eyes somehow turn into water fountains. It didn't help today when I saw my father and my uncle acting as pallbearers. They were carrying the coffin containing their sister. My mother (from whom I have inherited my moist eyes) was in bits. It was Molly who introduced her to my father fifty years ago. Indeed, had Molly and my mother not struck up a conversation on a train from Clare in Suffolk to Bartlow in Cambridgeshire, my parents would never have met and you wouldn't be reading these words.

Molly was a woman of her generation. She was born in 1931 and was educated in Ashdon, near Saffron Walden, at the same school I was to attend thirty years later. She worked as a railway clerk before marrying her husband, Percy. She immediately gave up work and had twins, my cousins Susan and Heather. Percy died seventeen years ago today and since then she has devoted herself to her grandchildren and caring for elderly people. She really was a woman who put others before herself. Six months ago Molly was diagnosed with three aneurisms, and it was from one of those she died. Susan, her daughter, discovered her body. I can think of nothing worse than discovering a dead parent. My sister Sheena rang to tell me. Sheena doesn't ring me that often and, when she does, I often fear the worst.

Why am I telling you all this? No idea really. I suppose it was an odd day and I just wanted to get it off my chest. But I was reminded of an exchange I had with one of the journalism students in Cardiff yesterday who made a remark about all politicians being on the make and somewhat inhumane. I countered that people have a similar view of journalists and made the point that politicians and journalists all have feelings, they all laugh, they cry, they shop in the same places as other people, watch the same TV programmes, suffer from the same illnesses. And everyone gets sad at funerals.

Funerals often provoke odd emotions in me and this one has been no different. One thing it has done is to make me question why I only really see my extended family at funerals. And it's made me determine to get my sister to ring me when she has good news – or even no news – so at least I don't always fear the worst when I see her name come up on my phone screen. Yesterday, possibly for the first time, I felt my age.

QUOTE OF THE DAY: NO. 94
SATURDAY 4 NOVEMBER

Shami Chakrabarti, Director of Liberty, on 18 Doughty Street:[†] 'I'm not a vegetarian. I just look like one.'
Class.

WHAT IT MEANS TO BE
SATURDAY 11 NOVEMBER

> It's easier to throw rocks at a house than build one
> – Congressman Matthew Santos

I heard this quote just now on an episode of *The West Wing* and it sums up to me the difference between commentating on politics and getting your hands dirty and taking part. Richard Nixon wrote a superb book called *In the Arena* in which he discussed what it takes for someone to make a difference in politics. Politics is hard. Devising political strategies is difficult. Building a political coalition is a nightmare. Writing, or commentating, about anything is a cakewalk by comparison.

There is only one way of effecting change, and that is to be 'In the Arena'. So if you're an aspirant political candidate who gets frustrated at not getting selected, or thinks about throwing in the towel, just remember why you're in it in the first place. You're 'In the Arena' because you want to change things, get things done, make life better – for others, not yourself. You don't just talk about what SHOULD be done and complain about what's NOT being done. You're a CAN-DO person. You ACHIEVE. The word CAN'T isn't one you like using. As Matthew Santos might put it, you prefer BUILDING a house, to throwing rocks at it.

PUBLIC HUMILIATION SHOULD NOT BE PART OF OUR LEGAL PROCESS
SUNDAY 19 NOVEMBER

Anyone who knows David Prior (former Tory MP for North

---

† Internet TV channel.

Norfolk) will testify to the decency of the man. His former constituents in North Norfolk and the staff at the Norfolk & Norwich
University Hospital will have been shocked at his very public arrest
this week. But let us remember that arrest does not imply anything.
What should shock us more is the very public way this was done.
Someone somewhere wanted it to be in the public domain, and I
don't think we have too far to look to know where the news was
leaked from. Whoever it was had an agenda.

This is not the first time it has happened. I well remember the
case of Neil and Christine Hamilton being arrested on suspicion
of rape and being put through months of hell before they were
completely exonerated. But in those few months the 'no smoke
without fire' brigade had a field day. The Metropolitan Police had
tipped off the press that they had been arrested and a phalanx of
cameras was waiting to greet them at Ilford Police Station.

The same thing happened more recently to Lord Levy, when he
was arrested in the cash-for-peerages inquiry. Whatever happened
to the concept of 'innocent until proven guilty'? It seems if you are
a public figure you have to put up with this sort of thing nowadays.

I don't blame the EDP for splashing the Prior case as a big story.
It is. But perhaps someone in Norfolk Police, or maybe the Norfolk
Health Service, should be hanging their head in shame this weekend for putting a transparently decent man and his family through
hell. And perhaps the rest of us should be asking ourselves what
their agenda is.

TOP TEN THINGS I WOULD NEVER DO
WEDNESDAY 22 NOVEMBER

The *Telegraph* has had a lot of letters lately suggesting clubs its
readers would never join. Today they even have a page-three feature
on it. So I thought I'd compile my Top Ten Things I Would Never
Do...

10. Join the Carlton Club until they admit women as full members
9. Take advice on social policy from Polly Toynbee (gasp...)
8. Take any notice of anonymous blog posters
7. Ever go to White Hart Lane again
6. Grow a beard (I tried once. Too ginger...)

5. Get a tattoo or a metal 'appendage' of any description
4. Vote to join the euro
3. Take any soft or hard drug
2. Shout 'Pardew Out'
1. Run for Mayor of London

RELATIVE POVERTY ISN'T AN ABSOLUTE
THURSDAY 26 NOVEMBER

Poverty is defined in an online dictionary thus: 'the condition of being extremely poor'. If you are in poverty, you are probably unable to pay your bills, are struggling to keep a roof over your head and are finding it difficult to feed yourself and your family. Indeed, that is how I have always thought of it. However, lingua-fascists have now redefined the word to include anyone who is earning less than 60 per cent of the median wage. Quite when this happened, no one's sure, but I trace it back to the 1980s when the Child Poverty Action Group tried to tell us that 3 million children in this country were living in poverty. It was rubbish then, and it's rubbish now.

Of course there are children, and indeed many adults, who are impoverished. No one denies that, and everyone would agree that it is a prime duty of the state to lift those people out of poverty, but to pretend that someone who is earning between £12,000 and £15,000 a year is living in poverty is a joke.

So the argument has moved on to a debate about whether we should be talking about absolute poverty (as per Churchill) or relative poverty (as per Polly Toynbee). The answer is that they are not necessarily mutually exclusive. In Churchill's day there was a huge amount of absolute poverty in the country, but this has almost totally gone. Sure, there are still pockets of poverty, especially in big cities and certain rural areas (this reminds me of a great line from John Gummer – 'poverty is considered quaint in rural areas, because it comes thatched') and the state has by and large failed to lift people in those areas out of poverty. The task is now falling to social entrepreneurs, outside the state machinery, to do this. So as the level of absolute poverty has declined to a small fraction of what it was half a century ago, it is only natural that politicians from all sides start to examine relative inequalities – note that I decline to use the phrase 'relative poverty'.

Polly Toynbee's analogy of a long train of caravans trekking through a desert, one behind the other is a good one. She is worried about what happens if the caravans at the back become detached from the rest of the group – for 'group', read 'society'.

I am not someone who believes that everybody must be equal. Like Boris Johnson I believe that society needs winners and losers. Winners must be rewarded, but society cannot function properly if we forget about the losers. But I actually regard it as a triumph of our society that we can even talk in terms of losers being people who earn 40 per cent of the median wage.

I don't know what the median wage is in Liechtenstein, but I suspect that under the current definition of 'relative poverty' a large number of very wealthy people would be caught in the poverty trap there. Conservatives must not be defined by the language of the left.

Perhaps we now need a real debate on what poverty actually means in the twenty-first century. Can we really equate poverty in this country with poverty in places like Darfur or Rwanda? Perhaps someone needs to invent a new word. Best that we do it before Polly Toynbee does.

CRIME WAVE HITS DOUGHTY STREET
WEDNESDAY 29 NOVEMBER

On Sunday night we had a break in at 18 Doughty Street. Last night I was broadcasting live and was told that my car had been broken into, as had those of YouGov's Stephan Shakespeare and MORI's Bob Worcester and two others cars. Makes you wonder what the MDs of ICM or NOP were doing, doesn't it?! Naturally we rang the police, but unsurprisingly they didn't want to know. This is a summary of the exchange...

18DS: So you're not going to come out then.

Police: No sir, we don't come out for car break-ins.

18DS: Not even when there are five cars damaged?

Police: No, but you are very welcome to visit any police station and report the crime, sir.

18DS: How kind.

And there you have it. A prime example of why many people have little confidence in the Metropolitan Police. If they're not willing to investigate five car break-ins, just what are they willing to do? Needless to say we just haven't bothered reporting it now, because there's nothing they will do about it anyway. And there's a prime example of why the crime figures aren't worth the paper they are written on.

TOP TEN POLITICAL CHAT-UP LINES
WEDNESDAY 20 DECEMBER

1. Would you like to see the contents of my despatch box?
2. Have you ever had a whip?
3. Hello, I'm David Mellor.
4. I've asked Angie to join us, you don't mind, do you?
5. I've asked Bobby to join us, you don't mind, do you?
6. I'm so depressed about the world crisis I really don't think I should spend tonight alone.
7. In your honour I'm naming 2007 the International Year of the Babe.
8. Hello, I'm Lembit Opik.
9. Ever done it in the lobby?
10. You know what they say about Black Rod?

Update: Dave's Part blog had the Top Ten Trotskyist Chat-Up Lines. The final four are...

4. That second-hand donkey jacket of yours would look great on my bedroom floor.
3. What's a nice girl like you doing in a lousy union faction like this?
2. Do you sell papers here often?
1. So, babe ... just how degenerate would your ideal workers' state be?

CHRISTMAS QUOTE OF THE DAY
MONDAY 25 DECEMBER

From my godmother: 'Your Christmas tree doesn't look as pretty as it did when I had cataracts...'

2007

DESPERATE HOUSEWIFE SAYS NO TO...
THURSDAY 4 JANUARY, 12.29 A.M.

One of the more bizarre evenings of the 2005 Tory leadership contest was when the two Davids presented an award at the ITV TV awards at the Albert Hall ... and were booed. On the way out I heard the two of them discussing *Desperate Housewives* and which character they both liked the best. At that point I hadn't ever seen an episode, so when they both agreed it was Bree Van de Kamp I didn't bat an eyelid. I was then given the first series on DVD and have been hooked ever since.

So when I watched the first episode of the third series tonight I laughed out loud at this fantastic line from Bree ... and then thought of the two Davids...

Picture the scene, Bree is about to have sex for the first time with her newly acquired fiancé, Orson (who also happens to be a murderer, but I digress). They rush upstairs into Bree's bedroom and both fall on the bed. Bree takes off her blouse and Orson moves slowly down her body towards ... well, you can guess. Bree looks mystified and then horrified as Orson's 'cunning' plan makes itself apparent. She blurts out: 'Orson, I don't do that!' Orson says: 'Why not?' Bree, still shocked, replies: 'I'm a Republican!'

Well, it made me laugh out loud, anyway. I suspect Messers Davis and Cameron did likewise.

TOP TEN TORY CHAT-UP LINES
SATURDAY 6 JANUARY

1. Yo Blair! Bend over, you're gonna love this...
2. Can I share the proceeds of this growth with you?

3. I've got a unique way of protecting the vulnerable.
4. Are you thinking what I'm thinking?
5. How would you like to shadow my portfolio?
6. Is your name Tamzin Lightwater?[†]
7. I'm so depressed about the 'A' List I really don't think I should spend tonight alone.
8. I'm really not gay, no really, no, no ... oh go on then...
9. Francis is always urging us to increase our members.
10. Would you like to come up and watch the Parliamentary Channel with me some time?

DOGGING IN THE WILDS OF NORTH KENT
FRIDAY 26 JANUARY

Tonight I went to speak to Chatham & Aylesford Conservatives Annual Dinner at a pub/restaurant, which appeared to be in the middle of a wood. The relevance of this will become clear. I must admit I have rarely received such an introduction as I got from the constituency chairman, Alan Sullivan. He said some nice things about Tracey Crouch, their election candidate, and then blurted out: 'And Tracey will then introduce Iain Dale who will be telling us about his experiences of "dogging"'. Cue raucous (but slightly nervous) laughter. I think he must have either mistaken me for Stan Collymore or become disoriented in the woods. But thankfully Alan recovered himself and admitted I would be talking about the marginally less exciting subject of 'blogging'. I couldn't help but notice the disappointment on several faces. For the uninitiated who don't know what 'dogging' is, I am sure a Google search will enlighten...

Public speaking is a really odd thing. Few people will ever have the guts to tell you that you've made a bad speech, so when people tell you you've made a really good one, you tend automatically to disbelieve them. I never look forward to making speeches, but once I'm in the swing of it and I get some laughs I am in my element. Laughs are the key to my speeches. If I don't make them laugh three times in the first two minutes, I then feel as if I am sinking

---

† Spoof columnist for *The Spectator*.

quickly and scrabbling for a lifejacket. Maybe I am just a frustrated stand-up comedian.

THE SPECIFIC SHOULD WIN OVER THE GENERAL
SATURDAY 27 JANUARY

I've been listening to *Any Questions* on my drive to Upton Park. Lynne Featherstone said something quite profound. On the question of gay adoption she urged people not to think about the generality of the issue but to concentrate on individual gay people you know and think about whether they would, as individuals, make good parents.

You can draw other parallels here. As a country, British people tend to dislike the French, yet individually we find them charming.

People think that politicians as a group are liars and untrustworthy, yet I've lost count of the times I have heard people say that their own MP is fantastic.

West Ham fans are reputedly all skinhead thugs, yet individually people rather like us (or have I just defeated my own argument?!).

THE CHANGING FACE OF FARMING
SATURDAY 3 FEBRUARY

I'm spending most of this weekend in Devon. The thing that has struck me here is how much I miss this kind of lifestyle.

I was brought up in a very rural area in North Essex and never imagined I would spend much of my working life in London. I come from a long line of farmers and it was expected that I too would become a farmer. Visiting some close family near Barnstaple last night it was good to see my cousin Richard again. We worked out that it had been seven years. He hadn't changed at all, yet he had been told this week that after twenty-seven years of working on the same farm he was being made redundant. The farmer was in tears when he broke the news. He said he just couldn't face carrying on due to all the regulations he had to comply with. So yet another farming family is getting out.

I made a decision at a very young age that I didn't want to go into farming and, as Neil Kinnock might have said: 'I was the first in a thousand generations of Dales to go to university.' My close family entirely supported that decision, even though it must have been painful for them to realise that their eldest son would never do what had been predetermined for him. Most of the rest of my family – also mostly in farming – didn't quite view it that way. They felt I was betraying my parents, although they never actually said so.

My parents own their farm. It's not a large farm and they do not confirm to most townies' view of a stereotypical farmer – they don't have a Range Rover, a mansion or wear tweed. But I had the chance in life that my cousin Richard did not, as his father (my father's brother) did not own land. Whenever I go home to my parents I often think how my life would have been different if I had been born twenty years earlier – because there's no doubt that I would have definitely gone into farming whether I wanted to or not.

It is a crying shame that Britain's farming heritage is disappearing. Small farms are being bought up by the big farming conglomerates. The care that farmers like my father have given to their land is being replaced by a very different culture. Those who know nothing about farming bang on about subsidies and how they've never seen a farmer on a bike. What they don't realise is that most farmers were doing quite well by themselves before the era of subsidies. All people need to do is look at New Zealand, a predominantly agricultural country that is self sufficient in food, pays no subsidies to its farmers and yet has a thriving farming community.

For my father's generation, farming is a vocation, a way of life. It's not about money. As long as he is earning a basic living he is happy. He hasn't had a new car since he bought a Cortina Super in about 1966. My parents just don't go on holidays. They rarely go out to dinner. But is their quality of life better than most? Are they happy and more content? You bet.

ANECDOTES FROM THE THATCHER STATUE UNVEILING
THURSDAY 22 FEBRUARY

A word of praise for James Hardy of the BBC. His report on last night's unveiling of Margaret Thatcher's statue struck just the right tone. Having been a journalist on the *Daily Mirror*, I suspect that

James is not a card-carrying Tory, but he captured the mood of the occasion beautifully.

Two anecdotes from the evening. My informant tells me that another person who acquitted himself well was Speaker Michael Martin. He led Lady Thatcher into the Members' Lobby from the chamber of the House of Commons. Assorted Tory MPs and 'old lags' from Thatcher Cabinets of years gone by were gathered to greet her. There was a touching moment when she saw Geoffrey Howe, who immediately held out his hand. Not a word was exchanged, but I'm told it was one of those 'moments' when words would have been superfluous.

It was also good to see John Major attending. A few years ago he wouldn't have been seen dead in her company. Time heals, I suppose.

An amusing exchange occurred when a Conservative MP questioned an 'Old Labour' MP as to why he was there. 'I would have thought you would rather anyone else had a statue erected here,' said the Tory. 'Look, mate, if it stops that bastard Blair from getting a statue, it's got to be a good thing,' said the Labour MP. 'No, no, you don't understand,' replied the Tory. 'In this new technological age, Blair won't be getting a statue, there will be a permanent moving hologram of him on the ceiling of the Members' Lobby.' Just for a moment the Labour MP believed it.

One final thing. Somebody in the Commons has a sense of humour. Were the statue of Lady T able to look down, what would she see? A small bust of Edward Heath on a shelf. How very appropriate.

MY STANCE ON CLIMATE CHANGE AND WHY I REMAIN A TORY
SUNDAY 11 MARCH

I suppose if you stick your head over the political parapet, you deserve to get it shot off from time to time. My comments on Al Gore have caused a certain frisson. Let's just look at what I said...

On Thursday, US climate-change hypocrite Al Gore will address David Cameron's shadow Cabinet. He will no doubt be instructing them all on the art of preaching climate change religion bollocks while at the same time creating a carbon footprint the size of a mammoth's. I wonder how many of them will find they have a subsequent engagement...

Al Gore is indeed a hypocrite. He tells the rest of the world to reduce their carbon footprint, while living in a house which has a carbon footprint the size of Tennessee. Gore's heating bill is dozens of times higher than that of virtually every other American. It's a little known fact that George W. Bush's Texas ranch is very environmentally friendly. Bush just gets on and does it without making a song and dance about it. Gore, meanwhile, flies to Hollywood and collects his ill-deserved Oscar from celebrities who have arrived at the ceremony in gas-guzzling stretch limos.

I used the phrase 'preaching climate change religion bollocks' for a reason, one which seems to have passed by the ninety or so people who have commented on the thread. It has indeed become a religion to those people who like to jump on the bandwagon of such causes. Their fervour reflects the CND marchers of the 1990s. If you speak out against their creed you're attacked as a 'denier', putting you on the same level as a Holocaust denier. I dislike the messianic side of those like Gore who treat climate change as a pseudo-religion which if you deign to question you're considered a 'nutter'.

I do question it, but I do it out of curiosity, not out of dogma. Let me make my position clear. I do believe climate change is taking place, but I have an open mind on the extent to which it is (if at all) man made. I am unconvinced both by the Stern Report and the IPCC report, which seems to change its evidence according to the conclusion. I am prepared to listen to the arguments of the climate change sceptics, just as I am to those I respect on the other side of the argument. The reason I railed against Al Gore is that he does not fall into that last category.

If I were to base all my views on climate change on either *An Inconvenient Truth* or *The Great Global Warming Swindle*, I certainly find the latter far more convincing. But it is not quite that simple. Both films perhaps raised more questions than they answered.

Al Gore's film should have had the subtitle *My Name Is Al, and I'm Running for President*. Why else would it have included the often emotional and tear-jerking autobiographical scenes which had little or nothing to do with climate change? As a docu-film it worked rather well and certainly held the viewer's attention, but its weakness stemmed from Gore's apparent obsession with one of his teachers.

We have all had teachers whom we revere, but Gore's reverence for one of his university teachers bordered on hero worship. You just got the feeling that the whole film was made with the intention of achieving an A grade and a pat on the back. On the face of it many of Gore's statistics were compelling, but you always got the feeling that they were being used selectively. The shots of glaciers breaking up pulled on the emotions until you learnt from the Channel 4 film that this has happened every spring down the centuries.

Indeed the Channel 4 film debunked many of the assertions made by Gore, not by polemics, but by scientists. And that was where it triumphed over Gore. Gore knows his script backwards. A polemicist he may be, but a scientist he ain't.

MEMORIES OF THE FALKLANDS
MONDAY 2 APRIL

Twenty-five years ago today I was on holiday, visiting friends, the Weber family, in the German spa town of Bad Wildungen. I was nineteen, and was on an Easter break from my degree course in German at the University of East Anglia in Norwich. After dinner, we sat down to watch TV. I watched incredulously as the newsreader told us of the Argentine invasion of the Falkland Islands. Unlike most people in Britain, I had a vague idea of where the Falklands were, due to my childhood stamp collection. My German friends assumed they lay off the coast of Scotland. Herr Weber, a veteran of the Russian front in the Second World War, said: 'It'll all be settled by diplomacy.'

I remember vividly replying: 'I doubt it very much. Margaret Thatcher is not known as the Iron Lady for nothing. I think there'll be a war.' 'No, no,' replied Herr Weber. 'There will be a compromise. They'll bring in the United Nations. People don't fight wars over small colonies any more.' 'Trust me,' I said. 'You don't know Margaret Thatcher.'

A few weeks later, back at university, I was asleep in my room one morning when there was a knock at the door. 'Oh, you're still alive then,' an anonymous voice said. Still half asleep, I didn't really think anything of it and dozed off again. A few minutes later, the same thing happened. 'Glad to see you're still with us,' said my next-door neighbour, Dave Larg. Strange, I thought. Later on in the communal kitchen someone asked if I had seen the papers yet. I said I hadn't. 'You ought to,' came the reply.

I remember as if it were yesterday: turning to page two of the *Daily Mail* and seeing my name. Killed in action in the Falklands. But it wasn't me. It was Welsh Guardsman Ian Dale, aged nineteen from Pontypridd. It was like being hit in the solar plexus. Tears streamed down my face, as they were to do many times over the next few weeks. Nothing else could have brought home to me the terrible waste of war like this did. I was the same age. It could have been me.

Not long afterwards, I attended a debate at the university between the President of the Students Union and leading light in the University Labour Club, Mark Seddon (who went on to become UN Correspondent with Al Jazeera), and someone whose name I now forget but who was also on the extreme left. I was horrified that such a debate could take place between the soft left and hard place with no other viewpoint being put forward. So up I stood and defended the sending of the Task Force and our right to retake British sovereign territory from a Fascist regime. That was my first real experience of the cut and thrust of political debate. And I enjoyed it. It was the catalyst for getting involved in politics.

For me, the Falklands War was a formative experience. My father was a teenager during the Second World War and even now he is happiest when he is reading about it or watching a TV documentary on it. I remain fascinated by the political, military and personal consequences of the Falklands War. I remember watching the TV pictures of HMS *Sheffield* in flames, of the helicopter rescues from the burning ships with tears welling in my eyes. I remember the sleep-inducing tones of the Ministry of Defence spokesman Ian McDonald at his daily press conferences. I remember the fury that overcame me as I watched the BBC's *Panorama* programme which sought to pour scorn on the war. I remember John Nott announcing the retaking of South Georgia late at night in Downing Street and Margaret Thatcher urging journalists present not to ask more questions but to 'rejoice' at the news.

But most of all, I remember the sense of relief, national pride and joy that most of the country felt as they watched the Union Jack being hoisted again over Government House in Port Stanley. It was a day that helped Britain regain its national pride, which many felt had been lost twenty-six years earlier in the depths of the Suez Canal. In my opinion, 14 June 1982 will be seen by future historians as a turning point in British history. It was a day which showed that Britain was no longer a soft touch and had the ability to stand up against aggressors. Most important of all, it demonstrated a resolve to the Communist world and the Soviet Union in particular that they thought we had lost years before.

IT'S ABOUT THAT OLD FASHIONED THING CALLED SHAME
WEDNESDAY 2 MAY

Lord Browne has had a very unpleasant twenty-four hours.[†] In some ways, for having lied to a court, you'd have to say he deserves it and that few should have sympathy with him. But – and it is a big but – that would be to ignore two facts. This story would not have taken up so much space in the newspapers if he hadn't been gay, but it is the second fact which few in the media have commented on, and this is why I am posting this now.

The only reason John Browne lied to the court – and I do not offer this as an excuse – was because of an old-fashioned thing called shame. He felt ashamed that he had resorted to a gay website to meet his former partner. For all I know he may have felt a sense of shame about his sexuality as well. It would not surprise me – he is, after all, fifty-nine years old. He comes from a generation of men who could never 'come out' in the way that people are able to today. While he may be comfortable in his own skin, he mixes in circles that still have difficulties with friends and colleagues who don't conform to society's norms. The City is sometimes not a comfortable place for openly gay people.

Shame is regarded as a bit odd in today's 'everything goes' society. It's almost regarded as quaint. It's no longer shameful to have a baby out of wedlock. It's no longer shameful to have a criminal record. It is no longer shameful to be unemployed. It is no longer shameful to

---

† John Browne, CEO of BP, lied to a court about his four-year relationship with his Canadian boyfriend.

be divorced. It is no longer shameful to be gay. For most of these, it's a very good thing too that shame has been partially banished from our society. However, we do have to recognise that for people of an older generation many of these things are indeed shameful.

So I don't excuse John Browne for not telling the truth to the court. But I do have some understanding for why he did it. He will now have to face the consequences.

The man I have total scorn for here is his former lover who sought to make money out of a kiss and tell. He is beneath contempt.

YOU KNOW SOMEONE LOVES YOU WHEN...
SUNDAY 6 MAY

Your two-year-old goddaughter sees you on TV, goes up to the TV screen, and then kisses it and hugs it. Bless.

READING GORDON BROWN

I was visiting a Tory MP in Portcullis House when I noticed the book by Simon Sebag-Montefiore, *Young Stalin*, on his desk. 'What are you reading that for?' I asked. 'So I can read the mindset of Gordon Brown,' came the reply. Boom boom.

DREAM, DREAM, DREAM, WHEN I WAS YOUNG
FRIDAY 18 MAY

I don't know about you, but I very rarely remember details of dreams. Last night, however, I had a very vivid dream and I can remember virtually every detail.

Before your imagination runs away with you, let me explain. Fifteen years ago a very dear friend of the family died of cancer. She died only four weeks after being diagnosed. Although she wasn't a relation she was one of my mother's best friends and my sisters and I called her Auntie Jean.

In my dream she suddenly reappeared in our lives and told us she had been living in Lincolnshire for the last fifteen years and hadn't died of cancer after all. It was a bit like Bobby Ewing reappearing in *Dallas*! I won't go into the details of the rest of the dream, but they were so real that when I woke up I really believed it all to be true for a second.

Often when you have a dream there is a reason for it. In this case, there was no reason. Why should Jean suddenly reappear in my thoughts after such a long time? Why can I remember this dream when I can't remember any others? It's a fascinating subject which I suspect there has been a lot of academic research on, but I know nothing about.

OVERHEARD...
FRIDAY 30 JUNE

Two young American females overheard on the tube:
Girl 1: Every girl would sleep with the President of the United States, wouldn't she?
Girl 2: Yeah definitely ... Well, not Bush.
Girl 1: No, definitely not.
Girl 2: And not Reagan.
Girl 1: No...
Girl 2: And I guess not Roosevelt...

RWANDAN DIARY: INTO AFRICA†
SATURDAY 20 JULY

Well, it's 7.30 a.m. and we are on a two-hour stopover at Nairobi airport before getting a flight to Kigali. There's a group of lobby journos with us too, so Alice (Head of Production and ace camerawoman at 18 Doughty Street) and I are not alone.

Having been told just before we got on the flight that Kenyan Airways have the second worst safety record of any world airline, I have to say it was an excellent flight. I still don't know if my leg was being pulled. I spent much of the flight reading more of Alastair Campbell's diaries but despite that didn't get a wink of sleep.

---

† Iain accompanied a group of more than fifty Conservative Party volunteers, led by Andrew Mitchell, to Rwanda, where they would work for two weeks on social action projects.

The guy in front of me kept reclining his seat, which was a bit annoying. Each time he got up to go to the loo I reached round and put the seat back up, which horrified Alice. Sadly he then reclined it again a few minutes after he got back.

Nairobi airport is like something out of a 1950s film set – lots of shouting, rather hot even at this time of day and dodgy decor. We just queued up at the transfer desk behind a man in a robe and the hairiest back you've ever seen. Alice nearly barfed her breakfast.

RWANDAN DIARY: DAY 1
SATURDAY 21 JULY

The flight from Nairobi to Kigali yesterday took an uneventful hour and a quarter. I expected to be hit by a massive heatwave as I got off the plane, but far from it. The heat has been pleasant and dry with no humidity whatsoever. We were met in the terminal and whisked off to our hotel in the centre of Kigali. Only an hour later, having had no sleep for a day, we started our tour of the Project Umbano schemes. We met up with Andrew Mitchell and his team who gave us a rundown of what we were about to face. There aren't exactly many spare hours.

We were then driven to an orphanage called Girubuntu, where Tobias Ellwood MP was leading a team of volunteers (including Brooks Newmark MP and blogger Vicky Ford)[†] to build a new classroom and renovate the existing buildings. It was a hive of activity. During our tour of the project more than forty locals turned up to join in. Word had travelled that white British MPs were building toilets – something guaranteed to attract people's interest.

I spent some time talking to a journalist from the only English language newspaper in Rwanda, the *New Times*. English has just been made an official language in Rwanda but literacy rates are very low and it doesn't have a huge circulation. This chap told me that it was quite difficult being a journalist in Rwanda. It's not a dictatorship but it's not easy to write articles criticising the government. His family were originally from Rwanda but left for Uganda in the 1950s. He had returned about a year ago as he wanted to help his country rise from the ashes.

---

† Later to become a Conservative MEP.

And that's the thing you notice here. There is a tremendous commitment from everybody to rebuild and renew. In only ten years since the genocide, a proper public administrative infrastructure has emerged. While there is still abject poverty, people can see with their own eyes what progress is being made. There is a law that on the fourth Saturday in every month everyone has to help on a community project.

We then went to visit the Rwandan Minister of Finance to discuss how international aid agencies were helping his country's development. The good thing is that everyone I have talked to says that there is very little sign of corruption in Rwanda and where they find it they deal with it quickly. This is good news as Britain is Rwanda's biggest giver of development aid, at £46 million last year. Germany gives only £1 million.

At 7 p.m. we all met up for dinner at the apartments where most of the volunteers are staying. Everyone had a story to tell and you could tell there was a real buzz about what was going on.

RWANDAN DIARY: DAY 2
SUNDAY 22 JULY

Another early start for a three-hour drive to the southern Rwandan town of Butare. Our first stop was at an orphanage school. We were treated to very enthusiastic singing by the 107 children. Their classroom was the size of one we would put fifteen kids in, rather than 107.

The school is clearly struggling to exist despite its excellent teachers' endeavours. They have started making Christmas cards and clothes to create an income stream. Because the school only takes orphans (of the 107 kids, thirty-five have HIV and fifteen are heads of family) there are many local children who don't get the schooling these kids get. It was quite heart-rending to see the other kids looking at us through the school fence.

Next stop was a nearby village for which Project Umubano is providing English teaching and helping with the re-roofing of a rabbit breeding enterprise. I have to admit I thought this was the poorest place I had ever seen in my life, yet one of the lobby journalists reckons there are far worse-off places than this. There are very few roads in Rwanda. Virtually every village is reached by treacherous dirt tracks in a sturdy 4x4. 18 Doughty Street's Alice became the village Pied Piper as all the local kids wanted to be captured on film. The look on their faces when she shows them the film and they can see themselves is a sight to behold. Just off to the right of this photo a man beckoned me over. He was holding a large jug, which contained the local beer, and invited me into his home. His house consisted of two rooms, one with a table and one chair and two posters on the walls and nothing else. No carpet, no other furniture, nothing. But I have rarely met a happier man. And that's the common theme. The people we meet are unfailingly happy despite the abject poverty they live in and their country's troubled recent past. Everywhere you go you meet happy, smiling people. They may be hiding deep sadness underneath, but they hide it very well indeed. None of the houses in this village has a toilet, but several outside latrines are being built at the moment.

Each latrine is shared by five families and they cost £170 each. I was given the honour of christening one of them. One of the journalists asked if I had brought a plaque. Ha ha. The rabbit breeding project is one which the Tory team is helping develop. The rabbits are meant to provide an income for the village. At first the villagers just treated the rabbits as food, but they are now trying to make it into a proper business. The roof needed to be replaced because the rabbits were getting too hot and not eating.

We then drove for an hour on an incredibly bumpy dirt track to a village which doesn't even feature on a map. It's where two British GPs (one of whom is Andrew Mitchell's wife, Sharon) are spending two weeks treating local people. We were warned that we would be crossing the 'Bridge of Death', which was a very rickety bridge with wooden slats. As we were in a Toyota 4x4 I didn't give much for our chances of getting across and wanted to get out and walk across. The driver wasn't having any of it and put his foot down. Well, we made it, although I am sure we dislodged a few slats while we were at it. The medical centre in the village is run by a group of nuns, but none of them has medical training. There are only 400 doctors in Rwanda which equates to one doctor per 200,000 people. In Britain we have one GP per 2,000 people. The task of the two British GPs is to train some local nurses and while they are there treat as many people as possible. In the first five days they treated more than 500 people. Word soon spread that they were there and they had to turn people away. Most people could be treated easily but there were at least three cases where I am sure they saved the people's lives. The nearest hospital is a four-hour walk away. There is no other way of getting there. If anyone breaks their leg or physically cannot walk, they are reliant on neighbours to carry them there on a stretcher. And when they get there they have to provide their own bed linen and food. Makes you think, doesn't it? At the medical centre there are a number of in-patient wards including ones for TB sufferers, a maternity ward and one for those suffering from malnutrition.

It is this project which has affected me most so far. The sheer hopelessness of the situation is appalling. Sharon and David, the two GPs, will leave at the end of next week knowing that they have probably saved lives. If they were there for the next two weeks they would be able to do the same. But they will leave a lasting legacy in the training they will have supplied to the nuns and other nursing staff. And they should be bloody proud of what they have done.

The running theme of the day was me thinking 'What can I, as an individual, do to make these people's lives better?' Now that probably sounds as if I have suddenly become a woolly liberal. Not a bit of it. But it is amazing how much very little money will buy here. And at the end of it, it is well-directed money which these communities need – money which if it comes through government agencies might never get to where it is most needed.

When I was at the first orphanage I did something which later I thought was incredibly crass. I gave the head teacher $50 to spend on provisions for the school. I just felt it was the only way I could show him that I was so impressed by what he was doing. I refuse to give money to charities who spend a vast proportion of it on admin. I want to give money directly, to an organisation I care about and where I know the money won't be wasted.

RWANDAN DIARY: DAY 3
MONDAY 23 JULY

Another very early start to head back down south to the village of Marambi, the site of one of the worst episodes of the 1994 genocide. It's also the site of a National Genocide Memorial. We were going at the invitation of Mary Blewitt, who lost sixty family members in the genocide. Since then she has started an excellent charity called SURF, a Rwandan genocide survivors fund. Andrew Mitchell is on its board and Mary has done brilliant work in raising the profile of Rwanda and its problems throughout the political spectrum in Britain. She's also raised more than £7 million to help survivors of the genocide.

The day did not start well, when after only an hour into the journey I started getting stomach cramps. Knowing that there were two more hours to go until we reached our destination I was facing the embarrassment of having to ask the coach to stop for, er, well, shall we call it a pit stop. Luckily the cramps gradually went away!

It took more than three hours to get to Marambi. None of us knew what to expect. What we experienced will affect every one of us for a very long time indeed.

As well as the mass grave, in which 50,000 Tutsis are buried, there are at least a dozen rooms with dead bodies laid out, all cased in lime. The smell was something which will stay with me for a very long time indeed. One room was full of bodies of children and babies. It was at that point I lost it. Alice, my cameralady, was extremely upset and tears were rolling down her face as she filmed. I did a piece to camera which was, shall we say, highly emotional. We were then shown a site where French soldiers built a basketball court on top of a mass grave. I cannot tell you how hated the French are in Rwanda. Their soldiers were sent to Marambi and actually protected the killers, who had hacked to death 50,000 Tutsis in forty-eight hours.

We then met one of only six surviors of the genocide at Marambi. Because he had a bullethole in his head the Hutu militias left him for dead. He escaped by walking through the hills to the border with Congo.

I then interviewed Mary Blewitt. She is such an inspirational figure. Her brother was one of the first to be killed in the genocide. She recently received a letter from the government asking her to exhume his body as they wanted to build on his burial site. So yesterday, thirteen years after his death, she had to rebury him. She agreed to talk about it in the interview, and as you can imagine it was fairly emotional.

Just to say, the reason I am in Rwanda is to make three documentaries for 18 Doughty Street – one on the Conservatives and Project Umubano, the second on the genocide and the third on life in Rwanda today. So far we must have filmed about five hours of footage in two days.

When we got back to Kigali, Alice and I had no way of getting back to our hotel so we decided to take our lives in our hands and hail two cabs. Why two, you may ask. Well, Rwandan cabs are motorbikes, not cars. So we were whisked through the streets of Kigali on the back of a couple of bikes. I can't pretend it wasn't slightly exhilarating, because it was. Alistair Burt MP has also taken to them apparently.

Tonight I had the somewhat odd experience of doing a live interview on *News 24*, from our hotel balcony in Kigali, but not on Rwanda, on David Cameron's apparent popularity problems. I don't know what it looked like on the TV, but it did feel as if I should have signed off by saying 'John Simpson, Baghdad', as the setting was very similar to that which the BBC use in Iraq!

RWANDAN DIARY: DAY 4
WEDNESDAY 25 JULY

This was our final full day in Rwanda. It started with David Cameron addressing the Rwandan Parliament. Apparently ITV News said that there was hardly anyone there. Not true. I counted around forty MPs, including the heads of all the leading committees, and there were a lot of press and NGO representatives present too. The speech didn't get off to a good start when all the lights went out for twenty seconds. Cameron made a good joke about it and moved on. It was a strong speech, launching the Globalisation Commission Report.

Next stop was the presidential compound where David Cameron spent an hour with President Kagame, who has led Rwanda since the 1994 genocide. Apparently they agreed that Kagame would address the Tory party conference in October. So with Governor Schwarzenegger there too, Blackpool will resonate to the Arnie & Kagame roadshow.

This afternoon it was back to the Girubuntu orphanage project which we visited on Day One. They've certainly made a lot of progress on building a new classroom and renovating the rest of the buildings. David Cameron was shown around and then did a series of media interviews including one for our film on the trip for 18

Doughty Street. We have nine hours of footage so far, so it's going to be quite a task to edit it down.

In the late afternoon Alice, my trusty camerawoman, and I hired a taxi to go out to a couple of villages to see what life is like outside the capital. At the first one I'm not sure that everyone was pleased to see us so we made a bit of a hasty getaway, but at the second one we were mobbed by both children and adults. Our taxi driver spoke excellent English. Both his parents were killed in the genocide and he is the head of the family, supporting his two younger sisters. He exists on $300 a month. He can't afford to buy a car (a Toyota Corolla costs $80,000 here!) so he rents one every day. But by comparison, he's well off. He said he was totally committed to rebuilding his country and was proud that everyone was pulling together.

One thing you notice here is that there is a total absence of litter in the streets. The government has banned plastic bags and on the fourth Saturday in the month everyone turns out to clear up their local neighbourhoods.

After returning to Kigali we found a local crafts centre, where I spent rather a lot of money on what I can only describe as shirts that Nelson Mandela would be proud to wear. I thought they'd go well with my Duchamp ties!

In the evening we all went out for a Chinese. Bearing in mind that most of us have got some sort of stomach upset (or worse) I wasn't sure that was a very good idea – especially as I don't like Chinese! The bill for eight of us came to $54. We tend to tip rather heavily here. Later on we met David Mundell MP and some of the volunteers at the Republika nightclub.

I had to get back to the hotel for midnight to do a Radio 5 Live interview on Gordon Brown's first month. It seems very strange to do interviews from Rwanda, but I think it went OK. I'll leave the last word on this blog post to *The Guardian*'s Will Woodward...

Mr Cameron's thirty-two hours in Rwanda may have looked bad at home; here, however, it has felt more positive.

Too right it has.

I SWEAR THIS IS TRUE...
FRIDAY 27 JULY

I just popped into Tunbridge Wells to pay some cheques into the bank. As it's a nice, sunny day I thought I would wear one of the shirts I bought in Rwanda. I was about to walk out the door when my partner said: 'You're not actually going out in that, are you?' Indeed I was. Anyway, I parked the car, went to the bank and was walking along Mount Pleasant when a woman approached me and the following exchange occurred:

Woman: Excuse me, but I hope you don't mind me asking, where did you get that shirt? I'd like to get one for my husband.

Me: I got it in Rwanda.

Woman: Oh, I don't know them. Have they got a branch in Tunbridge Wells?

Me: Er...

TOP TEN THINGS I LEARNT IN RWANDA
SATURDAY 28 JULY

---

1. Never break out in a chorus of the '80s hit 'Don't Mess With my Hutu'.
2. You're damned if you do, and damned if you don't.
3. David Mundell's taste in shirts is similar to my taste in ties.
4. I can exist without email on my Blackberry.
5. Rwandan women are the best dressed in the world.
6. France has a lot to answer for over the genocide.
7. It feels safer in Kigali than in parts of London.
8. No one in Britain understands the meaning of the word 'poverty'.
9. It is possible for one person to make a difference.
10. We should not try to impose our way of life on others.

CHARLOTTE ROBINSON
THURSDAY 30 AUGUST

Sometimes you hear a piece of news which knocks you for six. During the last election campaign I had some fantastic help from some teenagers from the village of Worsted in North Norfolk, one of them being a young lady called Charlotte Robinson.

Charlotte emailed me out of the blue in the spring and asked if she could come and do work experience at 18 Doughty Street for a week this summer. We emailed back and forth and I suggested she come last week. But I never heard back from her. I now know why. I've just been told that she died last week from an eating disorder. She can't have been more than eighteen. What a terrible waste of a life. Her wonderful family will be devastated. RIP Charlotte.

INDICATING TO THE RIGHT? RETURN TO A CORE VOTE STRATEGY? ER, NO...

At ten to seven this morning I woke to the sound of my mobile ringing. It was the *Today* programme. Oh God, I thought, who's died. Luckily no one had. They wanted to know if I could appear on their programme in the following hour to talk about David Cameron's *Newsnight* interview and what he said about immigration. Er, OK, I said, what did they want to do. Well, said the researcher, all the newspapers are headlining his words on immigration. Does this mean that he's reverting to a core vote strategy? Don't be silly, I said. Well, she continued, his people must have briefed it out. I doubt it, I said. He was asked a question and he answered it, and as far as I could recall he hadn't said anything particularly remarkable about immigration, merely repeated previously announced policies. But don't you think he's appealing to the right by saying this? Maybe, I said, but you don't have to be on the right to be concerned about uncontrolled immigration. But it does seem a bit of a coincidence that all the papers have led on his immigration comments, she said. Perhaps, I said, but it wouldn't be the first time the lobby had operated as a pack, would it, I rejoindered, reminding her of David Davis's conference speech.

By this time I could tell that what I was saying didn't really fit the line she was hoping I would take. But she seemed fairly adamant that she wanted me to go on. So rather than go back to sleep I waited for her call back. And waited. And waited. Anyway, I thought I would put the intervening time to good effect so I phoned one of David Cameron's press spokesmen and asked if the immigration answer was the one they were highlighting and briefing out. As I suspected, it was not. A journalist had asked if Cameron had said anything new in the interview and the line on transitional arrangements for EU nationals was one that was mentioned. And so the story grew. In a 45-minute interview it would be surprising if absolutely nothing new was said, and it was this that the journalists latched onto.

Cameron's spokesman denied absolutely that this was either a 'lurch to the right' or even sending a signal to the right. Anyway, back to the *Today* programme. I continued to wait ... and wait ... and, well, I went back to a deep doze until I woke at 8.30 to hear the dulcet tones of ConservativeHome's Tim Montgomerie explaining to the nation that that was indeed a signal to the right and the Tory grassroots would be very pleased indeed.

WHY CAN'T THESE DINOSAURS DEPART THE STAGE?
TUESDAY 4 SEPTEMBER

Before the last election Lynton Crosby told us all that we should ask ourselves every morning: 'What am I going to do today to help the Conservative Party win the next election?' These sentiments would of course be entirely lost on the Thirteenth Marquess of Lothian, who has let rip in the *Daily Telegraph* this morning. What on earth did he think he was doing by slagging off David Cameron in this most gratuitous way? And on the day that the party is publishing its Public Services Commission Report!

Michael Ancram is a delightful man in private, but he has the political judgement and timing of a blunderbuss. I well remember that in the Hague years he was the first to tear his hair out in frustration at the antics of Michael Portillo (see the Nick Kochan biography of Ann Widdecombe). He was no doubt also frustrated by those who went on TV to denounce Hague's apologies for what went wrong during the Thatcher years. And yet he is now doing exactly the same to David Cameron despite the fact that Cameron has never trashed Margaret Thatcher's legacy. He was, it should be remembered, deputy leader of the party when Iain Duncan Smith wrote a book called *There Is Such a Thing as Society* (I published it). I don't remember him speaking about that as an insult to Margaret Thatcher.

He criticises David Cameron for not paying enough attention to core Conservative issues like Europe and tax. Does he not realise that in the 2001 and 2005 general elections we lost in large part due to appearing to concentrate only on these core-vote issues?

Despite his history as a 'moderate' he appears unable to comprehend that elections are not won from the hard right – they are won from the centre ground, and, until recently, David Cameron was rather successfully reoccupying that centre ground. To revert to the kind of strategy chosen by Ancram would be electoral suicide. Yes, I would like a firmer line on issues like tax cuts too, and some of the Cameron programme leaves me reaching for the political smelling salts from time to time, but I recognise what has to be done. Careless talk like this costs votes and reinforces the view of a 'lurch to the right' which Gordon Brown would love the Conservatives to do.

Michael Ancram's pamphlet, which his article was intended to publicise, is called *Still a Conservative*. A Tory MP suggested to me this morning that it should be renamed *Still a Prat*. I find it hard to disagree.

Coming on top of yesterday's news on John Bercow and Patrick Mercer this sort of internal navel gazing is intolerable. The people I feel sorry for are the parliamentary candidates who have been slogging their guts out for months. They must look at this shower and wonder why they are bothering.

Politicians like Ancram have had their day. They should leave it to those who have a future ahead of them to plot the party's future.

POSITIVELY THE FINAL MENTION OF MICHAEL ANCRAM

Yesterday afternoon I asked for suggestions for a Top Ten List of Reasons Why Michael Ancram Should Be Taken Outside And Shot. Here is the final list...

10. So he knows how the grouse feel.
9. Because we need to discourage the aristocracy from overbreeding.
8. To put him out of my misery.
7. Because the House of Commons fossil collection is already large enough.
6. Because he believes in heaven, so we'd be doing him a huge favour.
5. Because it would make it easier to gain access to his lovely daughters.
4. Because his writing is staggeringly dull and pretentious.

3. *Pour encourager les autres*.
2. Because we couldn't lay our hands on Bob Crow.
1. And the number 1 reason Michael Ancram should be taken outside and shot is: Because shooting him inside would mean that you'd have to repaint the walls.

CRUNCH TIME
SUNDAY 16 SEPTEMBER

I am not a customer of Northern Rock. But if I were, I too would be withdrawing my money. For the elites to criticise those who feel their savings are at risk is stomach churning.

AN AUTUMN ELECTION ISN'T JUST POSSIBLE – IT'S PROBABLE
THURSDAY 20 SEPTEMBER

Everything in my gut tells me that an election will be called next week. There will be another couple of opinion polls in the next few days which will probably confirm a 5–8 point Labour lead.

Just do what I have done and draw a line down the middle of a piece of paper and write down the arguments for and against an autumn election from Gordon Brown's perspective. You won't find many in the 'against' column. Brown has written a book called *Courage*. If he fails to call an election soon – and the media momentum is gathering – he'll be accused of flunking it. Most other pundits and commentators still reckon that's exactly what he will do. I don't. I always thought an autumn election was possible. I now think it's probable. Indeed, I would go so far as to predict that he might even call it next Thursday, just to bugger the Conservative conference. It's just the sort of thing Brown would take great pleasure from.

GOD, GAYS, CHERRY-PICKERS AND CHEESEMONGERS
SUNDAY 23 SEPTEMBER

This exchange was heard recently on *University Challenge*:
Paxman: What is another word for 'cherrypickers' and 'cheesemongers'?

Contestant: Homosexuals?

Paxman: No. They're regiments in the British Army who will be very upset with you.

And in other news today, the Archbishop of Canterbury says 'homosexuality is not a disease'.

Well, that's a relief then.

Actually, what he said was this: 'I do not assume that homosexual inclination is a disease.' Which means he's keeping his options open. Nice to know our leading churchman is such a man of conviction, isn't it?

VICIOUS TYPING MEANS A NEW COMPUTER
SATURDAY 29 SEPTEMBER

Like most people in politics or the media I am totally reliant on my laptop. Despite various people trying to wean me off Sony Vaios and telling me how wonderful Apple Macs are, I'm a creature of habit, and like to stick to what I know. I've had my current laptop for a year, but I know I should get a new one. How do I know? Because I can no longer see the letters on the keyboard. I was introduced to typing at the age of ten when my father bought me an old iron typewriter from Cambridge market. I spent hours as a teenager bashing out football league tables with two fingers – hitting the letter keys for all they were worth. The trouble is, I still type as if I'm using an iron typewriter. I may seem a gentle sort, but when I type I can be vicious.

BORIS COMES OF AGE
MONDAY 1 OCTOBER

Today was the day I realised that Boris had it in him to be a first-rate politician. You see, in my heart of hearts I have always wondered if he had the self-discipline to get there, or even the passion. His speech this afternoon to the Conservative conference was a barnstormer, laced with humour (but not too much), with real substance. It was a speech which said to me: 'You can take me seriously. I'm in it to win it.' The delivery was good and the content was good.

What an odd day. Every person had only one subject on their mind – is there going to be an early election or not? Strangely, there seems to be a mood of eerie resignation to the fact that Gordon Brown will indeed call one.

However, there was one dissenting voice that I encountered on this – and one I have a lot of respect for. It was a private conversation so I won't say whom it was with, but it was one the country's leading political journalists. He's convinced Gordon Brown won't risk an election and thinks the polls are massively overstating the Labour lead. He reckons the lead could disappear as quickly as it arrived. The name of Ed Balls then came up. I remarked that I thought Balls was the most overrated politician in British politics and reminded me of Alan B'Stard's hapless assistant, Piers Fletcher-Dervish. No, no, no, said the political journalist. 'Ed Balls isn't the most overrated politician in British politician. That's Gordon Brown. He's a second rater.' I picked up my jaw from the floor and was about to ask him what he meant by that when someone interrupted the conversation.

Can it be true that we have all overestimated Gordon Brown? I described him in my *Telegraph* column last week as the greatest machine politician of his generation. Was I wrong? Perhaps we shouldn't all be so intimidated by him.

ZAC GOLDSMITH ADDS TO THE BUZZZZZZZZZ

Speaking at a fringe event last night Zac Goldsmith said that there are many misconceptions about the 'Quality of Life' report.[†]

He joked: 'I do quickly want to draw your attention to vibrators. According to a number of reports the report was going to recommend banning them. Given that today is a day about ruling things in and out I can rule out any more talk about banning vibrators.'

The Conservative Women's Organisation heaved a collective sigh of relief. At least, I think it was a sigh…

REFLECTIONS ON DAY 3
TUESDAY 2 OCTOBER

* Gordon Brown's trip to Iraq has gone down like a cup of cold

---

† A report commissioned by David Cameron and chaired by Zac Goldsmith, Tory candidate for Richmond Park and later its MP.

sick with the journalists here in Blackpool. They are as one in their outrage. Why? Because he very stupidly took only two broadcast journalists with him, and not a single dead tree scribe. Not a good PR move.

* David Davis's speech gets a slating on ConHome and in *The Sun* this morning. I must have been watching a different speech. But then again, so I was in 2005, so perhaps I am not the best judge. My partner rang me last night (and he's no great fan of DD – doesn't like it when he answers the phone at home and, without a greeting, DD just says 'Is he there?'!), raving about his speech – 'best one I've heard', 'Cameron will do well to better that' and 'told it how it is' were just three of the things he said.

* I was astonished at the number of people who said they had seen me do my little speech on Rwanda. Whenever you speak at a conference everyone always tells you how well you have done, even if they don't mean it, so I take compliments on speeches with a pinch of salt. However, virtually everyone said that it really came from the heart and they were glad I managed to hold it together. Luckily I took out the one line which might have made me lose it.

SPECTATOR DIARY
IAIN DALE'S BLACKPOOL CONFERENCE DIARY
FRIDAY 5 OCTOBER

Thank the Lord this will be the last time conference-goers have to endure the hellhole that calls itself Blackpool. The last time I stayed in a Blackpool hotel at a party conference was in the mid-1990s. I woke up at 2 a.m. on the first night covered in sweat. I hadn't been indulging in any, er, nefarious activity and didn't feel ill, but I eventually worked it out. The caring Blackpool hotel owner had thoughtfully put rubber incontinence sheets on the bed. Now I am sure some people would pay good money for that sort of thing, but I decided to check out the next morning. Each time I have gone to Blackpool since then I've stayed in the gloriously named Ribby Hall Holiday Village, a sort of modern-day Butlins without the red coats, located a few miles outside the town that even the locals dub Chav City. As a conference centre, the Winter Gardens remains stuck in the 1950s. As a blogger, an internet connection is a must for me at any conference venue. I rang the Winter Gardens to ask if they had WiFi. I really don't know why I bothered. I might as well have been asking for the availability of a nuclear physics lab. For the next few years the Tories are off to Birmingham and Manchester. I long for the day when Cardiff has enough hotel rooms to attract a conference of this size. It's one of the most vibrant cities in Britain.

Life as a blogger at a party conference can be weird. My blog has about 50,000 readers (nearly as many as *The Spectator*!) and all of them seemed to be in Blackpool. People find it odd when I say I'm actually quite shy, so I don't always find it easy to react to people who tell me how wonderful they think my blog is. I mean, how would you react when someone says: 'I think you're an absolute legend!' But in the blogosphere you make many enemies as well as new friends. You're either too sycophantic or too disloyal, too shrill or too friendly. You're too right-wing or not right-wing enough. There's only black and white, no grey. Virtually every day I get called a fascist **** or worse. My parenthood is regularly called into question. So why do I do it? Because blogging is a liberating experience and it's a way of saying what you want to say, when you want to say it, and without a media filter. Try it. You might like it.

A few weeks ago I had the bright idea of compiling a league table of the Top 100 Most Influential People on the Right. The *Telegraph* has been running the list all week, culminating with the Top 25 on the day David Cameron (the number one, natch) made his speech. A journalist rang me to ask why I was doing it. He wanted to know what was in it for me. 'Making a lot of enemies, I should think,' I replied. I spent the whole conference avoiding the half-dozen shadow Cabinet members who didn't make the cut, and ignoring the texts and emails of those who complained – in a good-natured way, of course – about their ranking. And you never know who's behind you when you're gossiping about the reasons so and so was number 62 or 69. Luckily Alan Duncan has a very well-developed sense of humour.

At every conference there's always one person who becomes your personal stalker. You see them everywhere. This year mine turned out to be the Thirteenth Marquess of Lothian, better known to you and me as Michael Ancram. Everywhere I went, he went. Every party I went to, he was there. Why should this bother me? It was I who took to the airwaves and the newspaper columns to denounce his recent pamphlet. I called him a dinosaur, Sir Bufton Tufton and God alone knows what else for breaking ranks on the eve of a conference and a possible election. But we never spoke. Either he hasn't a clue what I look like (probably) or he decided to blank me (unlikely – he's too polite). I wrestled with the dilemma of having a chat with him about it all, but then thought it best to let sleeping dogs lie. What a wimp.

Making a speech at a Tory conference can be a terrifying experience, especially if you discover just before you're about to go on that you have left your speech in your Ribby Hall Holiday Chalet, several miles from Blackpool. So it was with some trepidation that I approached the speaker's lectern to talk about Rwanda, having hastily scribbled it out again. I always think you should feel nervous before a speech like this. This time I didn't feel nervous at all, and it worried me. I was introduced by Nicola Blackwood, a Tory candidate from Oxford, who called me 'Britain's most famous blagger'. Nice. It got a laugh, though, and set me off to a good start. My mother rang me afterwards to tell me how well she thought I'd done — it's what mothers are for, after all. She said how nice it was to see Gillian Shephard in a TV cutaway during my speech. I had to tell her that it was in fact Edwina Currie. It's not the first time that mistake has been made.

I was followed by a Burmese lady, Zoya Phan, who made an impassioned speech urging international support for her country. I was not alone in having tears running down my face by the time she concluded. I was glad I didn't have to follow her.

WIDDECOMBE'S PARTY BLOWS MY COVER
FRIDAY 5 OCTOBER

I'm not going to blog much about Ann W's birthday do, as it was a private occasion, but I am sure she won't mind me telling you that we were serenaded by Aled Jones and treated to very funny speeches by Simon Hoggart and Ann herself. My stalker was there too, sat at Ann's top table and directly in my line of vision? Yup, Michael Ancram. I thought I had got away with it until Simon Hoggart started his speech and retold an anecdote about how Ann used to sell her books at the Politico's stand at party conference: 'No sex, no violence, no swearing!' He then added the words, 'And the man who used to run Politico's, Iain Dale, is here tonight...' I looked at Michael, he looked at me, winked and grinned. He later came over and we had a good laugh about it all. 'I thought Sir Bufton had better come and say hello,' he opened with. Respect.

FRIT!
SATURDAY 6 OCTOBER

Well, if Nick Robinson is right, Gordon Brown has bottled it. All summer he has wanted to call an election but at various stages he has chickened out at the last minute. I was told recently that he wanted to call an election in early September but in the end he decided not to. Oh how he must be regretting that decision. The recent polls, and internal Labour polling in the marginals, has persuaded Brown that calling an election would be too risky. And that is down to one man – David Cameron. No one, least of all Gordon Brown, expected such a dramatic turnaround in the polls. It demonstrates the volatility of the electorate. I always felt that for Brown, things could only get worse and this autumn would be the best time for him to get his own mandate. No one knows what is around the corner, but the economy looks very shaky indeed. The Northern Rock crisis is not over yet.

The last week has been incredibly damaging for Brown. The media has turned against him over the ill-judged trip to Basra and he has proved to be the spinner most of us always knew him to be. His attempt to portray himself as 'the change', someone who would conduct a new style of politics, has been revealed as a sham.

Make no mistake, David Cameron has got out of jail free. He has achieved the greatest political escape in modern history. Few of us would have been confident of a Tory victory, and Brown's decision has given the party a chance to fight another day.

Brown will give all sorts of excuses for not calling the election – state of the electoral register, blue tongue, foot and mouth, boundaries in Northern Ireland not ready, not in the national interest, blah, blah, blah, but no one will believe a word of it.

Because everyone really knows that the reason Gordon Brown hasn't called an election is because he couldn't be confident of winning it.

UEA: THOSE WERE THE DAYS
WEDNESDAY 10 OCTOBER

I am heading off up to Norwich mid-morning. In the evening I'm speaking to University of East Anglia Conservatives to mark the twenty-fifth anniversary of the setting up of the UEA Consoc in 1982 – and you can have three guesses as to who started it all. It's on days like this that I feel rather old.

I'm also going to have a drink with the Norfolk Blogger, Nich Starling, in the Maid's Head before the UEA bash. We used to hold a lot of our meetings there, and in a pub opposite called The Lawyer. A favourite hangout was a pizza restaurant a few yards away in Tombland called Pizza One, Pancakes Too. And another few hundred yards down the road is the nightclub – then called Bonds – where I first got totally off my head on Pernod & Blacks (yes, a real tart's drink, I know). I downed eleven in two hours – very Hagueish. Ah, the memories. Anyway, where was I?

One of my main memories of running UEA Tories was a meeting we held in 1985 with Cecil Parkinson as guest speaker. He was slowly being rehabilitated after his 1983 resignation and we expected a big crowd in Lecture Theatre 1. Little did I know that when we walked in it was full to overflowing, with 900 students.

He got a standing ovation, which I was a little surprised at, as UEA was a very left-wing university in those days. In fact his reception was so good that it provoked the Socialist Workers crowd who tried to invade the stage. They failed at that due to the skilful work of members of the UEA Rugby Society, so then the eggs started coming in. None of them hit Cecil. They all hit Ann, his wife, and me. My new suit was ruined. Cecil was furious and shouted, 'Which little lefty rat threw that at my wife?' The rest of the audience cheered and turned on the egg throwers who left without further incident. What a great meeting! Cecil loved it!

I have another memory of me and Caroline Flint at a student union meeting debating the pros and cons of taking VAT off tampons. She was Chair of the ~~Wimmins~~ Women's Society and used to dress in what looked like an old sack. How times change. She is a government minister and I'm, well, me. I agreed with her on tampons, by the way.

Among my other contemporaries was Mark Seddon, who I tried to get sacked as student union president for funnelling student union money to striking miners. Ann Taylor's former adviser Iain McKenzie was also there, as was former NUS President Vicky Phillips and Jo Gibbons, who now works for Tony Blair. She really didn't like me very much.

UPSETTING THE CHINGFORD STRANGLER
THURSDAY 11 OCTOBER

I shan't be walking down any dark alleys in the next few days. It seems I have upset Norman Tebbit. In my *Telegraph* column a couple of weeks ago I warned Tories that they should be disciplined during their conference. During the article I wrote this:

> A speech by Sir Bufton Tufton (the politician formerly known as Michael Ancram) hinting at the need for a different course will make front-page headlines in *The Mirror*. Be warned. It will happen... Every politician has a 'naughty brain', the one that craves attention. (Norman Tebbit, are you listening?) It's so much easier to say what you think and hang the consequences.

Michael Ancram thought it hugely funny, but not, I'm afraid, Lord T. He had, you may remember, given an interview to *The Times* on the eve of the conference in which he was not very complimentary about David Cameron and rather too complimentary about Gordon Brown.

Anyway, I got a letter this morning which was, well, very Norman-esque. It starts...

> I realise that in a desire to be noticed, little-known columnists write silly things to attract attention to themselves, but your remarks about me last week were really rather too silly...

Ouch. He continues...

> You may be unaware that any craving I might have had to be taken notice of has been more than satiated over my three or four decades of public life. Indeed, I sometimes find that being noticed can be a bit of a bore these days...

Well, that's me banged to rights. I should make clear that I adore Norman Tebbit. He's an icon to those of us who learnt our politics in the 1980s. Had things been different he could well have succeeded Margaret Thatcher in 1990. The point I was making was that interventions like Norman's can be highly damaging and that if, in 1987, when he was Party Chairman, Ian Gilmour had done something similar, Norman would rightly have strung him up from the nearest lamp-post.

I was sitting next to Lord T at a dinner a couple of years ago and the speaker was droning on about the Conservative Party needing to attract more celebrities like Jonny Wilkinson to support it. Norman leaned over and whispered in my ear, 'Yes, at least he knows how to kick balls.' Quite.

AND SO TO SLEEP
FRIDAY 12 OCTOBER

Very exciting. I went out and bought a new bed this afternoon, and decided to splash out on one that is 7 ft long. Being 6 ft 2 in. tall, I am fed up with sleeping in beds where my feet hang out the end. I've never understood people who deliberately buy cheap beds. After all, normal people spend a third of their lives in bed. Mostly asleep... I've noticed that as I get older I can survive on less sleep. I used to need a full eight hours but nowadays I seem to be able to survive quite happily on five or six. Am I alone in this?

THE DUKE OF EDINBURGH IN FINE FORM
SUNDAY 28 OCTOBER

A great anecdote from a speech by Gerald Howarth MP to the Young Britons' Foundation dinner. He was waiting in line to be received by the Duke of Edinburgh at a defence-related event and was rather surprised when the Duke looked him up and down and said to him, 'What does your party stand for nowadays then?' Unabashed, Gerald looked the Duke in the eye and said: 'For the defence of the Kingdom, sir.' The Duke of Edinburgh, looking doubtful, hit straight back with a single word. 'Bollocks.' There's no answer to that, really.

SAYING GOODBYE

Over the past week my beloved godmother, Eleanor Daniels, has been slipping away. Tomorrow I am going to Addenbrooke's Hospital in Cambridge to say goodbye to her. She's dying of cancer. Sadly, she has given up the fight and just wants to let go.

Eleanor has been more than a godmother to me and my two sisters. She was such an integral part of our childhood that we can all say she has played a major part in making us all what we are today. I remember all the wonderful day trips we went on as children. Off we'd troop in her Morris Minor (I still remember the number plate: 00 2163). Hunstanton, Walton-on-the-Naze, Wicksteed Park, Wells-next-the-Sea, Gosfield – the memories come flooding back. She never had her own children and has been like a sister to my mother. A kinder, more giving and caring person you could not hope to meet.

To be honest I am dreading seeing her in this state. I've never had to say 'goodbye' to anyone in this way before. The three of us[†] will go together. I suspect a lot of tears will be shed. If anyone deserves to go to heaven, she does.

Update: Monday 10 p.m.: Many thanks for all the wonderful messages in the comments. It has been a very traumatic day. I won't labour the details but Eleanor was very peaceful, recognised us all and we were all able to say our thank-yous to her and tell her we loved her. Saying goodbye was awful, but I am so glad I went.

ELEANOR DANIELS 1933–2007
SUNDAY 4 NOVEMBER

Eleanor Daniels, my beloved godmother, died last night in an NHS hospice in Cambridge. Three weeks ago she was admitted to Addenbrooke's Hospital. No one at the time could have believed that she would have been taken from us in such a short time.

Eleanor was born in 1933. From the age of two years old she became my mother's lifelong best friend. They attended the same school at Haverhill in Suffolk and their friendship endured when my mother moved to Norfolk. She trained to become a teacher and

---

†   Iain and his sisters, Tracey and Sheena.

spent more than thirty years teaching Domestic Science at my old school, the County High in Saffron Walden.

From the day I was born she became the most important person to me outside my immediate family. She stayed at our house every Tuesday night, and during the school holidays we'd all troop off in her Morris Minor for countless day trips to the coast or a visitor attraction. She was a second mother to my two sisters and me and we all worshipped her. She never married and we were the children she never had, I suppose.

She lived with her parents in a small village outside Saffron Walden, Little Chesterford. She was on the village hall committee, on the parish council and a leading light in the local garden club. It must have been her that John Major was referring to when he talked about old maids, cycling along the country lanes to church. She took her village duties incredibly seriously and it is a matter of huge regret that she never got to see the card which thirty villagers sent to her in hospital, each writing their own message of love and support.

Eleanor was a rock in my life. I could tell her things I could tell no one else. She bailed me out on several occasions in my younger years when I was on my financial uppers. She gave me wise advice which was always appreciated. In short, she was the perfect godmother.

When I went to see her on Monday to say goodbye I admit I didn't want to go. I was warned that she didn't look like the Eleanor we all knew and loved. I admit I was a coward, and just wanted to remember her as she always was – vibrant, laughing, funny, caring. I got to the door and didn't want to go into the room. My sister Tracey went in before me and as I was about to enter the room she gave me a look which said 'you will be shocked by what you see'. She was stronger than me.

Eleanor lay there and looked exactly like her mother, who died twenty-five years ago. She could barely talk. I hugged her, almost howling my eyes out. 'Stop it, stop it,' I thought to myself. 'For goodness sake, be strong.' Eleanor whispered in my ear, 'Don't upset yourself, don't upset yourself' – as ever caring for others before herself. I sat there for three hours holding her hand until my hand was almost numb. She drifted in and out of consciousness. From time to time my grief overwhelmed me and I would cry. My sisters cried too as we comforted each other. How could this world be so cruel, to make someone so good suffer like this? Tracey told her how much we loved her and how grateful we were for everything she had done for us. She played a huge part in making the three of us who we are today. It was then time to go. I hugged her, kissed her, told her how much I loved her. I got to the door, looked back and then did it all over again. I will remember that moment for ever. I got out into the corridor and howled my eyes out.

I never saw her again. But I did speak to her. On Thursday afternoon Tracey phoned to say they thought she was about to slip away. Sheena put the phone to Eleanor's ear and I said good-bye again. But she wasn't quite ready to go and hung on for two more days.

Sheena and Tracey both went to see Eleanor yesterday morning. They knew the end was near, but because they knew I was doing News 24 last night they didn't want to tell me how bad Eleanor's condition had become. I went to see Yasmin Alibhai-Brown's theatre show in Brentford on the way to the BBC. At 8.30 I saw I had a missed call from my parents' phone. I just knew.

It turned out that my sisters had taken their kids to the village fireworks. The call came from the hospice just as the first rocket whizzed into the sky. The symbolism was striking. Yes, there were tears last night, but they were tears of relief as much as tears of grief. None of us wanted Eleanor to suffer any longer. We wanted her to take her place among the angels. And as the rocket soared into the night sky, that's just what she did.

My sister Sheena has been an absolute heroine over the last three weeks. She still lives near my parents and has been with Eleanor every step of the way, sometimes for twelve hours at a time. Tracey and I know what she's had to take on and we love her all the more for it. And it's heartbreaking that she now has to cope with the fact that her partner's mother had a major stroke on Wednesday and may also have a very short time to live.

I know this blog is for political discussion, but it is also a diary. Some may regard this post as pure self-indulgence on my part. But you are my community. There are some things I feel the need to share. Most of you have never even met me. But because you read me most days we have some sort of bond. The messages on the thread earlier in the week, and your private emails, were of great comfort to me and my family. We all thank you for your kind words and good wishes.

AM I BEING TAKEN FOR A RIDE?
TUESDAY 6 NOVEMBER

I have spent much of the day dealing with undertakers, vicars and solicitors so I am afraid I know nothing about the reaction to the Queen's Speech. More on that anon. But I do want to share something that happened today.

I am the executor to my godmother's will, so went to see her solicitor this morning to establish what I have to do. At the end of the meeting I asked what the fees were likely to be. She informed me that her hourly rate was £185 and then added that it was her company's policy to charge (in addition to the hourly rate) 1 per cent commission on any cash sum left in the will and 0.5 per cent on the property, but this was of course subject to negotiation.

Once I had picked my jaw up off the floor I told her there would be no negotiation because I wouldn't be paying any commission at all. She agreed with no further discussion. I left the meeting with a very sour taste in my mouth, wondering if I should use my normal solicitor. It's quite clear to me that if they don't 'earn' the commission they will in all likelihood bump up the hours.

So my question is this: Are these commission charges normal practice nowadays and, if so, are solicitors trying to have their cake and eat it by charging a very high hourly rate AND a commission fee?

Update: Thanks to all those who have commented and offered advice. I have just told the firm that their services are no longer required, and I will do it myself.

AN ODD REACTION...
FRIDAY 9 NOVEMBER

I've just sat down in seat 15C on my flight to Malaga – I'm giving a speech there, bizarrely – to find the man sitting next to me reading my column in today's *Daily Telegraph*. Do you think...

A) I poked him in the arm and said, 'That's me, that is!'
B) He looked across and said, 'Fantastic article, mate.'
C) He turned the page having not made it to the end?

Well, the answer is none of the above. Bizarrely, I was rather embarrassed and proceeded to stick my head in Tony Benn's diaries.

WIDDECOMBE AND PRESCOTT
WEDNESDAY 14 NOVEMBER

Ann Widdecombe had a mildly embarrassing encounter tonight, although at the time she didn't realise it. She tells me that she was speaking at a dinner in one of the House of Commons dining rooms when she was asked by one of the guests if there had ever been a question she couldn't answer. She replied in a characteristically trenchant voice that indeed there was. The question was: what could any woman see in John Prescott that would make them want to have an affair with him? As she was saying this, guess who walked past the door? Yup, got it in one.

THE ALL-POWERFUL FRIENDS OF THE EARTH
FRIDAY 16 NOVEMBER

I got a letter from Friends of the Earth this morning asking for money. I was quite bemused by the second sentence: 'I am writing to ask you to join us in our vital and urgent campaign to stop climate change...'

Now FoE might be a powerful pressure group, but not even the Almighty can stop climate change. It is a naturally occurring and permanent phenomenon – always has been, always will be. Now I obviously know what they meant, but when they are this inaccurate in a fundraising letter one wonders about how accurate they are in other outlandish claims about global warming.

LORD, GIVE ME STRENGTH
SUNDAY 2 DECEMBER

This morning I have been to a christening. Here is a line from one of the hymns: 'And if I were a fuzzy wuzzy bear, I'd thank you Lord for my fuzzy wuzzy hair, but I just thank you, Father, for making me "me".'

And they wonder why the Church of England is losing its congregation!

At the christening party there were an unusual number of speeches from assorted parents, godparents and grandparents. Quote of the day was this, from the baby's maternal grandfather: 'Well at least we know who the father is...'

And then there was silence, followed by nervous laughter. The poor man carried on to say that he was referring to the growing number of single mothers. But I suspect his daughter will have been none too impressed!

50 IS THE NEW 65
MONDAY 10 DECEMBER

I've just read a piece about the new editor of *The Times*, James Harding. He's thirty-eight. Will Lewis, the editor of the *Daily Telegraph*, is also thirty-eight. George Osborne is thirty-six. David Cameron is forty.

At the age of forty-five, perhaps I should be considering retirement! It's quite a thought that in the political and media world forty-five is an age at which you might consider yourself a bit past it. The thing is, I don't feel any different to how I did when I was thirty – it's just that I have learnt a hell of a lot in the intervening fifteen years. Hopefully, that experience informs my decisions and means I make fewer bad ones. Hopefully.

But if I sometimes think that forty-five is beyond a sell-by date, I can hardly imagine what I will be thinking in five or ten years' time. Society is definitely becoming ever more youth-oriented, and in some ways you can see why. Newsreaders are rarely over forty. Our celebrity-obsessed media derides anyone who hasn't got the 'body beautiful' or has a few grey hairs and wrinkles. The BBC puts out to grass anyone who doesn't fit in with its 'right on' image. It's madness.

What we are doing is ignoring a huge group of talented people who still have a lot to give. I have written before about the fact that all political parties should be positively embracing candidates who are in their fifties, yet none of them considers it an issue they should even be thinking about. Newspapers also want ever younger writers and journalists – people who demonstrate hunger and ruthlessness, rather than experience and judgement.

I find it profoundly depressing that society now judges people over the age of fifty as a group who by and large have little to contribute any longer. And it's not just because I'm only five years off that age myself! Fifty seems to be the new sixty-five!

PUBLIC SERVICE ANNOUNCEMENT
WEDNESDAY 19 DECEMBER

I have news from the Maidstone & the Weald selection. There's no way of skirting the issue, so I'll just come out and say it. I didn't get past the first interview, which took place on Saturday.

I can't pretend that I am anything other than disappointed. God, I sound like a football manager after a 3–0 defeat. Seriously, I came out of the interview thinking I had performed really well. The selection committee was unfailingly polite and pleasant and I felt we connected. For the first time ever in a selection I spoke entirely without notes and felt I answered all the questions well, but I was clearly deluding myself. Or maybe they are looking for something very different from what I was able to offer. Whoever wins will have a fantastic career for one of the nicest seats in the country. Anyone who has been interviewed for a seat they really wanted and fallen at the first fence – regardless of party – will know how I am feeling now but, in the end, you pick yourself up, dust yourself off and just have to be philosophical about it. It just wasn't meant to be.

Now, where did I put that revolver?

THE RIGHTS AND WRONGS OF 2007
SATURDAY 22 DECEMBER

I've just been flicking through my blog posts for December 2006 and came across this one where I made my predictions for 2007. I was astonished to find that I had got 7 out of 10 (virtually) bang on the money!

1. More than one person will face charges in the Cash for Peerages Inquiry. WRONG

2. Sir Ming Campbell will not be leader of the Lib Dems by the end of the year. RIGHT

3. Ed Vaizey, Jeremy Hunt and Nick Herbert will be promoted to the shadow Cabinet. RIGHT (apart from Ed)

4. The Conservative Party 'A' List will be junked, having served its purpose. RIGHT

5. The SNP will become the largest party in Scotland after the May elections but cannot form a coalition. RIGHT

6. A Labour MP and a Lib Dem MP will defect to the Conservatives. WRONG

7. John Hutton will challenge Gordon Brown for the Labour leadership after John Reid wimps out. WRONG

8. In one of his first acts as PM, Brown will announce a timetable for troop withdrawal from Iraq. RIGHT

9. Depending on the opinion poll bounce from that decision and his honeymoon period, Brown will consider calling a general election within six months of becoming Prime Minister. RIGHT

10. West Ham will not get relegated. RIGHT

RELIVING RIVERDANCE
WEDNESDAY 26 DECEMBER

I've spent some of this morning watching Riverdance Day on Sky Real Lives. Believe it or not I was at the 1994 Eurovision Song Contest when Riverdance made its debut as the interval act. No one remembers anything about that evening apart from Riverdance. I had never seen anything like it. The whole audience was blown away by it. I then went to see it at the Hammersmith Apollo. I doubt whether I will ever see anything at a theatre which is so awe-inspiring. It's odd, as virtually all forms of dance leave me completely cold. This, however, is completely different. Maybe it's the music, maybe it's the story, or maybe it's because I was there at its birth, but whatever it is, I'm hooked. If you haven't seen it and get the chance, do go. I promise you won't regret it.

NOT IAIN DALE'S PREDICTIONS FOR 2008
MONDAY 31 DECEMBER

January

Daily Express runs front page with no picture of Madeleine McCann ... Boris Johnson apologises for comparing Golders Green to the streets of Gaza ... In a speech which shakes the political world, new Lib Dem leader Nick Clegg declares: 'I'm a Liberal.'

February

Kevin Maguire defects to the Conservative Party ... David Miliband denies rumours he is to star in *Harry Potter 8* ... Hillary Clinton quits presidential race after Super Tuesday disaster and proclaims: 'I back Osama 100 per cent.'

March

Lib Dem spring conference marred by Nick Clegg being caught saying to Lady Elspeth, 'It's not exactly helpful, is it?' after Sir Ming is caught buying back his classic Jaguar (petrol consumption 4 mpg) ... Tory blogger Iain Dale sacked from Tory 'A' List for proudly declaring he had bought a new Audi which emitted 300g of carbon per kilometre... Alistair Darling mysteriously disappears on Budget Day. Gordon Brown delivers the speech instead.

April

Guido becomes Director of the Smith Institute in a bid to scotch accusations of political partiality ... Government apologies for mislaying discs containing records of 85,000 prisoners. Jacqui Smith says it just goes to prove the case for ID cards ... Launching the Lib Dems' local council election campaign, Nick Clegg shocks his candidates by proclaiming: 'I'm a Liberal.'

May

Boris apologises for beating Ken Livingstone and is overheard at victory party saying to a key aide: 'Cripes, what now?' ... Government withdraws amendment on forty-two days and tables new amendment calling for twenty-eight-and-a-half days. Please ... David Cameron makes the Tory position on an EU Referendum absolutely crystal clear when he says: 'We are in favour of a referendum if the Treaty hasn't been ratified but even if it has we would still be in favour of it, whatever it is, oh yes we would, yes sirree. I couldn't be clearer than that.'

June

Home Secretary Jacqui Smith quits after clambering over the Despatch Box during Home Office Questions and slapping David Davis across the face, shrieking: 'I used to work on the beauty counter in Debenhams, you know!' ... Having got rid of his third Home Secretary, David Davis gets to keep the Home Office ... In mini reshuffle David Cameron promotes Nadine Dorries to the shadow Cabinet, telling friends it was the only way to get her to stop blogging. The next day Nadine blogs 'How dishy Dave popped the question and why I blushed' ... Lib Dem leader Nick Clegg appoints David Blunkett as his adviser on Home Affairs. Announcing the appointment on *Da Ali G Show*, he declares: 'Is it becoz I is a Liberal?'

July

ConservativeHome says 'Cameron must do better', as Tories score 74 per cent in YouGov poll. Lord Ashcroft widens his target seat campaign to include Bolsover, Rhondda and Bootle ... Home Secretary Liam Byrne says Early Release Scheme for murderers is the only way to free up enough prison places for really serious crimes ... David Cameron forced to cancel trip to Rwanda after his Witney constituency is affected by a plague of locusts. Andrew Mitchell is disconsolate.

August

Labour MP Tom Watson photographed delivering Christmas presents to the Miliband children ... Labour Whip Tom Watson resigns from government over 'complete misunderstanding' ... Much bitterness at CCHQ as Steve Hilton and Andy Coulson resolve their differences in a cage fight.

September

Professor Anthony King recovers from stroke after learning of the first Conservative by-election victory for twenty years ... Lib Dem leader Nick Clegg takes his party conference by storm by telling his party faithful to 'go back to your constituencies and tell them I'm a Liberal' ... The Labour conference gets off to a bad start when the police beat up the Police Minister Tony McNulty in a case of 'mistaken' identity. 'That'll learn him,' says Manchester Chief Constable Mike Todd.

October
In a bid to top last year's speech, David Cameron speaks to the Tory conference with no clothes on. 'What you see is what you get,' he tells the Tory faithful ... The Tories announce their Green manifesto and Simon Heffer self-combusts, live on *Richard & Judy* ... On a state visit to the Ukraine, French President Nicolas Sarkozy enters key Ugandan discussions with Prime Minister Yulia Tymoshenko.

November
Cherie Blair's memoirs cause a storm after she reveals the fishy present she left for Gordon Brown in the No. 11 curtains ... Mike Huckabee wins the US presidential election and declares: 'I won it for Jesus.' Jesus was unavailable for comment but is said to have wept ... Lib Dem Home Affairs Spokesman Chris Huhne arrested by House of Commons police officer for carrying a knife. Coincidentally, he was standing behind Lib Dem leader Nick Clegg at the time.

December
Electoral Commission forces Lib Dems to pay back the Michael Brown £2.4 million. Nick Clegg launches fundraising appeal across the nation with the slogan: 'I'm a Liberal, dontcha know' ... In final PMQs of the year David Cameron shouts to Gordon Brown: 'Why don't you just f*** off and let me have a go?' Brown replies: 'I'll take no lectures from the Right Honourable Gentleman ... 1992 ... Black Wednesday ... blah ... economic stability ... blah ... prudence with a purpose ... blah ... 586 quarters of economic growth ... well, apart from the last two ... er ... I'll take no lectures from the Right Honourable Gentleman ...' Iain Dale's debut appearance on *Any Questions* gets off to an unfortunate start when Jonathan Dimbleby introduces him with the words: 'And our fourth panellist is Britain's leading Conservative blogger, Tim Montgomerie.'

2008

Stuart Bruce has tagged me in a Meme on My Week in Media, so here goes...

What I've read
I tend to have a few books 'on the go'. The main one at the moment is Tom Bower's biography of Gordon Brown. It's frightening. If half of what he asserts is true, this country should be very frightened indeed. He paints Brown as a half-mad, half-psycho, full-on obsessive. I'm also trying to finish *The Reagan Diaries*, which I'm finding hard work. They are very poorly edited. I'm a newspaper addict. Every day I get the *Telegraph*, *Sun* and *Mail* delivered and I take *The Guardian* and *Indy* on Mondays for the media sections. I subscribe to virtually every political magazine on the market. I also take *Stuff*, the *Press Gazette* and *GQ*. This week I have mainly been reading back issues of *George* magazine to get some ideas for *The Politico*.

What I've watched
I probably watch less TV now than I have ever done in my life. I have weaned myself off the soaps I used to watch. I tend now to watch most things on DVD. Over Christmas I watched series three of *Lost* and am about to start on *Heroes*. As I type this I am watching a DVD of Ewan MacGregor's motorbike trip through Africa called *Long Way Down*. I was hugely disappointed by the Christmas Day TV. *To The Manor Born* was a total let-down. I watched a great series yesterday called *Torn*, all about a woman whose child was abducted and then eleven years later she recognised her in a shopping centre. I'm a sucker for things like that – and I love apocalyptic movies like *Independence Day* and *Flood*.

What I've listened to
Disaster has struck. I have 12,300 tracks in my iTunes library. This
morning I found that half of them have disappeared. I was bought
an iPod speaker thing for Christmas so I've had that on a fair bit
over the last few days. On the radio I'm a 5 Live fan. I hardly
ever listen to Radio 4. Sacrilege, I know. I've become a great fan
of Simon Mayo, who I believe to be one of the best interviewers
around. I love 5 Live Sport as well.

Where I've surfed
I have just started using the Google Blog reader, although I really
prefer visiting blogs directly rather than using RSS. This week I
have spent monitoring a new personal website someone is design-
ing for me to promote my media work – totally separate from the
blog. I look at NewsNow an awful lot to monitor political news
and West Ham stories.

SNOGGING SIMON HEFFER
TUESDAY 15 JANUARY

We recorded the first edition of *Confronting Heffer* for Telegraph
TV today. Simon had a raving cold, which was rather a shame as
the *Telegraph* photographer kept urging us to get closer and closer
until our noses were literally an inch apart. 'You're not my type,'
he muttered darkly. 'You're OK,' I said, 'I don't go for gingas.' We
had to keep terribly serious during these photographs, but in the
end I just burst out laughing. The thought of being the man nearest
to snogging Mr Heffer in the whole country was just too risible.
Perhaps I should have done it. I suspect it would have meant that
the intended series would have become a pilot, and no more.

THE JOBSWORTHS AT TV LICENSING

Readers of Charles Moore's *Spectator* column will be familiar with
the TV licensing authorities. He will be glad to know that he has
just recruited someone else to the cause. Me. Just before Christmas I
bought a new TV for my bedroom, which also doubles as my office.
A few days ago I received a very rude letter from TV Licensing

telling me they had no record of me buying a licence at my address and what was I going to do about it? They said that unless I could prove my address had a licence they would take me to court. Excuse me? Do they not have a computer? It would tell them, if they bothered to look, that my house does indeed have a valid licence.

I have absolutely no intention of co-operating with their petty bureaucracies, which only serve to protect jobs which should never exist in the first place. It's not up to me to prove my house has a licence. It's up to them to prove it doesn't. They might find that a tad difficult.

TRAIN ETIQUETTE
WEDNESDAY 16 JANUARY

I am typing this on a train travelling from Tonbridge to London. Sitting opposite me is Dr David Starkey. I need your advice. Should I...

A) Pretend I do not recognise him?
B) Tell him I just love his monarchy programmes?
C) Suggest Gordon Brown should appoint him Regis Professor of History at Cambridge?
D) Berate him for his recent criticism of the Queen?
    Or
E) Turn up the volume of my iPod just to provoke him into one of his rages...?

Update: I chose A.

DIABETES CAN BE BEATEN
FRIDAY 18 JANUARY

I got a bit of bad news on Wednesday, when I was told I had been diagnosed with diabetes. It wasn't a shock as – using my enormous medical expertise – I had already diagnosed myself. For some time I have had an unquenchable thirst and other symptoms. Luckily it is Type 2, so I won't have to inject myself every day.

I went to see my doctor yesterday evening who told me that it 'could be a blessing in disguise'. I must admit I wondered about her sanity when she said that, but she may be right. To have it diagnosed at my age means I can beat it if I adopt the right diet and exercise routines and get my blood sugar levels down. This will 'unfur' arteries and lessen the risk of heart or kidney problems in the future.

So I guess I am going to be harvesting lots of info about diabetes from various websites over the next few weeks and learning from other people about their experiences. My father was diagnosed with it seven years ago and my godmother (the one who died in November) had it too. She had to inject herself twice a day and had been doing it since the 1960s. I am now going to have to take ten pills a day for the foreseeable future. Even worse, I won't be able to drink Lemon Lucozade any more!

I must admit I was rather shocked by the reaction of a couple of people I have told face to face. They seemed to equate it with being told that I had a terminal illness. I don't see it that way at all. I count myself very lucky. I've had forty-five years of being totally healthy. In the last few weeks, a good friend of mine has been diagnosed with MS and another friend has been diagnosed with cancer. I'm the lucky one.

IT SHOULDN'T HAPPEN TO AN AUDI...
SUNDAY 20 JANUARY

Not happy, not happy at all. I'm typing this sitting in the BBC car park waiting for Audi Assist to come and rescue me, and my new Q7. Zac Goldsmith would say it serves me right for buying a one-man global warming machine. My response would be that I didn't buy it, my partner did! We got it nine days ago and during that time have been able to drive it for one whole day. You turn the key to start it and nothing happens. I think it's safe to say that Audi can have it back on Monday morning.

WHO WILL RID US OF THIS IDIOTIC PRIEST?
THURSDAY 7 FEBRUARY

Expect a mass walkout from the Church of England. We all know that Church of England bishops sometimes have difficulty with the concept of actually believing in God, but I never thought I would see the day when the Archbishop of Canterbury would advocate the implementation of another religion's so-called 'laws' in what remains a predominantly Christian country. He thinks the introduction of some sort of Sharia law is 'unavoidable'. According to the BBC report Dr Williams believes we should 'face up to the fact' that some of its citizens do not relate to the British legal system. 'He argues that adopting parts of Islamic Sharia law would help maintain social cohesion. For example, Muslims could choose to have marital disputes or financial matters dealt with in a Sharia court. He says Muslims should not have to choose between "the stark alternatives of cultural loyalty or state loyalty".'

So let's get this straight. The man who leads the Church of England doesn't believe we are all equal under the law. So what next: a different law for gay people, a different law for ethnic minorities? Where on earth would it end? I'll tell you where. Anarchy.

On several occasions in the past I have thought Rowan Williams unfit to lead the Church of England, but since I am not a member of it I kept quiet. But these remarks take his weakness of mind to an altogether different level. I imagine Cardinal Murphy O'Connor's doors will be open to many refugees from what used to be a fine Church. It has latterly become little more than a joke in most people's eyes.

WASHINGTON DC: A BLOGGING FIRST?
FRIDAY 8 FEBRUARY

I wonder if anyone has ever done a blog post from the Oval Office? I just have!

MIDNIGHT AT THE LINCOLN MEMORIAL

It's nearly midnight on my last night in Washington. Whenever I come here I always make a nocturnal visit to the Lincoln Memorial. It's a great place to sit and think – to contemplate the meaning of life, if you like. That's where I am now – sitting on the steps leading up to one of the most awe-inspiring memorials to a great American leader.

I'm looking down towards the Washington Memorial which glories in its own reflection in the waterway which separates it from the Lincoln Memorial. Over to the left is the tragic memorial to those many thousands who gave their lives in the Vietnam War. And way over to the right, just visible through the trees, is the Jefferson Memorial. Any of you who have stood where I am sitting now will realise what a special place this is.

It's a year since I last sat here, wondering what the next twelve months would bring. I sit here now thinking how lucky I am to live the life I lead, to have the family I love and the partner I will spend the rest of my life with. I look out at the Washington Memorial and see a great shining beacon of optimism. It's inspirational in its own rather abstract way.

I always leave America injected with the free spirit which is so prevalent here. It's as if I've had my annual fix of the 'Ameri-drug'. If you've ever been here you'll know what I mean. If you haven't, you'll think I'm babbling.

MY EVENING IN THE WEST WING
SATURDAY 9 FEBRUARY

At 8.30 p.m. yesterday evening a group of five of us had a privately arranged tour of the West Wing of the White House. To be honest, I wasn't expecting to see an awful lot, but boy was I wrong. Our guide was a friend of one of our group, who works in the next-door Dwight Eisenhower Old Executive Building (which President Bush calls 'The Ike'). We walked into the main entrance of the West Wing, next door to the swimming pool. You're immediately struck by the homely feel of the place. The corridors are bedecked with pictures of Dubya at work and at play on his Texas ranch. There is a particularly fetching one of him covered in dirt. It is the kind of picture that women of a certain age would go gooey over, I suspect.

Our first stop was the Rose Garden and the colonnade, which leads to the outside door of the Oval Office. I remember a great black and white picture of Ronald Reagan walking down the colonnade with George Bush Sr. We were then shown the Cabinet Room before being taken to the Oval Office.

To be honest I had doubted we would get to see the Oval Office, so it was a real surprise to walk up to the door and get a panoramic view of it. You're not allowed inside, but, kid that I am, I did put both feet inside the door under the rope and sent a blog post. Shane Greer did the same about ten seconds later. We both got a kick out of that!

The Oval Office was a bit smaller than I imagined and looked more like a living room than the replica in the *West Wing* TV series. The decoration was very light and airy – all creams and yellows, including the carpet, which I had imagined to be blue. We saw the Churchill bust given to Bush by Tony Blair. The only jarring part was George Bush's chair behind the famous desk. It was a high-backed leather chair which looked a bit plastic – totally out of kilter with the rest of the furnishings.

We then got to go the White House press briefing room, which has just been refurbished and had our pictures taken in front of the podium.

I have to say that the ninety minutes we spent there were well worth the cost of the entire trip. It was an honour to get to see the place where so much history has been made.

Afterwards, we went to a Brazilian restaurant. What superb food. They give you a plate and the waiters come to you with about fifteen different kinds of meat until you cannot eat any more. It wasn't cheap but it was certainly an experience.

This morning I was woken at 3 a.m. by a text message from my cab company who I had booked to meet me off the plane tomorrow. The driver was at Heathrow and was wondering where I was. I had given them the wrong day! Aaaaagh.

I went back to bed, then convinced myself I must have also booked the flight for yesterday. So I got up again, checked the paperwork and it said Feb 9. In my delirium I thought that was yesterday so started to ring Virgin to beg for a seat today – it was only then that I realised Feb 9 was indeed today. So I went back to bed and then of course couldn't sleep.

My morning got worse when I discovered that my iPod had given up the ghost and refused to work. Luckily I had just enough time to go and buy a Nano and download some music for the flight home.

And then I went to CPAC to interview Newt Gingrich. His minder cut me off after only three questions, so I'm not sure I'm even going to bother posting it. He did not impress me. Rude and charmless.

One hilarious tale from this afternoon. I got talking to a young girl from Alabama at CPAC and was explaining to her the differences between British and American Conservatives. I mentioned that neither abortion or gay rights were big issues in British politics. 'Oh,' she said, 'I've never met anyone who's gay.' I offered my hand and said, 'Well, now you have!' She roared with laughter and then added: 'We don't have any gay people in Alabama.' I told her the horrible truth and we joked that they had all probably left or been driven out of the state.

THE OLD ONES ARE THE BEST
THURSDAY 21 FEBRUARY

Tony Benn is reported in the *Telegraph* Spy column as telling LBC Radio: 'I got a death threat the other day. I haven't had one of those for years and I was so chuffed that someone thought I was still dangerous.' Cue chuckles. The only trouble is that Benn has been coming out with the line for several years. It's a good one and always goes down well with an audience. And he's not alone in wheeling out tried and tested laugh lines. Most politicians do it. I remember Michael Portillo got into trouble several years ago when at a dinner he told the exact same jokes as when he'd attended the same function a few years before. Ann Widdecombe has her 'Christian principles' joke, David Davis has his 'diamond ring' joke, and I have my 'Ann Widdecombe's knickers' joke. And if you haven't heard me tell that one before, I can guarantee you will, if you come to an event I am speaking at!

WE'VE BEEN BURGLED – AND SEVEN HOURS LATER, WHERE ARE THE POLICE?
SATURDAY 1 MARCH

Today has got worse. It started off well as I enjoyed my time with Suffolk Coastal Tories. We had a lively debate on the English Question, but I had to leave at 12.15 to get to Upton Park in time to watch West Ham play Chelsea. After twenty-five minutes I really wished I hadn't bothered, with the Hammers conceding three soft goals within five minutes. The only point to really cheer was seeing Frank Lampard get red carded. Anyway, I digress.

The real reason the day got worse was that we discovered we were broken into and burgled last night. Not the house, but some outbuildings which we rent out as storage units. About £400 worth of roof lead was missing, with various items strewn across the yard. My partner called the police sometime between 11 a.m. and noon. As I type this at nearly 7 p.m. they have still not bothered to come out. I suppose I shouldn't be surprised, but it galls me. It really does. It's clear from the items in our yard that the car used was stolen, as the contents of the boot were left behind. It's now dark, so any clues there might have been cannot be seen. If they had intended to do anything forensically, they now won't be able to.

They called back at 3 p.m. to say someone would be with us within the hour but they were coming a long way (!). A few minutes later someone called to say it would be longer. When I got back from football I called them again. They were unable to say when anyone would come. I'm afraid I lost my temper and told them exactly what I thought. You can probably imagine what I said.

So when I call them again in a few moments I'm afraid some even harsher words are going to be said. I do not pay taxes to fund them to be treated like this. I do not think it is unreasonable of me to expect them to attend a crime scene within seven hours of the crime being reported. They can witter on about resources all they like, but I'd love to know what is happening in West Kent today to mean they cannot attend a crime scene within seven hours. No wonder people aren't bothering to report crimes any longer. This is a major reason for the level of reported crime falling. And it's a terrible reflection of the level of service (if you can call it that) which rural areas now get from the police. Perhaps I should tell them I am holding the burglar at gunpoint.

Update 7.47 p.m.: Well, they turned up at 7.30 p.m., just as I was doing a phone interview with Steve Claridge on Setanta Sports about the West Ham game! I asked why it had taken seven hours and was told: 'That's quite good. It's normally longer!' We live in a village of 6,000 people a mile outside Tunbridge Wells and four miles from Tonbridge. Both these towns have relatively large police stations. So where do you think our policemen are based? Cranbrook, a town around half an hour's drive from here. These two policemen cover the area of Cranbrook, Lamberhurst, Pembury and Paddock Wood. Anyone who knows this area will realise how big an area that is. And it's covered by *two* policemen!

THE SORT OF INTERVIEW ED BALLS WOULD LIKE
WEDNESDAY 12 MARCH

A question from a press conference with the Chinese Foreign Minister this month (and I swear this is genuine):

> China Radio International: We saw you on television, singing Suzhou opera with other CPPCC members, making a deep impression on us all. Could you tell us about some of your other leisure-time activities? In addition, the media often describes you as scholarly yet witty and well-educated but humorous. Is this part of your natural personality or has it been shaped by your diplomatic career? Thank you.

I am sure Adam Boulton will learn from this.

THE 'PEOPLE LIKE US' PHENOMENON
SATURDAY 15 MARCH

Last night on Sky News we briefly discussed why the media gave a much higher profile to the Madeleine McCann case than the Shannon Matthews disappearance. There are, I'm sure, lots of factors, but one was the fact that for the media the McCanns were very much 'people like us' or, should I say, people like them. The Matthews family were nothing like the media classes in appearance, lifestyle and outlook. I really think there is something in this. Let's take the analogy further.

My fellow panellist, Peter Whittle, asserted that the reason David Cameron was given more or less a free ride by the media in his first eighteen months was because he belonged to the 'people like us' class. Was this part of the reason the media were so keen to promote him, and do down David Davis after his conference speech? Not consciously, but I do wonder if there was something subconscious about it.

Why was the coverage of the New Orleans floods slightly underdone by the US media? Might it have been different if it had happened in Manhattan, where 'people like us' live?

Harriet Harman was given a comparatively easy ride by the media when she sent her kids to a selective school. Could it have been because many media people were facing the same dilemma?

I could go on, but you see my point. That's where the internet comes into its own. It's more difficult in the blogosphere to go along with 'people like us' stories, because the truth is that there are millions of people out there who will expose the phenomenon's hypocrisy.

There is one positive effect of the 'people like us' phenomenon. In Dewsbury it brought a whole community together. The people on the estate where Shannon Matthews lived came together as one to try to help find her. It gave their community a spirit which it patently hadn't had before. Why did they come together like that? Because Shannon Matthews came from a 'family like us'.

A DIFFERENT KIND OF 'GROWLER'
WEDNESDAY 2 APRIL

This week's *House Magazine* has an advert in it for something called a 'Growler'. Apparently it is a giant-sized hip flask. When I was at school a 'Growler' was, er, something else... But best not go there.

I LIKE DRIVING IN MY CAR
WEDNESDAY 9 APRIL

Yesterday I took delivery of my new car, which I have been waiting nearly a year for. Boy, was it worth the wait. I make no apology for loving cars. And I absolutely adore this one. If you could drive a multiple orgasm, you'd be steering an Audi S5. Perhaps driving it to Upton Park was not the ideal first outing for it, but it survived to tell the tale. I did think about not blogging this momentous event, as I know what abuse I am going to get in the comments, but seeing as though this is a diary, it would be cheating not to. So let's get it out of the way...

* *How dare you buy a car which is a one-man global warming machine?* Easy. I wouldn't be seen dead in a Prius and it's my choice.
* *You're going through a mid-life crisis.* Yep. Since I was nineteen.
* *You're just showing off.* Yep. Well, wouldn't you?
* *It's just a penis extension.* You should see the gear stick.

There, I think that just about covers it. So go on, do your worst. [Battens down hatch and goes to bed.]

P.S. Am I the only one who gets emotional at seeing an old car go? I had my previous Audi for five years and loved it. Leaving it at the dealership seemed wrong. Almost cruel. Why did my eyes get a bit moist when I left it? Silly old Hector.

BACKSTAGE ON *THE ANDREW MARR SHOW*
SUNDAY 20 APRIL

A reader just emailed to ask what happens before and after *The Andrew Marr Show*, so I thought I'd share a few backstage secrets with you.

When you do the paper review, they normally send you the papers the night before to prepare properly. However, as I live in Kent I said not to bother (ever mindful of the need to save licence fee payers' money!) and I'd arrive a bit earlier. Anyway, when the alarm went off at 6 a.m., I did wonder why I was doing it. I arrived at TV Centre at 7.45 and was taken up to the green room with Caroline Lucas, where we started trawling through the papers. Andrew Marr and his producer Barney Jones were already there. I remember when I last did the paper review in 2003 when David Frost was presenting the programme that Frosty didn't turn up until a quarter of an hour before the programme was due to start. Andrew Marr has a more hands-on approach.

Caroline and I each chose five stories (although we only got through three on the show) which the ever-attendant researcher Ajay then marked up. When I do a paper review I normally underline the important bits of the story and write a few notes in the margins, but on this programme you have to hold the paper up to the camera so you're not supposed to write on the newspaper. At about 8.30 we were taken to make-up – they always spend far longer making up women, I find. I was done in about one minute flat. Perfect skin, you see...

By this time Jeremy Irons, George Osborne and Billy Bragg had arrived too. Alistair Darling arrived at the last minute, and at 8.50 we were taken down to the studio and mic-ed up. One trick I have learnt is that sometimes the back of your jacket can ride up and look very odd, so the way to avoid it is to sit on the bottom of your jacket. It's a bit uncomfortable but stops you looking a dick.

Osborne and Darling were brought into the studio to sit next to each other at the top of the programme (although on screen they looked separate) and were then wheeled off again while the paper review was taking place.

Caroline kicked off with her tax story and I then talked about 42-day terror detention,[†] making the point that a wise general doesn't fight on two fronts at the same time. We had a bit of gentle banter about the Tories' green credentials but after ten minutes it was all over – was it really ten minutes? Seemed like two! I then got whisked off to do a piece on News 24 (which is tomorrow being renamed BBC News) on the political stories of the day. Afterwards I returned to the green room and had a chat with Jeremy Irons. What a nice guy. He's playing Harold Macmillan in a play at the National Theatre at the moment.

The great thing about the Andrew Marr programme is the post-match breakfast. When David Frost was presenting it, the breakfast took place in the BBC boardroom. Nowadays it's eaten in the staff canteen, but very enjoyable it is too.

THE JOYS OF S&M

I had to laugh when I read this quote from Formula One boss Max Mosley in today's *Sunday Telegraph*. You will recall that he was exposed recently in the *News of the World* for enjoying the so-called delights of sado-masochistic sex. He said, 'As long as it's adults in private, and consensual, it doesn't hurt.'

Now, I may not be very well versed in the matters of S&M, but isn't the whole idea of it that it should indeed hurt?!

IF ONLY...
WEDNESDAY 23 APRIL

I have just got home, having spent an hour at Bloomsbury Police

---

† The Labour government wanted to lock up terror suspects for up to forty-two days without charge.

Station and two hours on the phone trying to freeze my bank accounts and cancel my credit cards. Why? Because our car was broken into this evening. Idiots that we are, we had locked our computer cases and laptops in the boot, and my wallet was in the case too. Worst of all, it contained my West Ham season ticket and four tickets for *Mamma Mia!* tomorrow night. God knows if I will be able to get them replaced.

The car was parked on Bloomsbury Square on a reasonably busy road, the kind of road you'd never think anyone would have the time to break into a car without being spotted. I feel as though a part of my life has disappeared with that laptop. We keep telling each other that at least no one was hurt – it's only possessions. But there's a part of you that feels personally violated. And then of course, there's the 'if only' aspect...

- If only we had left the office when we had intended to and hadn't had to wait for someone to lock up.
- If only I had parked the car in the space I had originally chosen but seemed a bit small.
- If only we had left the gallery viewing when we had intended, instead of staying for a good gossip with a friend.

So in March we were burgled at home and in April the car was broken into. Yes, crime really is on the decline, isn't it?

WERE YOU STILL UP FOR PORTILLO? I WAS...
SATURDAY 3 MAY

On local election night I laid into Michael Portillo, live on BBC1. Some bright spark has uploaded the video on YouTube. Let me explain why I did it.

Michael Portillo is a man of many talents. He writes well and is a brilliant presenter of TV documentaries. But he has been away from frontline politics for so long that he is out of touch with the modern Conservative Party. He lost his *Sunday Times* column recently and I am told that a large part of the reason was that it was felt he had little new to say and his Tory contacts were yesterday's men.

Portillo specialises in attacking the very party that gave him a national platform. He behaves now in the same way he behaved as a member of William Hague's shadow Cabinet – betraying those whose trust he ought to enjoy. It was very revealing to find out recently that until February this year William Hague hadn't spoken to Portillo since 2001.

Michael Portillo's trouble is that he clearly believes that it should be him, not David Cameron, who is about to lead the Tories back to No. 10. Having over the last seven years constantly predicted that the Tory Party is finished, he loses no opportunity to pour petrol onto any flames which happen to be licking around the feet of the Party.

I'm not asking for craven loyalty to the Party which made him – we're all entitled to express constructive criticism from time to time – but his constant snipings on *This Week* lack any sort of perspective.

Michael Portillo's behaviour at the BBC *Election Night* event at City Hall told me everything I needed to know. He slagged off Boris and then proceeded to say that 44 per cent was a pretty poor result for the Conservatives. He spent the rest of the evening on his own, reading a book called *Lost Boys*. He made no effort to talk to anyone there apart from Polly Toynbee and Fraser Nelson, who happened to sit down beside him on the same sofa. He ignored all the young people there and from what I could gather the BBC people didn't think much of his behaviour either.

His attitude on Thursday night went a long way to explain why he failed to win the party leadership in 2001. If you treat people with disdain, don't be surprised if they then react badly to it.

EXCLUSIVE: BORIS'S FIRST ACT AS MAYOR
FRIDAY 9 MAY

When Boris sat down at his desk on Monday morning he was presented with a huge press cuttings file, which included loads of articles from the *Morning Star*. 'Why on earth are you includ-ing these?' he asked one of his staff. 'Well,' said the staff member, 'Mayor Livingstone was keen to support the *Morning Star*.' 'In what way?' asked Boris.

It transpired that the GLA building had a subscription of forty – yes, forty – copies of the *Morning Star* delivered every day. Boris's first action as Mayor was to cancel all forty subscriptions to the lefty rag, thereby halving its circulation with one stroke of the mayoral pen. That's what I call the mark of a real Conservative – annoy the leftists and save the taxpayer £10,000 a year at the same time.

TEN SIGNS YOU HAVE JOINED THE ESTABLISHMENT
WEDNESDAY 14 MAY

One of these has happened to me this week...

10. You get a letter from No. 10 inviting you to accept a KCMG.
9. You start reading the Court and Social page of *The Times*.
8. You get invited to speak at the Reform Club.
7. You eat Welsh rarebit after dessert.
6. You believe William Rees-Mogg to be the world's greatest columnist.
5. You regard Nicholas Soames as a dangerous radical.
4. You don't remember the last time you had lunch without a fish course.
3. Your socks go up to your knees.
2. You are a member of more than one 'club'.
1. Your name is Robin Butler.

PSSST... CAN YOU (OR I) KEEP A TOTAL SECRET?
SATURDAY 31 MAY

Is it possible to keep a secret in politics? We all know that politicians and media people are terrible at keeping things to themselves (I am no exception) and that the collective catchphrase for the Westminster Village should be: 'Not that I'm one to gossip, but...' The concept of keeping something to yourself is almost alien to the political being. Politicos are very sharing people, at least when it comes to gossip.

On Thursday two of my colleagues interviewed the Prime Minister in No. 10 for the launch issue of *Total Politics*. As you can imagine, we were delighted to get the interview as it gets the magazine off to a flying start. Imagine my surprise, then, to read this in the 'Three Line Whip' column of the *Daily Telegraph* this morning:

Total Politics, the new magazine brainchild of Tory blogger Iain Dale, has landed a Gordon Brown interview for its first edition, out at the end of June. Brown reveals that he is not a good dancer, he would rather watch the new Indiana Jones film than the upcoming Bond film *Quantum of Solace*, that his favourite programme from his youth was *That Was The Week That Was*, and the last film that made him cry was *Hotel Rwanda*.

Now, don't run away with the impression that this interview was full of personal interest pap – these were a few throwaway questions at the end. Anyway, we now have three choices. Do we...

A) Launch a *Yes Minister*-style leak inquiry?
B) Think of a unique form of torture to make Jonathan Isaby reveal his source?
C) Accept the suggestion you are about to make in the comments?

Now, I suppose you're all gagging to know what was in the rest of the interview? Well, I'd love to tell you, but I'd have to kill you.

BAN SMOKING OR LEAVE SMOKERS ALONE

I hate cigarettes. I loathe smoking. But if smoking is legal, then surely the consumer has the right to choose the brand of cigarette he or she wishes to smoke, and the cigarette companies have the right to design the packets in any way they want to, as long as they include the government health warning.

The proposal to ban any form of branding of cigarette packaging is a ridiculous overreaction by cowardly nanny staters. They also want to ban the public display of packets of cigarettes and for them to be sold from under the counter on the basis of what the eye doesn't see...

The real agenda of the people behind these authoritarian proposals is to ban smoking outright. At least that would be an intellectually honest position. As it is, the constant chipping away of the rights of smokers is typical of the authoritarian drift among so-called health professionals.

Either ban it outright or leave people to make their own decisions.

DAVID DAVIS RESIGNS
THURSDAY 12 JUNE

Earlier today I had decided to have a three-day break from blogging, for reasons which I will explain later on today or tomorrow. Just as well I didn't.

David Davis is resigning from the shadow Cabinet, resigning his seat and will fight a by-election on the 42-days issue.

More later...

DAVID DAVIS'S WALK INTO THE UNKNOWN

So, now that the dust has settled, what are we to make of it all? The news media is in meltdown mode as they struggle to come to terms with the enormity of what David Davis has done. Instant conclusions are naturally being drawn, but many of them are very detached from reality.

I should perhaps make clear that I did not know about this decision until this morning. I am glad I didn't for several reasons. I still haven't spoken to him so what I am about to write is my take on the situation and my take only.

During my six months working for DD in 2005, Tony Blair introduced his ninety-day detention proposals. I saw first-hand how passionately David feels about this issue. It's not a matter of political conviction, it's almost as if it is in his DNA. He genuinely thinks that extending pre-charge detention to forty-two days will make the country less safe. It will give the terrorists a propaganda victory.

Up until the weekend he believed the 42-day proposal would be defeated. He hadn't reckoned on the duplicity of the DUP or the fact that so many Labour MPs would be bought off by offers of goodies for their constituency or the chairmanship of this or that committee.

Labour is spinning away that David's decision is a kind of emotional reaction to the loss. They could not be more wrong. David Davis doesn't make emotional decisions. He makes them with a military precision. He won't have done this on the spur of the moment, he will have thought about it deeply and played some war game scenarios. In the end he will have come to the conclusion that the only way to defeat the 42-day agenda is to start a massive public debate. And that's what a by-election will do.

This isn't about one man's vanity. It is about the ability to sacrifice personal and public advantage for a greater cause. As he said in his statement, Sunday is the anniversary of Magna Carta. Over the last 800 years people have fought and died to protect our civil liberties. If it falls to one man to sacrifice political advantage to try to make a stand against their further erosion, then so be it.

David would have been Home Secretary in the next Conservative government. He has consistently been the party's best media performer over the last two years. He has played a major part in the revival of Conservative fortunes, and while many people have tried to drive wedges between him and David Cameron they have failed to manage it. Quite obviously, they come from a different background and have certain different priorities – so do any two politicians. But during the leadership contest they grew to respect one another greatly and a good working relationship was established. For David to sacrifice his political future in this way, effectively to be a single-issue campaigner, says a lot about his moral compass.

I don't pretend that David Cameron will be pleased at today's turn of events. He would obviously have wanted to keep David on board. But he is where he is. We are where we are. How's that for being profound!? He's made an excellent appointment in Dominic Grieve, someone who regular readers know I believe should have been in the shadow Cabinet ages ago.

The Lib Dems are to be commended for deciding not to stand in the by-election. Labour is showing all the signs of following suit. If they do, they will be treating the issue (and voters) with contempt. The 42-day issue can now be debated fully during the by-election campaign. Sure, there are 69 per cent of people opposed to David's stance, but they oppose it with their hearts not their heads. Most of us can have sympathy with banging terrorists up for as long as it takes, but when you think about the actual consequences of doing so without charge, you slowly begin to think with your head, not your heart.

I see that well-known by-election Labour campaigner, Stephen McCabe MP, thinks that David is 'treating Parliament and the voters with contempt'. They really don't get it, do they? They don't get the fact that out there, voters are crying out for politicians who take moral stands, who stand up for what they believe in, even if it is temporarily unpopular. They are fed up with politicians who are on the take, or can be corralled into a voting lobby by a government whip offering them sweeties for their pet cause. Ann Widdecombe took a courageous stand when she made her 'something of the night' speech. She did so in the full knowledge that it could be the ruination of her political career. She did what she thought was right. And that's what David Davis is doing.

As many of you will have seen, I have been on various media outlets during the afternoon giving my views. It's been like flying blind to be honest. Dangerous but fun!

WESTMINSTER VILLAGE V. THE REAL WORLD
FRIDAY 13 JUNE

One thing in particular has struck me over the last fifteen hours or so – the vast gulf between the Westminster Village bubble and the real world. While political pundits and politicians have spent the time searching for weird motives behind DD's decision, the rest of the country has given a different verdict. Let's ignore the reaction on political blogs for the moment (even though it has been far more positive than from the mainstream media commentators) and look at what's been said by BBC viewers on the Have Your Say website, or the *Telegraph* website, or the *Mail*, or *The Guardian*, or *The Independent*. Reaction on most of those sites is running 80–20 in favour of David Davis. Why? Because they see someone standing up for what he believes – a refreshing change from what they see as the political norm.

This by-election could mark a watershed in British politics. It could be the first by-election in living memory run outside the wet blanket of party politics. I hope all the fundraising will be done on the internet, with a maximum campaign contribution of £100 – contrast that approach with Kelvin MacKenzie's campaign which will be funded by Rupert Murdoch. A by-election campaign like this doesn't need to cost huge amounts of money.

So perhaps the media pundits who are perplexed this morning might like to get out of Westminster for a change and talk to some real people. But I am not holding my breath.

OUR PERFECT DAY
MONDAY 16 JUNE

Yesterday I got married. Well, John and I entered into a civil partnership, which is the nearest I shall ever come to it. The event took place at the magnificent Wadhurst Castle in East Sussex – a perfect setting for an event like this.

I have to say that it was a perfect day. Everything ran smoothly, everyone turned up and I think all who attended had a really good time. The day started at 1.30 p.m. with drinks before the ceremony. One guest had left Norwich at 4 a.m. and had turned up at 10.30 just to make sure he was on time! Indeed, many people turned up very early, which was good as it meant there was a chance to speak to everyone properly.

The ceremony was due to start at 2.30 and rather worryingly there was the odd hint of rain in the air. We had decided to do the whole thing outside as it was such a nice day. Very Southfork! We had to actually sign the register inside the castle, in the room licensed for such occasions. Luckily the rain held off. We had gone to some trouble to ensure the ceremony was as 'yuck-free' as possible and asked three friends – Mark Fox, Rena Valeh and Alex Rosoman – to do three readings. The setting was amazing with stupendous views out over the East Sussex Downs.

Gyles Brandreth was one of the guests, and it was he who took the 1994 Marriage Act through Parliament, which enabled places like Wadhurst Castle to hold marriage ceremonies. The ceremony itself was more moving that I had perhaps expected. Having never been to one for a civil partnership before, I wasn't quite sure how it would be or how I would react. John is fairly inscrutable, but at one point I did feel I was about to 'lose it' and had to do some deep breathing to get back on track! There was a real sense of occasion about it all. Nadine captures it well:

> We began with drinks on the terrace, which is where Iain and John exchanged vows – at which point everyone suddenly went quiet. Not quiet in the normal way – the fact that something special was taking place hung heavily in the air. It was very emotional.

We then seemed to spend an age taking photos of different groups of people – the one I particularly enjoyed was the West Ham fans group photo where we broke into a rendition of 'I'm Forever Blowing Bubbles'. Classy, eh?

Then there was a picture with all the women wearing what they called 'fascinators'. Fascinating. For some reason, I wanted to call them 'fluffers', until I remembered what Emily Maitlis told me a 'fluffer' was.

Then it was time to sit down for an absolutely wonderful meal, prepared by a fantastic caterer called Amuse. I cannot recommend them highly enough. Because it was a Sunday, we decided people wouldn't want to leave late, so instead of evening entertainment we had a six-course meal!

Each course was interspersed with a reading or speech. Keith Simpson was Master of Ceremonies, my niece Issy read a poem my sister Tracey had composed for John and myself that morning:

> We try to make our mark in this life
> Scratch our names in the sand
> Then watch, unprepared, as the real world
> Washes up and fills the grooves
> Where our dreams had been
> If you find a love in this life
> Where acceptance and truth
> Are not fleeting or fickle
> Then watch the waves break
> Don't run from the shore

My other sister, Sheena, then proposed a toast to absent friends and paid a short tribute to my godmother, who died last year, and John's brother Roger, who was killed in a road accident in Thailand in 1994. There wasn't a dry eye in the house. Tracey then made the speech of the day, which even seasoned speechmakers like Gyles Brandreth and Christine Hamilton said was the best speech they had heard this year. Naturally, I was the butt of most of her jokes. She also pointed out that it was thanks to Tony Blair we were there at all (she's a Lib Dem). I clapped. Here's an extract from Tracey's speech:

It surely has to be a sign of advancing years when sentimentality for one's own brother replaces the need to crack a bloody good joke about toilets and vicars in a fabulous Kenneth Williams accent! I mean, I am talking about a man who has single-handedly kept my daughter's school PTA raffle superbly stocked over the years with gifts I have passed on of such unbelievable bad taste they are almost kitsch collectors' items! I am talking about a man ... yes, a grown man ... who still wells up when he remembers Amy Turtle leaving *Crossroads* and Benny's unrequited love for Miss Diane. A man who likes – no, who adores – Steps and ABBA and for whom surely the song 'Dancing Queen' was written. Well, on second thoughts the words – Disco Dancer, Rhythm, and Co-ordination – do not apply to my brother! Iain is so obsessed with this beloved pop group that he became hugely upset when, having asked people to vote for their top ten ABBA songs (I know ... who would do that? ... and why?), their choices did not match his own. That reminds me of his mania for lists when we were growing up. He would categorise his impressively eclectic collection of 45s so fastidiously it was bordering on an OCD! He would continually be asking me and my sister Sheena infuriating questions during car journeys to Frinton, like 'Name your top five favourite TV programmes' or 'Rank these in ascending order of educational value: *Pogles Wood*, *Hector's House*, *Trumpton* or *Hammy Hamster's Tales From the Riverbank*' and 'Would you rather star on the *Galloping Gourmet*, *Opportunity Knocks* or *Dallas?*' His hankering for TV fame began at a very early age!

And surely Iain must be the only person ever to manage to get a dog run over whilst walking him on a lead! Ah Gio, Iain and John's little barrel of a dog, fondly named after Iain's favourite aftershave, Aqua di Gio, or more commonly known in the Dale/Simmons household as Gio's Piss. If Gio were a child, he would almost certainly be in a reform school for delinquents by now, but I guess his thieving and gluttonous behaviour can really only be blamed on the parents! And John ... looking so dapper today (no hint of the used-car salesman about him at all) ... but I have to say I have my suspicions about his links with the dark side – his nocturnal habits and absolute fear of rising before noon surely point to something a little sinister (more garlic anyone?). In fact I believe I am right in saying that he realised the life of a sales rep for a drugs company was not for him when his boss found him asleep, mid-morning, on the job.

Now after that massive digression, let's get back to the wallowing in sentiment predicament I alluded to earlier... My brother is so clever that he has grabbed the time he has been given so far, ignited it, turning the flicker into the brightest of flames. And a flame will keep burning safely if it has some protection around it and that is what John has provided for the last thirteen years. Iain has pursued his dreams like a tenacious terrier, realised most of them, but not got overly depressed when the reality is maybe not living up to expectations. He moves on and is sanguine about the experience.

John has had to cope with a terrible tragedy. He has done this with a quiet, commendable dignity. And I, for one, am proud to now be able to call him my brother-in-law. (Not so sure how he feels about officially becoming part of the Dale Family ... very scary business!) I am a hopeless internet-phobe, but finally, this weekend, I actually looked at Iain's website and his blog diary for the first time. I was suitably impressed and actually, though it pains me to say it, I was staggered when I read his biography page and was reminded of all that he has done. It is also simply quite amazing to see his picture, taken by David Bailey, in *GQ* magazine alongside the great and the good. I was even tempted to post a comment on his blog along with the hundreds of other well-wishers ... I particularly liked the comments about the Labour government making this event possible ... However, I don't want to make any new nerdy friends or start a bun fight today when we're all behaving so well.

John and Iain have forged a partnership that works brilliantly on many different levels – they balance out each other: John with his impeccable taste, Iain with his... well... let's just say 'individual taste'. Iain with his fiery nature, John with his placid and calm temperament. Iain's impulsiveness and John's reticence to make hasty decisions. Iain's love of the limelight and fame (he was recently on two BBC channels simultaneously, I mean when is he not on the television or radio), John happier in the background. Iain with his work ethic, John with his 'I'd rather be polishing my balls' ethic – oh, you are a filthy audience ... I'm referring to his glass collection of course! In fact, John has spent years trying to educate Iain in all things Art Nouveau, but without success: Iain still thinks that Lalique is a French vegetable!

But joking aside, their partnership is one based on trust and companionship. One that has endured much already, not least the prejudice of people who should spend time judging their own lives before passing judgement on others. Jane and Garry, my mum and dad, and Enid and Roland, John's parents, would want me to say, I'm sure, how proud they are of their sons and all they have achieved in their lives so far. Ultimately, though, happiness surely is what every parent wants for their offspring. And I too hope that

Iain and John have many more happy years ahead of them together. Please join me in raising your glasses to love, to happiness, to Iain and John.

Donal Blaney relates the funniest moment:

In an innuendo-laden series of speeches, Iain's sister Tracey (who delivered a truly Herculean speech for someone genuinely unaccustomed to public speaking) caused the greatest mirth of the day. She made some obtuse reference to masturbation – only for the throng to dissolve into giggles when an eight-year-old child asked, a little too loudly, 'What's masturbation, Daddy?' Priceless.

Keith Simpson followed at the end of the meal with a host of hilarious imagined telegrams from guests who couldn't attend. And then it was my turn. My rhetoric certainly didn't match that of my sister. Here's an excerpt:

John and I have been blessed with many gifts in our lives, but the gift of loving parents is one that we will always cherish. So few children get to adulthood nowadays without some degree of family upheaval. We both can honestly say that we had more or less perfect childhoods – loving parents, a nice home, brought up in nice areas – in my case in an idyllic village in Essex – yes there are idyllic parts of Essex – and John a few miles away in Tunbridge Wells...

We could not have hoped for a better start in life. So what went wrong afterwards I hear you ask! But, seriously, we know how lucky we have been. On behalf of John and myself I want to say a big public thank you for supporting us both in whatever we have done in our lives, and whatever we have become. I know we have both done our best to make you proud of us. I also know that at times we have both let you down. But even then you have been there for us and guided us. We both love you all very much, even if we might not say – or even show it – often enough...

Now, seeing as John really is unaccustomed to public speaking, I can safely talk about him in the full knowledge that he won't stand up and get his own back. John and I met way back in the summer of 1995. It was Princess Diana who brought John and I together. I mean, how gay is that? John was far more interested in the fact that I owned Princess Diana's car than he was in the fact that he was meeting the future ex-Tory candidate for North Norfolk. Can't think why...

I think our relationship is a perfect exemplification of the hackneyed old cliché of opposites attract. I love my football, John precedes every mention of the word football with the prefix 'bloody'. I love my politics whereas John views it as a bit like tiddlywinks, a game played predominantly by little boys. He is incredibly tolerant of my never ceasing phone conversations with political friends, but less tolerant of my good friend David Davis. David's timing is sometimes not all it might be. On Friday night I overheard John on the phone saying to my mother: 'All I know is it's bloody typical of David Davis to pick this weekend to do it...'

You may not believe this given what many of you know of my temperament and occasional volcanic temper, but in thirteen years we have never had a row. I have to admit we did come close to it over the seating plan here, but John did eventually agree to sit next to me...

Let me finish by saying two things – first of all a quote from Robert Sexton: 'In a time when nothing is more certain than change, the commitment of two people to one another has become difficult and rare. Yet, by its scarcity, the beauty and value of this exchange have only been enhanced.'

We all live in uncertain worlds, none more so than the kind of life we lead. So to find someone who has felt able to stick with me for thirteen years, has made me feel very lucky indeed. John, today we have committed the rest of our lives to each other. I'm sure there will be some turbulent times ahead, but today, to misquote Winston Churchill, I feel I have won first prize in the lottery of life.

And that was it. A remarkable day, spent with family and friends, enjoying a spectacular setting and wonderful food. Neither of us could have asked for more. I apologise for the length of this post, but so many people have been so kind in their good wishes that I wanted to share our day with you.

IT SHOULDN'T HAPPEN TO AN MP
WEDNESDAY 2 JULY

There's an old saying in Parliament: never write something to a constituent you wouldn't want to see on the front page of your local newspaper. *The Sun* reports this morning that after receiving an abusive letter from a constituent, Labour MP David Clelland sent back a reply telling his constituent to 'stick your vote where it best pleases you'. The constituent says he is 'very offended'.

Most MPs would have sent back a reply full of the usual platitudes and ignoring the abuse in the original letter. Good for David Clelland for standing up for himself.

THE FONZ IS SQUARER THAN RICHIE CUNNINGHAM
WEDNESDAY 2 JULY

In my youth the cool hero of choice was The Fonz, played by Henry Winkler in the US TV sitcom *Happy Days*. He wasn't just cool, he was ice cool. He was the guy who always got the girl, played the hard guy but in reality was an old softie. And Richie Cunningham's mother fancied the pants off him.

So it was with some degree of shock that I turned to page twelve of today's *Telegraph* to find a picture of him reading a kids' book with Ed Balls. And he looked like the definition of the word 'uncool'. He looked squarer than Richie Cunningham, wearing a David Davis-esque stripy tie.

Somehow I felt old. Part of my childhood died in that picture.

AN INSTITUTIONALLY INCOMPETENT POLICE FORCE
TUESDAY 8 JULY

A man goes into a police station and tells the receptionist: 'I have just killed two people.' He's told not to queue jump and wait his turn. That's what happened to the man who turned himself in yesterday for the killing of the two French students in New Cross. He then waited for several minutes in the reception area of the police station until someone would see him. At any time he could have changed his mind and walked out of the police station.

No doubt the policeman on reception was too busy filling in a diversity awareness form to be bothered by a self-confessed murderer. Is it any wonder that people are increasingly wondering what the police are there for? They refuse to investigate car crime, their attitude to house burglary is generally laughable, but if you defend yourself against an attack it's you who is liable to be arrested.

Yes, cases of recorded crime are falling. I have no doubt at all that it is in large part due to the fact that people just don't bother to report many crimes any more. Too many people just don't see the point.

Last night on BBC *South East News*, the lead story was of a group of people whose houses had been repeatedly burgled, yet the police refused to even visit the crime scene initially. It was only when the media got involved that they did so – four days later. As the reporter said at the end of his report: 'People are asking, if the police won't investigate burglary, what is the point of them?' Indeed.

YOU KNOW YOU ARE A POLITICAL CHAV WHEN...
WEDNESDAY 16 JULY

What an utterly ridiculous debate. And no, I am not talking about the debate on parliamentary expenses in the House of Commons, I am talking about the Fabian Society publicity stunt policy document which reckons the word 'chav' should be banned as it is kind of, well, racist. Utter bollocks. And as a linguist, can I just say that it is impossible to ban words. Language evolves and it evolves for a reason. The word 'chav' was invented to portray a social phenomenon. It could have been a different word, but it wasn't. Get over it. Anyway, by way of a bit of fun, read on...

You Know You Are A Political Chav When...
10. You prefer *Heat* magazine to *The Economist*.
9. You don't merely hug a hoodie, you wear one.
8. You sprinkle your party conference speech with a liberal use of the word 'innit'.
7. You have more than three metal appendages.
6. You wear your trackie bottoms in the division lobby.
5. You start your maiden speech with the words, 'Well, I mean like...'
4. The Speaker awards you an ASBO for heckling at PMQs.
3. Your drink of choice in the Pugin Room is Red Bull.

2. You enter a bulldog in the Parliamentary Dog of the Year contest.
1. You are a former Member of Parliament for Peterborough (and we're not talking Brian Mawhinney here...).

GORDON'S IMPERFECT ECONOMIC STORM APPROACHES
FRIDAY 18 JULY

An economic shudder has just run down my spine. I just read *this* on the BBC website:

> In June public borrowing reached a massive £9.16 billion.

That's 9.16 billion of Her Majesty's Pounds. It's also 24 per cent more than Treasury forecasts. In the first quarter of this financial year, the government borrowed more than £24 billion. Annualise it, and the government will be borrowing close on £100 billion this year – a seventh of all government spending. No wonder Alistair Darling is seeking to rewrite his own rules. In case you think I am being over-dramatic, government borrowing is at its highest since April 1946.

Inflation is set to rocket. Unemployment is increasing. The balance of trade is at its worst level ever. The PSBR is out of control. And this is all before the recession has really started to bite. Have I missed anything?

If this sort of financial management goes on, I dread to think what kind of financial situation the Conservatives may inherit in May 2010.

A SUPERMARKET TALE OF TWO NORFOLK MPS
SATURDAY 26 JULY

Norwich North Labour MP Ian Gibson was on the *Today* programme this morning bemoaning the fact that he now gets shouted at in supermarkets by angry constituents and it's all Gordon Brown's fault.

Later on this morning, Mid Norfolk Tory MP Keith Simpson was dragooned into shopping by his lady wife at the local Tesco.

He was eyeing up a nice bottle of Pinot Grigio when a rather attractive lady ran up to him and exclaimed: 'Ah, just the man I need!'
Preparing himself for some political praise, he straightened his back
and drew himself up to his full 6 ft 3 in. 'Yes,' the lady continued,
'would you reach up and get me that bottle on the top shelf, there's
a good chap?'

Cue instant deflation, and a gimlet glare from Mrs S.

THE *ANY QUESTIONS* EXPERIENCE
SATURDAY 16 AUGUST

I don't normally get nervous before appearing on radio or TV, I
must admit, but yesterday was different. There's enormous potential
to make a complete dick of yourself on *Any Questions*, and the
idea of the four-hour drive home afterwards thinking I had done
really badly nagged away at me all day. As the panel walked on to
the stage at the King's School in Ottery St Mary, I whispered to my
fellow panellist Sarah Sands: 'I'd rather be interviewed by Paxman.'

We were all asked to meet at the Bowd Inn, near Sidmouth, for
a pre-programme dinner with Jonathan Dimbleby at 6 p.m. Sarah
Sands and Mary Beard were already there when I arrived, having
travelled down by train. I had left Tunbridge Wells at 10 a.m. and
had a good drive round the M25 and down the A30. I got to the area
at around 2 p.m. and spent the afternoon relaxing and reading the
papers. I kept asking myself if I had done enough preparation, while
all the time knowing in the back of my mind that I often perform
best when I have done absolutely no preparation whatsoever.

The pre-programme dinner was very jolly, with Jonathan Dimbleby
entertaining us with anecdote after anecdote, and telling us of his
new job chairing Index on Censorship. Although I had met Sarah
Sands before, I didn't know Mary Beard (a left-of-centre Cambridge
don) or Tim Smit from the Eden Project. Attending the dinner before-
hand was very useful in that it enabled us all to build a little bit of
a rapport and size each other up. It was clear from the outset that
Tim and I might well have a major disagreement on the programme.
Jonathan left the dinner before the rest of us to head to the venue and
choose the questions with his producer, Lisa Jenkinson.

There wasn't much discussion about the likely question areas,
although we were all obsessed about the final 'funny' question.

But we did agree that GM foods was a definite possibility, given Jonathan Dimbleby's position as the recently retired Chairman of the Soil Association.

At 7.30 p.m. we were taken the five miles to the school and spent ten minutes in the library, while the audience was warmed up by a man from BBC Radio Cornwall. There were about 350 people packed into the Assembly Hall. The local paper took a group photo of us as 'show time' approached.

As we walked out onto the raised stage, I looked out to the audience, almost willing them to be responsive. I know I perform best when there is audience reaction – it's almost immaterial whether it's positive or negative. At 7.55, Jonathan asked a member of the audience for the warm-up question, which was: 'Forty years on from Woodstock, which Woodstock Act would you like to see in a 2008 Woodstock?' Oh bugger, I thought, I haven't got a clue who sang at Woodstock. I was called on last, and explained that my musical knowledge didn't extend back before 1974 and Abba, but the only '60s act worth hearing again would, of course, be Sir Cliff Richard. The men in the audience groaned, and all the 'women of a certain age' cheered!

Before we knew it, we heard the Radio 4 pips and, after the news, off we went. That empty feeling in my stomach was disappearing... Jonathan finished introducing me by saying that I host the theatre show *A Night With Ann Widdecombe*. He mischievously looked at me and asked: 'Is that a whole night?' I rolled with the audience laughter and replied: 'That's for me to know and you to guess.' Cue more audience laughter. We were on our way, and having got an audience reaction, my nerves had gone. It was a good way for Jonathan to put me at my ease.

We had three questions which I had predicted – on Georgia, Policy Exchange and GM foods – and two questions which I hadn't. One question asked if we agreed with the judge who said that a broken society was equally as apocalyptic as global warming, and the other one posed the question of how we could encourage boys to read more books. The final 'funny' question asked what alternative career path we would have taken had we not chosen to do what we currently do.

I had a good spat with Tim Smit on global warming. I expressed some scepticism about man-made global warming, which both Tim and Jonathan seemed rather surprised by. Tim asserted that not a single scientist disagreed with the fact that global warming is entirely man-made. I took issue with that and quoted the example of the UN report, for which many dissenting scientists had lost their jobs and were considered almost heretical. Tim had to agree I was right. I also laid into Greenpeace and others for refusing to debate the issue because they regard the argument as already won. Jonathan then asked the audience if they shared my scepticism and, rather to all our surprise, found that half of them did. Greenpeace clearly haven't won the argument if the Ottery St Mary audience is anything to go by.

Anyway, it all seemed to go by very quickly and I found the whole experience most enjoyable. I think I avoided the 'making a dick of yourself' factor – unless of course you tell me different! – although I think there were a couple of questions where I missed a trick or two.

After the programme we had a drink with the Ottery St Mary town councillors who had hosted the event and I left at around 9.30 p.m. to drive back to Kent.

Much of the journey was spent thinking about how I could have done better, but also wondering if I had hogged it a bit. Sometimes saying less is more. Hopefully I did well enough to be invited back. Time will tell!

AN EVENING WITH DON BLACK
MONDAY 18 AUGUST

A few weeks ago my partner suggested we get tickets for a concert at the Palladium, organised by Radio 2. My heart sank. It was a tribute to Don Black to mark his seventieth birthday. 'Who's Don Black?' I said. I got a contemptuous look, which in itself is nothing unusual.

It was then explained to me that Don Black is one of the world's most famous lyricists and that he has penned the lyrics to songs like 'Diamonds are Forever' and 'To Sir with Love'. Apparently some very famous people would be singing. OK, I thought, anything for a quiet life. So I duly booked the tickets for the two of us and a couple of friends – in fact, I thought, why not splash out and get the Royal Box – that ought to win me some brownie points. I knew not what I was letting myself in for...

Anyway, we got to the Palladium in good time and although the view from the box was a little restricted, it was nice to have the extra leg room and comfy chairs. Michael Parkinson introduced the evening and the musical accompaniment was by the Royal Philharmonic Orchestra. We got underway with a song performed by Peter Grant, who was followed by the likes of Marti Webb (take that look off your face), Mica Paris, Jonathan Ansell (from G4), Hayley Westenra, Lee Mead, Elkie Brooks (Sam), Raza Jaffrey (who I recognised from *Spooks*, but was apparently the lead in *Bollywood Dreams*) and, believe it or not, Joe Longthorne who, it has to be said, looked a bit like a waxwork. I have to say the whole first half was hugely enjoyable.

As the second half was about to start, the door to the box opened and a woman with a head mic appeared along with a man. She asked would it be all right if Mr Black watched the second half with us in our box! To be honest I hadn't even realised the man was Don Black – he looked about fifty, rather than seventy. So she brought in an extra chair and we watched the likes of Lulu, Craig David (who murdered the Michael Jackson song 'Ben'), Maria Freedman and Gary Barlow (who sang 'Born Free') alongside the man who had written all the songs they were performing. Lulu did a brilliant rendition of 'To Sir with Love'. Michel Legrand conducted the RPO at one stage and Mica Paris rounded off the show with 'Diamonds are Forever'.

It was a truly memorable evening and it really set me thinking. We always associate songs with individual people who sing them, rarely giving a thought to the person who actually wrote the music or the lyrics. Don Black has penned hundreds of songs, which we are all familiar with, yet I didn't know his name. That may be due to my philistinic ignorance, but I suspect I am not alone.

I MISS MY COMBINE HARVESTER
FRIDAY 22 AUGUST

This weekend, weather permitting, I hope to be driving a combine harvester on my father's farm near Saffron Walden. I suspect that there are many farmers around the country who, like him, are extremely concerned by the terrible weather we have been having and its effect on yields. There's nothing quite like driving a combine harvester. I know it sounds stupid, but you can become quite attached to them. I was quite emotional when in the mid-1990s my father pensioned off an old Massey Ferguson combine which we had bought in 1966. In fact, I was furious. I knew every inch of that old hulk like the back of my hand and I still miss it!

The other thing I miss about harvest is stubble burning. My dad still hates John Gummer with a passion for banning it in the early 1990s.

HAS CAROL THATCHER INTRUDED ON HER MOTHER'S PRIVACY?
SUNDAY 24 AUGUST

I'm struggling to decide what to make of Carol Thatcher's book, serialised today in the *Mail on Sunday*. If my mother had dementia, would I be inclined to tell the world about it in this manner? Probably not, but then my mother is only an iconic figure within her own family, not all over the world.

The downside of making all this public is that the media will now obsess about the issue. Up till now, most newspapers and journalists have been quite respectful of Lady T's position and have been careful not to be prurient. I hope the publication of Carol's book will not change that, but I fear otherwise.

Dementia is a terrible disease. I've seen the effects it can have on partners and families. It's also a disease that people find embarrassing to confront and talk about. By being open about the fact he was suffering from it, when he wrote his famous letter to the American people, Ronald Reagan did a huge amount of good. Dementia charities were deluged with money to plough into medical research. If Carol's book has the same effect, it will have achieved a positive result.

But I can't sweep from my mind the thought that I wish she had kept her counsel. It's as if she has intruded on her mother's privacy.

BLOG MEME: WHAT WERE YOU DOING WHEN...?

It's a long time since I started a blog meme, and what better time to do it than a very boring Bank Holiday Sunday? Every few years there's an earth-shattering event which you remember for the rest of your life – and you remember where you were and what you were doing when you heard about it. Here are four of mine...

Princess Diana's death – 31 August 1997

I was asleep in my flat on the Isle of Dogs when the phone went. 'Princess Diana's been in a car crash. Switch on the TV,' I was ordered by my partner. I did so and kept it on. I had a feeling of foreboding. I was watching when Martyn Lewis broke the news and broke down himself. I picked up the phone. 'She's dead,' I said to my very sleepy partner, who struggled to take in the news. He refused to believe it.

Margaret Thatcher's resignation – 22 November 1990

I was working in my office in 36 Grosvenor Gardens. I was in the process of setting up a lobbying company. There was no TV and no radio. Just a telephone. I was stunned and felt as if I was experiencing one of those 'what if' moments. Somehow it didn't seem real.

England's World Cup semi-final v. Germany – 4 July 1990

Gazza's tears. Lineker's signal to Bobby Robson to have a word with him. The two penalty misses. This game had it all, and where was I? Watching it with several hundred insurance brokers in Nottingham. I was covering their conference for my then employers Lloyds List. Three hundred insurance brokers and me in floods of tears. You had to be there.

President Kennedy's assassination – 22 November 1963

I was in my pram gurgling and wetting myself.

MEME: CAN THIS REALLY BE HAPPENING TO ME?
FRIDAY 5 SEPTEMBER

In her book, Carol Thatcher relates a story about attending a dinner to celebrate the 250th anniversary of No. 10, and finding herself sitting with former Prime Ministers and descendants of the likes of Lloyd George and Disraeli. She describes it as a 'Can this really be happening to me?' moment.

Quite often in my life I've been at an event, or met someone famous, and thought to myself: 'Can this really be happening to me?' Here are five of those occasions...

1983: At the age of twenty, attending a reception at No. 10. I remember walking up the famous stairs to be met by Mrs T at the top, and thinking to myself, 'I can't believe how tiny she is.' Later on in the evening, I nearly threw up at her feet, but that's another story.

1985: On my first day working at the House of Commons, walking along the corridor between Central Lobby and Peers' Lobby encountering former PM Jim Callaghan and former US President Gerald Ford coming the other way. We nodded, with me thinking to myself, 'What's a lad from Essex doing mixing with these people?'

1991: I had an SAS guard while I was in Beirut, speaking at a conference. Being driven through downtown Beirut in a convoy of armour-plated Land Rovers with SAS soldiers pointing their machine guns out of the window was an experience in itself. The hotel was also heavily guarded by the Lebanese army. It turned out I was the first British visitor there since John McCarthy had been released from captivity. I hadn't known that in advance...

2002: Meeting the Queen at Buckingham Palace with my partner. We talked to her for several minutes about Politico's. We were surprised (although I don't know why) that she didn't know where Artillery Row was, even though it is only a quarter of a mile from her home! Contrary to our expectation, she was very easy to talk to.

2008: Visiting the White House and blogging from the Oval Office.

ON THE GAME IN CHELMSFORD
WEDNESDAY 17 SEPTEMBER

From the show with Ann Widdecombe in Chelmsford last night:

> ID: So when ITV ask you to do these programmes, how do you judge whether to do them?
> AW: Well, when they asked me to do prostitution, I readily agreed...
> [cue audience collapsing with laughter]

It really was a cracking evening last night. The theatre was sold out, with more than 500 people packed in. The repartee worked a treat, to the extent that one man said to me afterwards: 'You are so easy together. Are you an item?' Miss W was a bit too quick to reply: 'We most certainly are not!' He didn't look convinced...

TOP TEN CHAT-UP LINES OVERHEARD AT LABOUR CONFERENCE
SATURDAY 20 SEPTEMBER

10. Close your eyes and pretend I'm Tony Blair.
9. You know what they say about guys with huge portfolios?
8. Is that a composite motion in your pocket, or are you just pleased to see me?
7. Something's rising, and I'm not talking about the PSBR.
6. That's not my hand, but don't stop shaking.
5. I'm a close personal friend of Ed Miliband.
4. I'm stiffer than Des Browne.
3. Would you like to see my inflation package?
2. I'd love to give you a standing ovation.
1. Hi, my name's Jack Straw.

IT'S WACAWEEK!
SUNDAY 21 SEPTEMBER

I thought the *This Week* sofa had plumbed the depths when Jade Goody's posterior was invited to grace it. I was wrong. I've just caught up with this week's show. I am still trying to recover from the fact that Timmy Mallett was a guest. Here's his opening piece of insightful analysis:

> Andrew Neil: Are we good in this country or bad at positive thinking?
> Timmy Mallett: Wow, I've no idea. I don't really think about that particularly.
> AN: Are we a nation of pessimists?
> TM: No, I'd like to say, er, we like to say the glass is half full except when we're at the bar I suppose, when we're at the bar and someone else has got the round in, in which case we say it's half empty and I'll have another pint please...

Do you think the *This Week* producers meet up each week and have a competition to decide: Who is the most ludicrous person we can invite on? Whoever had the bright idea of Timmy Mallett must have won by a landslide! Coming next week: Tyrone from *Coronation Street*.

AND THE MOST QUALIFIED PERSON IS...
WEDNESDAY 24 SEPTEMBER

Gordon Brown makes much of the fact that he is the only politician who is remotely qualified to get us out of the economic mess he has landed us in. Using his logic, I wondered about some other similarly 'qualified' people, who might have overseen similar reconstructions/revamps...

1. Hitler – uniquely qualified to oversee the postwar reconstruction of Germany
2. Graham Taylor – uniquely qualified to rebuild the England team after their failure to qualify for the 1994 World Cup.
3. Adam Applegarth – uniquely qualified to bring the glory days back to Northern Rock.
4. Robert Maxwell – uniquely qualified to rebuild the *Daily Mirror* pension fund.

I could go on.

A DAY WITH THE FAMILY
SUNDAY 28 SEPTEMBER

It might seem a bizarre way to spend your golden wedding anniversary, but my parents didn't want a party. They just wanted their three grandchildren and three children at home. In the end we all went out for a pub lunch in Great Yeldham and then spent a couple of hours at the Colne Valley Railway at Castle Hedingham. They were having a Thomas the Tank Engine day, so my nieces were in their element. One of them, though, was a little frightened by the Fat Controller! The steam railway only has a mile of track, and I did think £11.50 per ticket was a bit steep (!), but it was all a very enjoyable experience.

The best part of the day was that on the way there, as a surprise, we took my parents to the church where they got married, in nearby Linton. It was all rather touching.

Yesterday evening, before I headed up to Birmingham, my sisters decided we would do something we hadn't done for about twenty-five years – play a card game called Racing Demons. I used to love this game – it's incredibly fast-moving, and provokes a lot of swearing. Nothing had changed, and I found myself calling my fourteen-year-old niece, Issy, things which would be banned on this blog... Disgraceful.

It was a lovely day.

AND ANOTHER THING... THE SACKING OF TOM HARRIS
SATURDAY 4 OCTOBER

The news that Tom Harris has been sacked from the government – he was a junior Transport minister – came as a bit of a shock last night. Regular readers will know that I like Tom and have been relentless in promoting his blog as a brilliant example of how an MP (and minister) should blog. But as he wends his way around Sainsbury's this afternoon, Tom may well be regretting setting foot in the world of blogging because it may have cost him his job. Perhaps.

He doesn't say if the Prime Minister gave a reason for his dismissal, but there has indeed been a perception that his blog has, on the odd occasion, strayed over the edge.

Perhaps Nadine Dorries was right when she said at the Tory conference that it is impossible to be an MP and to blog without consequences. As my friend Shane Greer continually points out, perception is more important than reality in politics, and if people perceive you as a maverick, or a troublemaker, you will never climb the greasy pole. Nadine is seriously contemplating abandoning her blog. Tom, on the other hand, will have more time for his. I wish it were not so.

More than a few people have asked me over the years if I thought my blog was harming my political prospects. I would like to think not, but if I am honest I am sure it has created more than a few enemies I otherwise would not have had. So be it. People in politics cannot go round constantly thinking about the effects of every word they write or utter. That way lies stultifying boredom and political mediocrity. If the only way to get on is to grease up to your party's political establishment and parrot a party line at every opportunity then it is clear that it is pointless having a blog. Not only would it be pointless writing one, but no one would bother reading it.

I wouldn't blame Tom Harris for feeling rather angry today. It's a pity he hates football – a visit to Parkhead for a bit of shouting might do him good. When I was excluded from the first tranche of the 'A' List I don't mind admitting that I felt a bit angry too. I didn't write this at the time, but I knew why it had happened. I knew that someone who I had written something disobliging about in a newspaper column had exacted revenge and put the black spot on me. But instead of letting my anger win, I managed to exact something positive out of a potentially very damaging negative.

I hope that Tom manages to do the same.

IF YOU DON'T HAVE A DOG, YOU MAY NOT UNDERSTAND

Watching one's dog suffer in pain is a dreadful experience. Five years ago, our Jack Russell, Gio, jumped off a sofa and broke a ligament in the knee of one of his back legs. On Friday he did the same thing to the other one. You always know Gio is in pain as he puts on an incredibly sheepish look and sits in a corner looking plaintive.

We took him to the vet, hoping that he hadn't broken anything, but the vet thinks he has. He's given him some painkillers but we have to take him back on Monday and he may well have to be operated on. He's nearly eleven years old and an anaesthetic at his age can be very dangerous. I'm already an emotional wreck just thinking about the worst-case scenario. I don't expect the non-dog lovers among you to understand, but I would do literally anything to ensure he gets better.

GIO IS BACK HOME
MONDAY 6 OCTOBER

So many of you have been kind enough to leave messages or email me about Gio, that I felt I should give you an update. His operation went very well and John collected him from the vet at 6.30 (£420 worse off!). He's now fully conscious, but not particularly enjoying his collar, which he must wear to prevent him trying to undo the stitches in his leg. He's just had some chicken and rice so he must be on the mend!

As you can imagine, we are all relieved that he came through the anaesthetic and operation unscathed.

A SURE SIGN OF AN ECONOMIC SLOWDOWN
WEDNESDAY 15 OCTOBER

Most mornings I catch the 8.02 from Tonbridge station. Six months ago I had to get the 7.52, and six months before that it was the 7.42. The reason? Because if I had arrived at the station any later than that the car park would have been full. Nowadays, the car park rarely fills until mid-morning. Today at 8 a.m. there were more than eighty free spaces.

This surely has to be a sign of economic slowdown. Fewer and fewer people are making the daily commute into London and I can think of no other reason than that.

WHEN IN ENGLAND...
TUESDAY 21 OCTOBER

I've just had one of my more bizarre broadcasting experiences with Press TV. I was invited on to do an hour's discussion on the presidency of George W. Bush. When I got there I discovered that the title of the programmes was *Is George W. Bush the Worst President in US History?* and that it was to be presented by Yvonne Ridley. Ridley is the former *Sunday Express* journalist who was captured by the Taliban and then converted to Islam.

I had never met Ms Ridley before so, being the polite lad I am, extended my hand to shake hands with her. She recoiled. 'I don't do that!' she exclaimed. 'What do you mean, you don't do that?' I asked, slightly nervously. 'Have you never been to an Arab country?' she asked. 'Not many,' I said. 'Well, if you had, you'd know that Muslim women don't shake hands with men,' she informed me. 'Well, all the Muslim women I know not only shake my hand but usually kiss me,' I retorted. And then I added for good measure, 'And anyway, I always go by the maxim: When in England...' So we didn't get off to a very good start.

KILLING TIME
SATURDAY 25 OCTOBER

I'm writing this somewhere over the Croatian coast, essentially because I have nothing better to do. I had forgotten how much I hate flying. There's always that sense of excited anticipation but the reality is usually a disappointment. A bit like a one-night stand. I have a long memory...

I'm sat here in 28E, crammed in like a sardine. I've tried to sleep but can't. Even James Blunt on my iPod has failed to make the Sandman come. I've been reading Frank Skinner's book, but I can't get into it. I like a knob joke as much as the next man but the book hasn't got the warmth of his autobiography, which was one of the best books I have read in years. And seeing as I don't like watching so-called in-flight entertainment, I am spending my time being transfixed by the screen at the front which charts our progress. We don't seem to be getting far. Still two-and-a-half long hours to go. I think I shall spend the next few minutes making a voodoo curse on the man in front of me who insists on reclining his seat with the clear purpose of crushing my legs. In a vain attempt to allow my left leg a little room, I edge it out into the aisle ... only for it to be crushed by the food trolley.

The stewardess seems affronted that I decline the no doubt delicious meal she is offering to me. Like I care. She shouldn't have tried to crush my leg. She makes me feel guilty by asking the man in front to put his seat upright. Once she's out of sight he reclines again. Tosser. I now debate whether I should tap him on the shoulder and a) ask him politely to put his seat up as it is going to give me a blood clot or b) treat him to one of my special withering looks. Of course I do nothing. I'm British, innit?

At the moment I'd happily storm the cockpit and ask the pilot to let me get off in Dubrovnik. Update: 1,238 miles to go.

The fact that I am typing this when I should be at Upton Park watching Craig Bellamy score a hat-trick against Arsenal hardly improves my mood. When I planned this trip, the match was being played yesterday. However, while I was at the airport someone from Israel left a comment on my West Ham blog to say he'd tell me a bar where I can watch the Hammers play Man U on Wednesday evening. I gently enquired with the lovely Nathalie, my CFI[†]

---

† Conservative Friends of Israel.

travelling companion, what our itinerary had in store for us, and she thought Wednesday evening would be free. Result! I suspect it might also have something to do with the fact that her boss, Stuart Polak, will be keen to see his beloved Liverpool at the same time ... and presumably in a different bar.

I suppose we should be grateful we are even on the plane. El Al were kind enough to let us use their lounge at Terminal 1 (excellent smoked salmon bagels, by the way). We kept asking them if they would call our flight. Yes, they said, don't worry. But they never did. By the time we went to the gate the flight was closing. That happened to me once before, in the USA and I did miss my flight and had to wait a day for another one – in Bangor, Maine. Don't ever do that. Bangor makes Tunbridge Wells look like a metropolis.

Update: 1,112 miles to go. Just flying over Tirana. I always wanted to go to Albania when Enver Hoxha ruled the roost. Never made it though, apart from a holiday in Corfu in 1985 when we looked at the Albanian coastline a few miles away and wondered about storming it. We decided against.

Twenty minutes later: Just as we sat in our seats, Nathalie asked if I had ever flown with El Al before. 'No,' I replied. 'It's, er, different,' she said. Wondering what she could mean, I tentatively asked how. 'It's quite noisy,' she said. I now know she means. I have never been on a plane where as many people seem to delight in getting up and wandering around. Half of them seem to delight in bashing against my left shoulder as they do so. Charming.

Oh. My. God. The woman on the other side of the aisle is standing up and doing some sort of exercise routine. And at her age. Hmmm. Back to the knob jokes for a few minutes, I think.

Sixty minutes later (over the Sea of Crete): I have never had the pleasure of joining the Mile High Club. Indeed, I have never quite understood how two people can emerge from a plane loo unnoticed. But on this El Al plane there are four loos in a sort of two-by-two area in the middle of the plane (a 747–400) so anything would be possible. Mind you, looking round me, I doubt there will be much illicit activity on this particular flight. And being a married man now... Talking of scoring, my mind turns back to Craig Bellamy. I just know he scored today. Please let it be so. Assuming my Blackberry works in Israel I should find out in less than an hour. The excitement mounts...

By the way, thank you to Richard, who emailed me suggesting

a visit in the Golan Heights to a cafe called Coffee Annan – get it? Kofi Annan! Honestly, this Hebrew humour is side-splitting, isn't it? Three hundred and forty miles to go.

Ten minutes to landing: Reading this back I wonder whether to post it or not, but I know I will. I suspect it will be some time before the call comes from the *Sunday Times* to be a travel writer...

ISRAEL DIARY: DAY ONE
MONDAY 27 OCTOBER

I'm so tired I can hardly type, so we'll see how far I get with this. Today was spent travelling through northern Israel in a huge American nine-seater 4x4. We set off from Tel Aviv just after 8 a.m. The traffic heading out of the city was New York-esque in proportion. We ended up making a detour to avoid a huge traffic jam not far from Nazareth, as we made our way up to the Golan Heights. The further north you head, the more spectacular the scenery becomes. We headed for a Kibbutz just over the fence from the South Lebanon border village of Adaisseh. If you look on the map it's right at the northern tip of Israel. Looking over into Lebanon I felt in a time-warp, as I remembered the first time I had been to the East/West German border thirty-one years ago. As our guide told us all about the history of the area, we suddenly heard distant gunfire. We were told it could be cross-border gunfire or it could be a wedding. A few minutes later there was a huge bang not that far away. Our guide told of a cross-border attack by Hizbollah terrorists who, one night, attacked the Kibbutz and kidnapped several children. A three-month-old baby was shot in the head. The baby's twin brother is now a friend of our guide. It was from Adaisseh that many of the rockets were launched in 2006 that did so much damage to Israel.

From there we travelled across to the Syrian border. The Golan Heights were annexed by Israel in 1967 and have remained a bone of contention ever since. There are very few settlements in the area as there is great uncertainty over its future. Rabin was apparently ready to hand the Heights back to Syria as part of a wider Middle Eastern peace deal, but he didn't live to take it further. Looking down over the border, there are many villages and towns visible in the valley below. Again, memories of East Germany came back to me.

From there we travelled south to the Sea of Galilee. It was this part of the day that told me what the expression 'Holy Land' means. All of us were truly humbled by what we saw and experienced this afternoon. We visited three holy sites which figure prominently in the Bible – all of which were within a stone's throw of each other on the shore of the Sea of Galilee. First on the agenda was the site of the feeding of the 5,000, then to the point where Jesus is said to have walked on water and finally – and most memorably for all of us – the Mount of Beatitudes, where Jesus gave the Sermon on the Mount. On the site of the feeding of the 5,000 it almost appeared to us that there were 5,000 German tourists there expecting a reprise.

We all know these stories from the Bible, and I suppose I have always considered each of them a work of fiction. But when you actually stand on the very ground that Jesus was said to have stood on, it makes you re-evaluate some very long-held views. I have to say, though, that bearing in mind its historical significance, the Mount of Beatitudes is a rubbish dump. Literally. It's astonishing that the Israeli government doesn't seem to worry about the upkeep of many of its historical gems.

This evening we went out for a meal on the beachfront in Tel Aviv. It was in a restaurant not far from Mike's Bar, which was bombed by two Britons not long ago. Perhaps I should not have been hugely surprised to be security swept as I walked into the restaurant. But I was.

ISRAEL DIARY: DAY TWO
TUESDAY 28 OCTOBER

The day started with breakfast at our hotel with the British ambassador to Israel, Tom Phillips. It's his second tour of duty here and he gave us an overview of the situation as he saw it. I asked him about Tony Blair's role here, which I hadn't realised was purely related to economic development in Gaza and the West Bank. For some reason I had thought he had a role in the peace process.

We then spent the morning at the rather impressive University of Tel Aviv. The campus is incredibly well kept, possibly due to the fact that the students haven't returned yet.

Our first meeting of the day was with Professor Asher Susser, the former Director of the Dayan Center for Middle Eastern Studies. He taught me more about the Middle East in half an hour than I thought possible. He believes that, for the first time since 1967, Israel now suffers from an existential threat. He said Egypt has declined in importance and influence, especially with regard to Gaza and the Sudan. In his opinion there are now only three important players in the Middle East peace process, none of which is an Arab state. Arabs are not calling the shots any longer, he maintained. The three states are Israel itself, Turkey and Iran. I questioned him about this and asked why he failed to mention Syria or Jordan. He said Syria was now just the frontman for Iran and played second fiddle. Iran had replaced the Soviet Union as the main influence on the Syrian regime.

Professor Susser maintains that the future of Lebanon is up for grabs between the Sunnis and the Shias, but because the centre of gravity in Middle Eastern politics has shifted from Cairo to the Persian Gulf and Iran is now establishing a Mediterranean presence through Lebanon, there is a retreat of secular politics and Islamists are shaping discourse and politics in the area.

He does, however, believe that Iranian expansion may well be contained in 2009 because of the dramatic fall in the price of oil. Every dollar fall in the oil price means $1 billion fewer dollars in revenue for Iran. This may well provide the opportunity to open a proper dialogue with Iran. He says you cannot boycott Iran out of existence. Pressure must be ratcheted up on the Iranian regime as a precursor to negotiation. He says Israel should prepare for a US–Iranian dialogue because it is surely coming. The US should concede Iranian pre-eminence in the gulf in return for full Western recognition – but that's where a line should be drawn. The US must make it clear that the Iranians cannot be allowed to interfere in the Mediterranean.

He likened the Iranian nuclear situation to that of Japan, which has the capability to make a bomb but hasn't actually done so. He said it was up to the four great powers, plus maybe Russia, to supervise and verify any Iranian nuclear programme.

Later in the morning we had an economic briefing from Professor Dan Ben-David from the university's Department of Public Policy.

He is a leading Kadima supporter and had been set on a political career, but next week he is starting a new job as head of the Israeli equivalent of the Brookings Institution. He started off by giving us a set of very impressive figures about the Israeli economy. Foreign investment has gone up from $600 million in 1993 to $13,500 million in 2006. He was keen to stress that Israelis are some of the most innovative people in the world, with patent applications on a level with those of America. But then the good news stopped. Living standards are not as high as those of other nations with equivalent economies, poverty is higher and so is inequality. All have been getting worse since the 1970s. Labour productivity is a quarter lower than in the USA, with only 71 per cent of males in employment (UK figure is 81 per cent). Professor Ben-David clearly believes Israel has the potential to become a thriving market economy, but is not quite there yet.

Our third session of the morning was spent at the Aerodynamic Lab, where we received a talk about, well, aerodynamics. Quite honestly it might as well have been in Hebrew, as I didn't understand a word of it. I got an ungraded Physics O Level, so I wasn't entirely surprised.

The last engagement of the morning was an hour-long tour of the Israeli Diaspora Museum. The museum explains how Jews have come to move to various countries throughout the world.

We spent the afternoon at the Institute for Counter-Terrorism. I'm going to come over all Jack Bauer now and say that I would love to tell you what we talked about, but then I would have to kill you. There were some fairly bleak messages about the rise of radical Islamic terrorism and what the West, and mainstream Muslims, will need to do to counter it.

Due to being extremely tired I wasn't particularly looking forward to going out tonight, but it really was an evening to remember. They say you can't really get to know a country until you get to know its people. Well, tonight we were invited to dinner at a private house in Tel Aviv by a lovely lady called Evelyn. There were about fifteen of us altogether, including a journalist from the *Haaretz* newspaper and a senior official from the foreign ministry. We talked about all sorts of things, but I was keen to learn what they all thought of Benjamin Netanyahu. He seems to me like a politician who talks tough in opposition but is then rather more liberal in power.

ISRAEL DIARY: DAY THREE
WEDNESDAY 29 OCTOBER

> I do not know what a Jew is, we only know what human beings are.
> – Pastor André Trocmé, 10 August 1942

It's been such a full day I am not quite sure where to start. We left the hotel in Tel Aviv to spend the whole day in Jerusalem. The traffic there has to be seen. The morning started with a briefing by one of President Peres's advisers. We talked about the history of Jerusalem and its very confusing geography. For those who haven't been here, it's almost impossible to explain without being on the ground. We were taken to a vantage point high up on a hillside overlooking the Mount of Olives and the old city. From there you can also see the security fence and the West Bank.

We then took a tour of the Old City with an absolutely superb tour guide. It was great walking through the Suq – row upon row of shops. The variety was astonishing. They don't do political correctness in Jerusalem. I nearly bought a supply of T-shirts with VISIT ISRAEL BEFORE ISRAEL VISITS YOU for some of the anti-Jewish commenters who have infested this blog of late. There were also T-shirts of Yasser Arafat.

To stand where history was made – rather like when we went to the Sea of Galilee on Monday – was an absolute privilege. To trace the path to the crucifixion and see the spot where Jesus died was incredible. We then visited the holy wall just under the Mount of Olives. It was bizarre to hear the Muslim call to prayer while looking at the Mount of Olives, but people should realise that Jerusalem is a city which welcomes people of all religions. I suppose I had thought of it as primarily a Jewish place, but it is far from that, with peoples of all backgrounds and religions finding it a place of religious significance.

After that we headed off to Yad Vashem, the new Holocaust museum and memorial. It was only opened in 2005 and is a very impressive building. I have to say though, having been to a couple of concentration camps, I found it less emotional than I was expecting. On visits to Buchenwald and Dachau I found it incredibly harrowing, but here – perhaps because of the crowds – I didn't. Even typing that, I feel slightly guilty.

We then finished the day at the Knesset, where we were due

to meet the Israeli Deputy Foreign Minister, who is Druse, but he couldn't make it. Instead, we had an hour with a fascinating member of the Knesset, Binyamin Elon. He is the leader of the National Union party, which holds nine of the 120 seats in the Knesset, and was Minister of Tourism under Ariel Sharon. His party is certainly right wing, but he holds some very unconventional views on the future of the West Bank. He is firmly against a two-state solution and favours a confederation on the West Bank, with Jordan and Israel holding joint sovereignty of the area. He argues that there has never been such a thing as a Palestinian nation and that up until recently, the inhabitants of the West Bank have always been called Arabs.

We didn't get back to Tel Aviv until 8.30 p.m. I tried to find a bar showing the West Ham v. Man U game but failed lamentably. Just as well, considering the result.

Before I came here, several people told me that Israeli food was awful. They could not be more wrong. The breakfast in the Carlton Hotel has to be seen to be believed (the Carlton is highly recommended – one of the best hotels I have ever stayed in), and every single meal has been memorable. And for all the right reasons! Today in Jerusalem I had the best smoked salmon and cream cheese onion bagel I have ever had.

ISRAEL DIARY: DAY FOUR
THURSDAY 30 OCTOBER

Another early start, leaving the hotel at 7.45 a.m. for the 75-minute drive to Ramallah. For those who don't know, Ramallah is on the West Bank and houses the headquarters of the Palestinian Authority. In order to get into Ramallah we had to change buses as our Jewish driver is not allowed to cross into the West Bank. During the short drive to the Palestinian Authority HQ we drove through the streets of Ramallah, which is one of the more prosperous West Bank towns. Indeed, it looked little different to most Arab towns. We arrived a bit early and had to sit outside the PA compound. Eventually we were allowed in and had the opportunity of viewing the morning marching by PA soldiers. Not sure their marching technique would quite make Sandhurst!

The security, it has to be said, was lax in the extreme. We were let into the building which houses President Abbas's office and we could have gone anywhere we wanted. We were shown into a waiting area before our meeting with Rafiq Husseini, Abbas's Chief of Staff. The waiting area was opposite Yasser Arafat's old office.

We were with Mr Husseini for forty-five minutes but left the meeting wishing it could have lasted the whole morning. What an impressive man. You got the feeling that if they were all like him, peace would break out in an instant. Calm, collected, authoritative and non-dogmatic – an ideal man to be one of the Palestinian Authority's chief negotiators. We had hoped to meet the Chief Negotiator for the Palestinian Authority, Saeb Erekat, but unfortunately he proved to be otherwise engaged. Husseini made clear that little progress was likely to be made in the immediate future, due to the forthcoming Israeli elections, the change of US President and also the fact that there might well be Palestinian elections at the beginning of January. So while there is an Arab Peace Plan up for discussion the week after next, it is not likely to get much traction. Olmert can't deliver the Israelis and it's doubtful whether Abbas could deliver wholesale support from the PA at this time, especially given the position of Hamas in Gaza. We asked him about Hamas, and his hope is that they will lose electoral ground at the next elections after people have experienced the horrendous way they have governed Gaza over the last two years. He doesn't think they are getting much traction on the West Bank. He made the point that aid money can never replace the freedom to live in your homeland. He felt the economy of the West Bank was starting to revive after a very difficult few years, but poverty was still a real problem. Travel rights would remain a problem for families who have been split up. As we left, we visited the tomb of Yasser Arafat, which forms an impressive part of the PA compound. For some he remains a hero. For others, he was a man who led a completely corrupt regime.

In the middle of the morning we left the PA compound to travel the short distance to the UNWRA refugee camp. We arrived in Ramallah at around 11 and met the head of the camp, a very charming Palestinian who was born there and has lived there all his life. We talked to him for forty-five minutes about the camp and the problems he has. Six thousand people live there. It's certainly not got the worst conditions of the various camps but there's little doubt that housing issues are the main area of concern. He told us he had ten children, earns $800 a month (far more than most of his compatriots) and they all live in three rooms – one for boys, one for girls and one for him and his wife. We kept asking him what measures could best improve the living conditions for him and the other 6,000 people who live in the camp, but he repeatedly told us that nothing could alter the fact that they are refugees and have been driven out of their homes. Even though he was born there, and his children are third generation, they all still class themselves as refugees – even though they have never even seen the place they regard as home. And this is surely the nub of the whole refugee problem. Until there is an acceptance that there is no going back, it is difficult to see how life in the West Bank can be normalised. We can throw as much money at the area as we like (and British aid alone is a massive $500 million over three years), it will never solve what the refugees believe to be the main issue.

We were then taken on a tour of the camp. Conditions were not as bad as I was expecting, to be honest, and I suspect things are very different elsewhere. Everybody we met was keen to shake our hands – at no time did we feel under threat. Yesterday we were told we would have to stay in the bus as it was too dangerous, but that went by the board. Several passers-by told us their stories. We then went to visit an elderly man and his wife in their own home. And as we walked in we could hardly fail to see the massive picture of Saddam Hussein on the wall! The couple had been driven out of their village on the coast in 1954 and had lived in the camp ever since. They have four children, the oldest one being in Gaza. They haven't seen him in ten years as they cannot travel there without a permit. As we left, Nick Boles[†] pointed up to the picture of Saddam and did a throat-slitting gesture while saying 'very bad man!' The woman found this very funny – luckily!

We then had a late lunch at the American Colony Hotel in East Jerusalem with the British Consul to the Palestinian Authority, before spending a couple of hours having briefings with two female diplomats from the Israeli foreign ministry.

This evening – the final evening of the trip – we went to a restaurant in Jaffa with two young journalists from *Haaretz* and another newspaper, the name of which temporarily escapes me.

So that's it. I have to get up at 5.30 a.m. to catch the 9.05 El Al flight in the morning. It's been a real eye-opener of a trip.

---

†   At the time, Conservative candidate for Grantham; now its MP.

THE TEN QUALITIES OF A GOOD PRIME MINISTER
SUNDAY 2 NOVEMBER

In his profile of Tony Blair in GQ, Matthew d'Ancona says this:

> [Blair] has told allies that you need ten qualities to be a good Prime Minister but Brown only has six.

This set me to speculate on what those ten qualities might be. Here's my list.

1. Decisiveness
2. Conviction
3. Understanding the motivations of Middle England
4. Being a good negotiator
5. Being a good conciliator
6. Having a good TV presence
7. Being a good parliamentary performer
8. Having a thick skin
9. Being able to cut through civil service bullshit
10. Having a non-political hinterland

IS IT COZ HE IS BLACK?
WEDNESDAY 5 NOVEMBER

I could hardly believe my ears this morning, listening to my old mucker Yasmin Alibhai-Brown on 5 Live, talking about the US election. Shelagh Fogarty quoted a poll saying that 97 per cent of black voters in America are supporting Obama. She asked Yasmin if she thought it was OK for black people to vote for him purely because he is black. Yasmin said yes, she thought it was absolutely fine.

I wonder what she would have said to white voters voting for McCain purely on the basis that he is white. Sadly, that question wasn't asked.

And I say this as an Obama supporter.

A MEDIUM (AND RARE) EVENING WITH A PSYCHIC
SATURDAY 8 NOVEMBER

Tonight I am going to Hastings Theatre to see, believe it or not, Sally Morgan, the TV psychic and medium, do her thing. I have always been extremely sceptical of psychics, but when you know people who have had their minds read – and then had it done to you yourself – you tend to re-evaluate things. I saw a programme on ITV2 a few weeks ago where Mrs Morgan 'spoke' to the dead relatives of various celebrities. On the face of it, it was amazing stuff. Anyway, my partner and my sister fancied going, so I thought, why not?

My only experience of this sort of thing was at university when we had one of these shows in one of the lecture theatres one evening. I got called on stage and had my mind read. I can't remember the psychic's name but he asked if I had a library card on me. I produced it and he proceeded to read a fifteen-digit number off it without being able to see it. He then asked me to think of my favourite TV character and to keep thinking about the person as I wrote it down. He correctly guessed it was J. R. Ewing. My sister went to a similar evening recently and the medium spoke to her via my godmother, who died last year. She was completely spooked by it as there were a number of things which the medium said which she could not possibly have known.

One of my colleagues at *Total Politics* told me a story the other night. His father broke down in the middle of nowhere, but there was a telephone box nearby. As he was walking past it the phone rang. He went into the phone box and picked up the receiver. 'Hello darling, what time will you be home?' said the person at the other end. It was his wife. When he asked her how on earth she could phone a telephone box without knowing where he was, she said she hadn't, she had phoned his mobile. When they checked their phone bill a few weeks later, the number which was shown was that of the phone box. How spooky is that?

Anyway, in case you think I am going off my rocker, I intend to treat the evening as a bit of fun. Have any of you had any experiences with mediums or psychics you wish to share?

Update: 10.30 p.m. What a load of old bollocks. She may be hugely convincing on TV, but in the theatre she's rubbish. The polite applause at the end told the story of the evening. But the number of people who were hanging on her every word and willing her to play with their emotions was astonishing. After the second person she reduced to tears I felt like leaving, but the sheer mawkishness of it was somehow too gripping. 'I'm getting Justin, or Justine ... Maybe justice. Has anyone had a problem with the law?' she asked at one stage. Half the audience then looked at their feet. Well, it was in Hastings... She finished by telling a story about a 23-year-old British soldier who came to her for a reading. 'I fitted him in on a slack day between TV filming,' she informed us. He wanted to know if there was an afterlife. Three days later he killed himself. 'His mum came to see me,' Sally told us. I bet she did.

TOP TEN MOST IRRITATING PHRASES HEARD ON RADIO PHONE-INS
MONDAY 10 NOVEMBER

1. As I said to your researcher...
2. I'm not a racist, but...
3. With all due respect, Stephen...
4. At the end of the day, Alan...
5. Know what I mean, like? (Said in fake West Indian accent.)
6. Shouldn't of...
7. He's got to go (as in 'Alan Curbishley, he's got to go').
8. It's got to be said, Richard...
9. I'm working class, I am...
10. You've got to be 'avin a larf...

PRISONERS' EDUCATION: JACK STRAW JERKS HIS KNEE
FRIDAY 21 NOVEMBER

So Jack Straw has banned prisoners at Whitemoor Prison from learning about how to write a comedy script or do stand-up. They were taking part in an eight-day course as part of an education programme. What harm can possibly be done by learning about comedy scriptwriting and improvisation? I'd have thought learning how to diffuse potentially harmful situations by the use of humour was a good thing. Instead, Jack Straw has jerked his knee and responded to synthetic tabloid outrage. Not only that, he's ordered an inquiry! You couldn't make it up.

Prison is a balance between punishment and rehabilitation. I don't believe in going soft on people in prison – but nor do I believe that activities which make them want to learn and develop should be discouraged.

I FANCIED ESTHER RANTZEN: WHO'LL RAISE ME GAIL TILSLEY?
WEDNESDAY 26 NOVEMBER

I seem to have created a bit of a stir with my latest Twitter/Facebook status update. For those who missed it, this is it:

> Iain is wondering if it is wrong to admit that, as an eleven-year-old, he fancied Esther Rantzen.

Now, perhaps it deserves a little – but not too much – explanation. Well, so it might, but who can explain these things properly? Was it her teeth? Was it the way she looked over to the old man at the edge of the studio and said, 'Cyril'? Was it her billowing evening dresses in which she presented *That's Life?* Who knows, but as I watched her this evening on *I'm A Celebrity* buried in a coffin with maggots and cockroaches crawling over her prostrate body, well, those old stirrings kind of returned. [Enough info – Ed.]

And then someone on Facebook wrote:

> Iain, if it helps, I'll raise you Gail Tilsley

DISGRACING MYSELF IN THE KREMLIN AGE 13 ¾
WEDNESDAY 10 DECEMBER

This afternoon I am flying to Moscow to speak at a conference organised by the Moscow School of Political Studies. The audience is around 150 Russian journalists and politicians, all under the age of thirty-five. I will be speaking about the role of blogging in politics and the media, but I am far from being the only Brit speaking. John Lloyd of the Reuters Institute of Journalism and the *Telegraph*'s Iain Martin are also on the programme.

The last time I was in Moscow was in April 1976 when I was a mere thirteen years old. It was a trip organised by my school and we spent five days in Leningrad (as it then was) and five days in Moscow. For a thirteen-year-old it was quite a trip – the first time I had been abroad, or indeed away from home for any length of time. I remember I took £14 spending money – and returned with £7 unspent. A ride on the immaculately clean underground cost a mere two kopeks.

Leningrad was spectacular. The River Neva was full of huge chunks of ice. The Hermitage was fabulous. Even as a youngster with no great love of art I could appreciate it.

I have many memories of that trip which I could relate (or bore you with) but perhaps the most vivid is one which, if you have just had your breakfast, you might want to avoid reading...

One evening we were taken to see the opera *Madame Butterfly* in the Hall of the Supreme Soviet in the Kremlin. I have to say that we did not view the prospect of sitting through three hours of an Italian opera sung in Russian with any degree of enthusiasm – especially as we were in the front row and going to sleep would have been a bit obvious. Ever since then I have viewed opera as lovely music interrupted by raucous screeching. Anyway, I digress.

In the interval, we were treated to Russian ice cream covered in a blackcurrant sauce. Russian ice cream is just superb – probably the best I have tasted anywhere in the world. Unfortunately, however, halfway through the second half I felt decidedly ill. I leaned over to our teacher and whispered, 'I need to go to the loo, and I need to go now.' 'Shut up and wait,' he hissed back. 'No,' I said, 'you don't understand. If I don't go now, you'll live to regret it.' We made our way out but couldn't find a loo anywhere. I was becoming increasingly desperate and almost doubled up with pain. Eventually, he located a loo and I ran through the door and... well... how can I put this? Suffice to say that by the time I got into the cubicle nature had already taken its course.

Now I am sure there are many Russians who had cause to shit themselves in the Kremlin, metaphorically speaking. I, on the other hand, managed to actually do it. I have often wondered where those lovely red underpants ended up...

There is a postscript to this story. A dozen of us had contracted a terrible virus called giardia lamblia. At the time it was very rare. It was so serious that we were not allowed to use the same toilet as the rest of our families. We all lost a lot of weight. Before that I had been an incredibly good swimmer and I was about to be entered into some championships. It took six months to be cured, and by that time I was never the same swimmer again.

So if you want to know why I never won a swimming gold medal, blame the Commies!

HOW DOES ONE EXPLAIN 'FISKING' IN RUSSIAN?
THURSDAY 11 DECEMBER, MOSCOW

This morning I delivered a 45-minute talk about blogging. It all seemed to go off OK, although I don't mind admitting that it was a bit odd having consecutive translation. Anyone who has seen me speak at this sort of thing will know that I try to inject a bit of humour into it – especially if it's a talk lasting for forty-five minutes, followed by another forty-five minutes of questions. But humour very rarely translates well and, even if it does, you have to wait a bit too long for the punch-line to come.

When I do talks like this, I always know if they have gone OK by the quantity and quality of the questions which follow. Today's were exceptional. I was particularly taken by a question about so-called 'killer blogs'. In Russia, blogs are often set up with one aim in mind – to kill off a politician's career. There are no real libel laws here, so you can make any allegations you like on a blog and the subject of the attack has little means of redress. I explained that this sort of blog doesn't really exist in Britain and that if I wrote on my blog that a politician had been caught having sex with a sheep, I would be sued. I think it got a little lost in translation. I went on to explain the concept of 'fisking' and 'Twitter'. At this point the translator had a nervous breakdown.

The organiser came up to me later and told me that one of the female participants from Siberia had told her that my presentation had 'changed her life'. At this point I realised that not only must the translator have had a nervous breakdown, but must also be taking hallucinogenic drugs!

MR DALE'S CHRISTMAS DIARY: PART 94

I've noticed two things in my subconscious today – behaviour patterns which have changed without forethought, but both of which are direct results of the recession. The first one is that I now regularly read the business pages of newspapers – something I never used to do. And secondly, I am spending far less this Christmas on presents than I have done in previous years. I haven't deliberately decided to spend less. I just have. I wonder how many others are doing the same.

...

I just went down to Curry's to buy a 160GB iPod. No luck. Apparently they only make a 120GB one now, or so they told me. That's no good to me. I have more than 30,000 songs on my hard drive. So I went next door to PC World. Excellent. They had one on display, although no stock of them. Here's how the conversation went...

> Me: I'll have the display one, please.
> PCW: Sorry, but we can't sell you the display one.
> Me: Why not? You can't get any more. It's a discontinued line.
> PCW: It's our policy.
> Me: Well it's a stupid policy. I want to give you £200 you are unlikely to get from anyone else for it. Don't you want my money?
> PCW: Sorry, it's our policy.
> Me: Can I speak to the manager, please?
> I then explain the position to the manager...
> Manager: OK, but I can't give you any discount and we haven't got a box for it.
> Me: Thanks. I don't need a box and I didn't ask for discount.

The manager then asks a sales assistant to get it out of the cabinet for me. After ten minutes he comes back saying I can't have it because there are no cables with it. I explain that I already have cables. Five minutes later he returns and says he can't work out how to get it out of the display cabinet anyway, but if I'd like a discount of £15 on the 120GB version they'd happily offer me that. I calmly (and politely!) explain that, no, if I had wanted a 120GB iPod I'd have asked for one. He suggests I try Argos, over the road. I do, and needless to say they haven't got any either.

What's a boy got to do to spend money this Christmas?!

MY BOOK OF THE YEAR
MONDAY 22 DECEMBER

I feel a bit bereft. You know that feeling when you finish a book that you wished would never end? I've got that now. This instant. Four years ago I bought a book I probably thought I'd never end up reading. You know, one of those books which looks quite interesting, but there's always another book which seems to take precedence over it. *Blue-Eyed Son* by Nicky Campbell was one of those books. Until last week.

For those who don't know him, Nicky Campbell presents *5 Live Breakfast* and *Watchdog*. He made his name as a DJ on Radio 1 and presenting a game show called *Wheel of Fortune*. I've been interviewed by him perhaps a dozen times, but never really spoken to him outside the confines of a live radio studio. He can be quite a sharp interviewer and is always ready with a witty one-liner. He's one of Radio 5 Live's star presenters. Like most media people, he has his fans but he also has his detractors. But even his detractors could not fail to be moved by his wonderful book.

The book has a simple aim. To tell the story of Nicky Campbell's adoption and how he found his biological parents and wider family. I won't spoil the story here, but he tells it with such an emotional intensity that it is sometimes difficult for the reader to cope with more than a few pages at a time. The conflict between wanting to discover where he came from and not wishing to bring any pain to his family is starkly presented.

I can't remember reading a book which has had such an emotional effect on me. Barely a page would go by without my eyes moistening, or a tear running down my cheek. Maybe it's because Nicky and I are more or less the same age. Maybe it's because family clearly means as much to him as it does to me. Maybe it's the way he describes his hopes, fears and insecurities which brings on the waterworks. I don't know. All I know is that reading this book had exactly the same impact on me as watching *Band of Brothers* did when I saw it on DVD a few years ago. I was unable to watch more than one episode at a time. I know it sounds pathetic, but there will be enough of you who know what I mean.

I am not adopted and I suppose no one who isn't can quite understand the inner tortures which Nicky Campbell clearly went through as he went on his journey. He needed to know where he came from, and the discoveries he made along the way were not always comfortable ones. But he is searingly honest about his own weaknesses, ego and selfishness. At times his wife probably felt she deserved a medal. 'You do have a family. It's us,' she blurted out once.

Yes, this book is primarily about Nicky Campbell. But it is so much more than that. It's a book about the power of family as the cornerstone of our society. It's a book which celebrates family history, warts and all. And it's a book which I am so glad that I ended up reading. I'm now going to give it to my mum for Christmas. Because she is the only person I know who cries more easily than me!

REVISITING CHRISTMAS WAY BACK WHEN
WEDNESDAY 24 DECEMBER

I find that as I get older I find it far more difficult to get into the Christmas spirit. Not because I am at all Scrooge-like, before you get the wrong idea, but more because I suppose I'd quite like Christmases to be exactly how I remember them as a child. Not going to happen, is it?!

I've just got back from a Christingle service at our local village church at Ashdon, near Saffron Walden. It brought back a lot of childhood memories, even though such services didn't exist way back when. Then there was quite a feudal set-up, with the Vestey family, who own most of the local land, always sitting right at the front. Our family also used to sit in the same seats (much further back!) and I was irrationally disappointed to find they were already taken when we arrived today.

The local church doesn't have a full-time vicar any longer. Today's could have been in *Dad's Army*. His eyebrows were bushier than Denis Healey's and I imagined that at any minute he might shout out, 'Don't panic, Mr Mainwaring!'

I have rarely seen the church so packed. There were around 200 in the congregation, which in a village of around 800 is quite a lot. There were lots of 'yummy mummies' with their kids, who all took part in the service.

As you may have gathered from previous posts, I am not at all religious, but I do love all the Christmas traditions and rituals.

Sitting here with my parents, by the fire, I'm taken back to Sunday afternoons in the early 1970s when we'd play a card game called Spite 'n' Venom, then watch *Catweazle*, the *Clangers* and *The Golden Shot*, followed later on by *The Brothers*. That's if there wasn't a power cut, which there often was.

Those were the days.

TEN PREDICTIONS FOR 2009
TUESDAY 30 DECEMBER

1. There won't be an election.
2. Unemployment will top 3 million by the end of the year.
3. Damian Green will not face charges.
4. Ed Balls will be Chancellor by the end of the year.
5. Ken Clarke will join the shadow Cabinet. David Davis won't.
6. *The Independent* will go out of business.
7. There will be a second massive recapitalisation of the banks.
8. Lynne Featherstone will be promoted to a major job on the Lib Dem front bench.
9. Jonathan Ross will leave the BBC.
10. The economic growth rate will be three times worse than the Treasury has predicted.

2009

TEN THINGS I'M DREADING ABOUT GOING BACK TO WORK
SUNDAY 4 JANUARY

1. Getting up at 6.45 a.m
2. Scraping ice off the windscreen
3. Train being late or not arriving at all
4. Forgetting my iPod
5. People continually asking: 'Did you have a good Christmas?'
6. People continually asking: 'Did you have a good New Year?'
7. People continually saying: 'Yes, there's a lot of it about.'
8. Freezing my nads off walking from Charing Cross to the office
9. Ringing someone and getting an answerphone message saying: 'I'm not back until 12 January.'
10. Getting to Charing Cross in the evening to find all trains to Tonbridge are delayed/cancelled

MEETING MARGARET THATCHER
WEDNESDAY 14 JANUARY

I went to the Carlton Club this evening for a drinks party hosted by Liam Fox. I was delighted to see Lady Thatcher arrive and looking fantastic. For a woman of eighty-three and supposedly in frail health, she looked absolutely stunning.

I had a couple of minutes talking to her and told her it was twenty-six years to the day that I first met her at a reception for Conservative students at 10 Downing Street. 'I think I remember that,' she said. 'It was so nice to see so many young people in the building. That didn't happen very often.' We talked a little about newspapers and she said, 'I never read them. I had Bernard to do it for me.' Everyone needs a Bernard...

As I left the Carlton Club, a thought struck me. If Lady T were in her heyday and had to take over as Prime Minister now, what would she do? If I had asked her, I know exactly what her reply would have been: 'Restore sound money, dear.' And you know what? She'd have been dead right.

NEW STATESMAN DIARY
TEA WITH TONY AND MAGGIE'S ACID HOUSE PARTY
SATURDAY 17 JANUARY

If you have a blog and are worried that few are reading it, let me give you a piece of advice. Write a post about Israel. Or abortion. Or climate change. Or homosexuality. Watch those hits! And if you can write a single post containing all those subjects within three paragraphs of spiteful prose, you will really hit the jackpot. But it is the subject of Israel that seems to make normally sane and rational people lose all semblance of reason. I have expressed unreserved support for Israel's action against Hamas on my blog and, in consequence, have experienced all manner of threats and allegations. Apparently I must be in the pay of the Israeli government or being blackmailed by Mossad over some past indiscretion. Neither happens to be true. I just subscribe to the rather old-fashioned belief that Israel has every right to defend its population from the 5,000 rocket attacks it has suffered over the past three years. The Israeli response has been attacked as being 'disproportionate'. Rubbish. What would be 'proportionate'? Lobbing 5,000 rockets back into Gaza?

•••

It's not just the British economy that has been going back to the 1970s. For Christmas 2007, I was given a machine that lets you convert vinyl recordings into MP3 files. It sat in its box for a year because I feared I wouldn't be able to figure out how to make it work. Last week I finally plucked up the courage and linked it to my laptop. And what do you know? It's easy to operate and I have started putting all my 1,500 singles and 200 LPs on to my iPod. I have discovered records I had forgotten I possessed, and which I last played more than twenty years ago. I still can't find a record that the Liberal Party released for the 1964 election called 'The Jo Grimond Song', though. Or a 12-inch acid house track from 1991 called

'Maggie's Last Party', with Lady Thatcher's dulcet tones dubbed over house music – an *NS* reader offer if ever there was one.

•••

Thirty years ago I regarded Tony Benn as the greatest threat to Britain outside the Soviet Union. Nowadays we agree on Europe, the constitution and threats to civil liberties. I interviewed him last week for the next issue of *Total Politics* in the endearingly ramshackle basement office of his Holland Park home. I don't go in for Paxman-style interviewing, but I quickly learnt that you have to challenge some of Tony's wilder assertions. 'Thatcher made trade unions illegal.' Er, no, she didn't, actually. 'The Soviet Union posed no military threat.' Come again? On most subjects he is incredibly persuasive, and it is easy to see why he continues to fill theatres up and down the country. But he still attracts incredible bitterness from those on the Labour right who blame him for the party's eighteen years in opposition. When I solicited questions for the interview on my blog, I was taken aback by the venom unleashed by people who are normally quite meek and mild. He clearly has something in common with Israel.

•••

OK, I hold my hands up. If I hadn't lunched with Derek Draper he might never have embarked on his one-man crusade to provide competition for the right-of-centre blogosphere. This week he launched LabourList.org as a lefty rival to ConservativeHome. com. I wish him well, but fear he underestimates the task ahead. Group blogs are damned hard work, especially with no external funding or mainstream media back-up.

My advice to Derek was to start his own blog – Dolly's Diary has a certain ring to it – and see how it went. People kept suggesting Labour needed its very own Iain Dale (flattery or insult?). He fitted the bill perfectly. LabourList's problem is personified by its roster of contributors, which on the face of it is a list of people you wouldn't answer the door to: the same old faces that have come to embody the New Labour years. Sure, there are a few aged lefties thrown in, too, but where is the fresh thinking, where are the new kids on the block who are going to inherit the ashes of what remains of Labour after the next election? The site also faces the prospect of being so slavishly loyal it becomes irrelevant. Irritated by the disloyalty of many ConservativeHome contributors, the Cameroons set up a similar blog called Platform 10 about eighteen months ago. But it was so 'on message' that it failed to attract a large enough audience to make a real impact. I'm afraid I foresee the same fate for LabourList if it isn't careful.

• • •

Those of us on the right who broke the habit of a lifetime, as well as our Republican tribal allegiances, and supported Barack Obama are now in a bit of a bind. We want him to prove us right, if only so we can salve our consciences, but we're also keen for the Republicans to find a moderate voice to challenge Obama in 2012. That can't happen while Sarah Palin remains the de facto leader of what is rapidly becoming a narrow right-wing sect rather than a big-tent political party. Like Tony Blair, Obama will go through his first term with no serious opposition. Let's hope he achieves more than Blair did.

THERE'S PROBABLY NO ALLAH

The row over the 'There's Probably No God' adverts took a new twist today. The *Telegraph* reports that a devoutly Christian bus driver in Southampton has refused to drive his bus because it has the advert pasted to the side. The bus company has given him another bus to drive.

Personally, I have no issue with the ASA passing this advert. But the thought does occur to me. If the advert had said 'There's Probably No Allah: Now, Stop Worrying and Enjoy Your Life', would it have got through the ASA's censors? I think we all know the answer. And if it had, somehow, got through the ASA, would the bus company have touched it with the proverbial bargepole? Of course not.

HOW TO CUT PUBLIC EXPENDITURE: PART ONE
WEDNESDAY 21 JANUARY

Over the last three months my mum has noticed that, every week, £30 appears in her bank account. Despite numerous phone calls she has been unable to find out what it is or where it has come from. Yesterday, she spent more than an hour at her bank and they finally found out.

It seems that Her Majesty's Government thinks she is a sixth-form student, and is paying her £30 a week to attend school. I kid ye not. Mrs Dale may be many things, but a sixth-form student ain't one of them. Naturally, she is taking steps to ensure that the money is stopped and she repays what she has been paid. So, OK, we all make mistakes and I am sure that this is a one-off mistake (actually, I'm not, but that's not the point I want to make with this post).

I have no idea how much it is costing the taxpayer to pay £30 a week to all sixth-form students, but I suspect the figure runs into hundreds of millions of pounds. I was against the grant when it was first introduced, and I see no reason to change my mind. My point is that it is this sort of public expenditure which is going to come under very close scrutiny in the coming months when government is forced to rein in its spending horns whether it likes it or not.

The Conservatives should be looking at every scheme like this and evaluating its economic and social worth. I would axe it tomorrow, if it were down to me, but politically it may well be difficult to do.

SHOULD GORDON BROWN COPY ANN WIDDECOMBE?
SUNDAY 25 JANUARY

A reader has pointed me to Matthew Parris's column in today's *Times*. He reckons we're stuffed. Economically, anyway. Reading his prose about the kind of hopeful language that politicians deploy in these circumstances made me think back to a question Ann Widdecombe was asked last night during our theatre show in Bournemouth: 'If you were Chancellor of the Exchequer, what would you do to get us out of recession?'

The audience was expecting Ann to announce a series of economic initiatives which would rescue the economy. But her answer was rather different: 'Haven't a clue,' she said. 'And the trouble is, nor has anyone else.'

She accused politicians of announcing initiatives for their own sake, rather than because they were sure to have an effect. They were keen to be seen to be doing something, even if it turned out to be the wrong thing.

She has a point. No politician in government or those in the senior echelons of the opposition can be seen to be shrugging their shoulders in despair or admitting they really don't know what should be done because we are in uncharted territory.

But that's exactly where we are. So when we hear Gordon Brown repeatedly saying that we're 'doing everything we can' or 'using all the weapons at our disposal', what he's really saying is: 'Frankly, we ain't got a clue what to do either, but we can't be seen to admit it.'

PICKLES 1, PAXMAN 0
MONDAY 26 JANUARY

Jeremy Paxman: Eric Pickles, you've been uncharacteristically quiet.
Eric Pickles: Generally when I come on this programme, I like to respond to questions.
Love him.

QUOTE OF THE DAY
FRIDAY 30 JANUARY

Campaigning is like sex – if you're not enjoying it, you're not doing it right. It should never be a drudge.
– Hazel Blears

TWENTY-FIVE RANDOM THINGS ABOUT ME
TUESDAY 3 FEBRUARY

1. I worked for a year as a nurse in a German spinal injuries hospital after leaving school.
2. My first car was an orange Cortina Mk III, which became known at university as the Big Jaffa.
3. On my twentieth birthday I wrote off my Cortina after hitting a Transit van head on at 50 mph.
4. My parents lost me at the 1964 Essex Show when I was two. I was found picking up cigarette butts and eating them.

5. As a baby I somehow fell out of my pram. I still have the mark on my forehead.

6. I was bottom of my German class aged fourteen. I went on a three-week school exchange and then came top.

7. I lived in London from 1985 to 1997, in Fulham, Putney, Walthamstow and the Isle of Dogs.

8. Our Gio is a Battersea dog. We went in for an adult spaniel and came out with a Jack Russell puppy.

9. Gio got run over once, while still on his lead, while I was walking him.

10. My first West Ham game was at the Abbey Stadium in Cambridge in 1974. We lost 3–2.

11. I was an ace hockey player at school, scoring several hat tricks.

12. I won the 1992 Medway Ports Authority Golf Championship – my greatest sporting achievement. I play off a ridiculous 13 handicap, when it should be at least 20.

13. As an eleven-year-old I fancied Esther Rantzen something rotten. Explains a lot.

14. I have 31,589 songs on my iPod.

15. I have been to three US Presidential Libraries – JFK, Ronald Reagan and Richard Nixon.

16. In 1984, I met and spoke to Franz Josef Strauss.

17. I once completely dried up doing an early morning Sky News paper review.

18. Frank Dobson once called me 'dear' when I was presenting *Sunday Service* on 5 Live.

19. I once appeared on 'Beat the Jock' on Radio 1 with Mike Read.

20. I own more than 120 Cliff Richard CDs, yet when I met him I was completely tongue-tied.

21. I first drove a combine harvester at the age of eight – unsupervised.

22. I was the first Briton to go to Beirut after the release of John McCarthy. It's a long story.

23. I was at university with Caroline Flint. And David Grossman, so he tells me. I once debated the issue of VAT on tampons with Miss Flint.

24. I am on my twelfth Audi. The first was an Audi Quattro Coupé in 1989. D52 VJN.

25. Neil and Christine Hamilton once threatened to sue me.

Tweet of the Day: Tom Harris MP

> Walking back from the gym feeling as smug and self-satisfied as a Lib Dem on 'Thought for the Day'.

CAROL THATCHER: WHY CAN'T THE BBC BE CONSISTENT?

Chris Moyles is Radio 1's star DJ. Two years ago he was involved, on air, in an incident which led to him being accused of racism. Halle Berry, no less, felt that he was indeed being racist. In December 2008 he faced another allegation, after he asserted that 'Polish women make good prostitutes'. On neither occasion did the BBC fire him, let alone discipline him or even make him apologise. On both occasions the BBC said he was 'poking fun'.

Today, despite issuing a full apology, Carol Thatcher was fired by the BBC – not disciplined, but fired – from *The One Show*, after she likened a tennis player's hair to that of a golliwog. It was a jokey remark made off air in the green room.

The logic of the BBC's argument is that the very mention of the word 'golliwog' is considered racist. Utterly preposterous.

Whatever Carol Thatcher said off air should not have been made public by the BBC. By firing her in this manner and allowing all this to enter the public domain, they have branded her a racist when she is patently nothing of the sort.

When dealing with the BBC, having the surname of Thatcher is not an advantage. However, if you are a fat, loud-mouthed git with a surname of Moyles (or Ross, or Brand) you can get away with anything.

TODAY: THE CAROL THATCHER INTERVIEW
WEDNESDAY 4 FEBRUARY

I'm not sure that the *Today* programme got the dust-up they were looking for this morning. I was supposed to be on with Amanda Platell, but she was replaced at the last minute by Michael Eboda from *New Nation*. He duly took the line that it [the Carol Thatcher firing] seemed to be a bit of a fuss about nothing and had got over-blown. He was right.

I won't relate the whole discussion, but right at the end John Humphrys posed an interesting question: Should you say exactly the same in private as you say in public? I wasn't sure how to answer that at first so I deployed a delaying tactic and had a bit of a rant about Adrian Chiles instead. Humphrys, of course, was having none of it and put the question to me again. I ended up by saying, 'In theory yes, but we don't live in a theoretical world.' A bit lame, but it was the best I could think of! But it is a very interesting question. I am sure none of us can say we haven't said things in private which we wouldn't want made public, although theoretically we should all operate on the basis that anything we say could indeed be made public.

BANNED BY DRAPER: MY LIFE'S WORK IS NOW COMPLETE

Derek Draper should take some of his own psychotherapy. Having spent yesterday ranting at junior interns at the Taxpayers' Alliance, it seems that his Victim of the Day today is me. This is what he has just tweeted:

> LabourList has suspended Iain Dale from our blogroll until he clears up remarks he has made about 'Golliwog' being an acceptable term.

On his piss-poor website he says this:

> 10.00 a.m. Ashcroft sock-puppet Iain Dale has defended Carol Thatcher and the use of the word 'Golliwog'. See, even the nice-seeming ones are nasty underneath. On the *Today* programme he said Adrian Chiles must hear worse every day. No, Iain, he doesn't. Because he doesn't make a habit of hanging out with racist Tories. Until Dale thinks again we are suspending his listing on our blogroll. Come on Iain, do the decent thing and admit you got this wrong.

As my readers can imagine, I am truly bovvered. Inconsolable. Bereft. My blog won't be able to survive without the thirty visitors LabourList has sent its way. Believe me, it's his site which loses out if I don't link to it, not t'other way around. And with fewer than a thousand visitors a day, he needs all the links he can get.

There's just one thing that Derek might have to explain. Just where, exactly, have I ever said that the use of the word 'golliwog' is acceptable. Not here, and not on the *Today* programme. I have indeed tried to explain why the BBC is guilty of hypocrisy and has overreacted, but that is not the same as saying the word is nowadays 'acceptable'.

The 'R' word is a very easy one to throw around as a diversionary tactic. It is totally inappropriate here, and yet again Draper looks a fool.

IAIN DALE'S POLITICAL DICTIONARY
THURSDAY 5 FEBRUARY

Liquidity (n): When you look at your investments and wet your pants.

DON'T BLAME THE COUNCIL – CLEAR YOUR OWN PAVEMENT!
SATURDAY 7 FEBRUARY

Geoff Hoon has come under fire for his rather tactless comment that people should stop whinging about the snow, and that if motorists are so concerned they should buy snow chains. However, I have some sympathy with this viewpoint.

When I lived in Germany motorists always had snow chains. They had to. They would also have winter tyres fitted. Clearly the expense of this in this country would be ludicrous, unless your car was absolutely vital to you in all weathers. Councils do have a duty to grit roads, but there is a balance to strike. Should they really invest millions of pounds in grit, gritter lorries and snow ploughs when they might only be needed once every ten or so years? If I were a councillor I doubt whether I'd vote to spend money on that over and above providing new education facilities.

But one thing which does annoy me about this weather is that people in Britain seem to take no responsibility for keeping the pavement clear outside their own houses. In Germany and Switzerland it is a legal requirement for people to do that* – and not only that, but to grit the pavement too, if I remember rightly. In this country we just moan about the fact that the council has failed to get the snow off every inch of our pavements. Surely it isn't too much to ask to get people to clear their own part of the pavement each time snow falls?

*Ah, but what if you are old or disabled, I hear you cry? Simple. You arrange for a neighbour to do it. It's called community spirit.

TWENTY-FIVE (MORE) RANDOM THINGS ABOUT ME
SUNDAY 8 FEBRUARY

1. When I was nine I stuck a pitchfork through my big toe.
2. My Saturday job was mucking out my dad's pigs. I was paid 10p per hour.
3. At primary school, my friend threw a lump of plasticine at me from the other side of the classroom. It went straight into my mouth.
4. If I could buy a 20-tog duvet, I would. I like to sleep under two duvets.
5. I have blogged from the Oval Office.
6. Quite unbelievably, I have done fashion shoots for both *GQ* and *Esquire*.
7. I once compèred a wrestling match.
8. I once grew a beard, but it was a bit ginger so had to come off.
9. I was once interviewed by Giggle the guinea pig for the *Sheringham Independent*.
10. The first time I ever got drunk, I downed eleven Pernod & blacks in two hours in a Norwich nightclub.
11. I have never tried any illegal drug.
12. I once won a pig, playing bowls.
13. On my first visit to America in 1987, I insisted on visiting Southfork ranch. I now wish to go to Dollywood.
14. The best hotel I ever stayed in was the Serena Hotel in Kigali, Rwanda.
15. The worst hotel I ever stayed in was a guest house in Blackpool. The bed had rubber sheets.
16. The first speeding ticket I ever got was in South Dakota.
17. I once had blonde streaks in my hair. It was a mistake.
18. I appeared on the *Multi-Coloured Swap Shop* in 1978 with a

photo of a funny road sign in Cambridge which said SHORT STAY – TOILETS – P.

19. The only time I have sung in public was when I played one of Mack the Knife's henchmen in Brecht's *Die Dreigroschenoper* and had to sing 'Soldaten Wohnen'. Not pretty.

20. I once got hit by several eggs which had been meant for Cecil Parkinson.

21. I failed Biology O Level and got ungraded in Physics.

22. I owned an Audi Cabriolet formerly owned by Princess Diana. I sold it a year too early, if you get my drift.

23. In 1994 I took my father to visit the Normandy war cemeteries. I found a grave with my name on it.

24. On local-election day 1985, the day before my finals, I knocked a Labour-voting motorcyclist off his bike while driving three Tory-voting old ladies to the polling station.

25. I was stopped for speeding in North Norfolk on the night of my selection as candidate. I was, ahem, let off with a warning.

PRESCOTT JUST WOUNDED ME
WEDNESDAY 11 FEBRUARY

I was walking along Millbank, minding my own business, whistling away to Roxette on my iPod (actually, I can't whistle, but that's another story), when who should I spy coming the other way but John Prescott.

We shook hands, I congratulated him on his blog and then he told me his RBS petition gadget had broken and couldn't take any more signatures. Apparently he was off to present the petition to John McFall. He then looked me up and down and said, 'I can tell you're a Tory by your coat.' I returned the favour and told him mine was probably far older than his, and it may be a Loden but it was made in Yorkshire – eight years ago. He looked doubtful.

'Anyway,' I said, 'keep up the good work.' He looked quizzical. 'Keeping the spotlight off Draper, I mean,' I replied with a smile. He gave me what I like to interpret as a knowing look.

P.S. Douglas Hurd used to wear a Loden too. One day he was approached by Carol Mather, an old-school Tory MP who said to him, 'Douglas, the last time I saw a man dressed in a coat like that, I shot him!'

MY SUNDAY NEWSPAPER SHAME
SUNDAY 15 FEBRUARY

On Friday I caused a bit of havoc on my Twitter feed by saying this...

> Oh dear, looks like I am going to be exposed in a Sunday newspaper for a misdeed of my youth. Gulp. It's all rather embarrassing.

I was inundated with messages on email and via Facebook of the 'We'll stand by you' variety. All very touching. The trouble was, it was just my little joke. It referred to a conversation I had just had with *Sunday Times* journalist Richard Woods who was writing a story on the 25 Random Things About Me meme which has been going round. This is the relevant extract...

> ... It was this potential insight into character that lured Iain Dale, a British political blogger, to take part in '25 Random Things' even though he is wary of internet crazes. 'Some of these things that go round the internet are incredibly boring,' he said. 'But the way some people have done these lists is really interesting.'
>
> When Dale compiled his own thoughts he admitted at No. 13: 'As an eleven-year-old I fancied Esther Rantzen [the former television presenter] something rotten.' He grew up to be gay. And at No. 20, he confessed: 'I own more than 120 Cliff Richard CDs.'
>
> Surely that can't possibly be true. Nobody would buy 120 different Cliff Richard CDs. 'Er, well, yes I did,' Dale explained yesterday. 'Strangely, I went to see him at the London Palladium in 1978 when he re-formed with the Shadows and, um, I'm the sort of person that if I buy an album of somebody and I like it, I end up buying everything. So I have got virtually everything he's ever done – compilations, the lot.'
>
> It could be worse. At least it wasn't Bucks Fizz.'

Is this the time to admit that not only do I have Cliff's entire back catalogue, but I also have Bucks Fizz's? Probably not.

AN EVENING WITH TWENTY FIREMEN
SATURDAY 21 FEBRUARY

Well, if you've been following my Twitter feed you'll know that it's been quite an evening at Dale Towers near Saffron Walden. We've been spending the weekend with my parents at their farm (where I grew up) in Ashdon.

At about 9 p.m. my partner, John, went out for a smoke and came rushing in saying he thought there was a fire at the back of the farm, where my father lets one of the villagers work on his stock cars.

We rushed round there – it's about 300 yards from the house – and the flames were leaping thirty feet in the air and were threatening a barn and a mobile phone mast. I phoned 999 and within about ten minutes three fire engines carrying about twenty firemen arrived from nearby Linton and Saffron Walden. They soon had it under control. Around half an hour later two police arrived.

I shall be careful what I say, but it is pretty clear it was arson. People were seen running away from the farm. Villages are small places. People know things. The stock car guy knows who did it. I know who did it. The police know who did it. Will they be charged? Will they buggery.

Still, the evening did have some consolation for my two sisters. They spent the entire time trying to snog the firemen and making jokes about helmets and sliding down poles. I, of course, maintained my decorum at all times.

RWANDA: THE SHAME OF DONALD STEINBERG
TUESDAY 24 FEBRUARY

I was going to write this blog post last night, but I was so angry I decided it was best to sleep on it. Bad decision. I'm still fizzing with anger. Yesterday evening I was invited by *Time* magazine's excellent London Bureau Chief Catherine Mayer to attend a screening of an important film about Rwanda, *Shaking Hands with the Devil*.

The screening took place at BAFTA and was followed by a panel discussion. The participants were Gordon Brown's foreign policy adviser Justin Forsyth, Bob Geldof, Col. Bob Stewart, Mark Malloch Brown and an American diplomat, Donald Steinberg.

Mr Steinberg served in the White House during the Clinton administration at the time of the Rwandan genocide. He advised Clinton to keep well out of it – possibly one of the worst pieces of advice given to an American President in the last twenty years. He was rewarded for this failure in the classic way bureaucrats are usually rewarded for failure. He was promoted.

He ended up as ambassador to Angola and then – get this – became an adviser to the UN on Darfur and, even more unbelievably, is now a Deputy President of the International Crisis Group. You couldn't make it up.

This man had the bare-faced cheek to sit on a panel which sought to comment on a film about a genocide which he had the power to stop. He then had the cheek to berate the current Rwandan regime for being repressive, and accused it of trying to shame the international community into providing foreign aid as recompense for their inaction during the genocide. It was all I could do to keep my temper. I have rarely felt so angry.

Steinberg is Jewish. He grew up in the shadow of the Holocaust. When he had the influence to stop a repeat in Rwanda he funked it. I don't know how he looks himself in the mirror each morning. But he is representative of a class of so-called public servants who make a career out of supporting appeasement and failing to stand up to aggression. They're people who feel quite at home in the United Nations and thrive on making excuses for that organisation's terrible failures. And when they have finished with failing, they go on the international lecture circuit to lecture us on what should happen in the future. Or they do what Mark Malloch Brown has done and become a *goat*.

The only ones to talk any degree of sense on this panel were Bob Geldof and Justin Forsyth. Which tells you what an excruciating experience it was to listen to the rest of them pontificate in their oleaginous 'I know best' manner.

I can highly recommend the film, though. It graphically depicts how the Canadian UN General on the ground in Rwanda, Dallaire, was totally let down by his masters in New York. I'd like to think the UN has learnt its lesson, but I doubt it very much.

WHERE WERE YOU WHEN YOU HEARD MARGARET THATCHER HAD RESIGNED?

The *New Statesman* has a Thatcher Special this week – yes, you did read that correctly. One of the features is a 'Where were you when you heard she had resigned?' They have edited my contribution, so I thought I'd give you the unedited version here:

The night before Margaret Thatcher's resignation, I remember having had rows with two Tory MPs who owed their seats to Margaret Thatcher, yet intended to switch their votes away from her in the second ballot. I went home to my dingy flat in Walthamstow feeling angry and let down – almost tearful. Watching the news, my left-wing flatmate came home and started crowing about what trouble Mrs T was in. I'm not prone to physical violence, but I was tempted to hit him. By the time *Newsnight* finished I had realised she was finished.

The next morning, I was at my desk in Grosvenor Gardens (I had just set up a lobbying company) when I heard the news. The world stood still for a moment. I wasn't surprised that she had stepped down, but it was still a shock. Only a few days before my three-year-old niece, Emma, had asked: 'Uncle Iain, is it possible for a man to be Prime Minister?' We were about to find out.

I don't mind admitting I could barely talk and that my eyes were moist. It really was the end of an era. A candle went out that day. The woman who had inspired my interest in politics, saved the country from trade union control and done so much to win the Cold War had gone. For ever. Politics for me would never be quite the same.

THIS IS A QUESTIONNAIRE I FILLED OUT FOR THE NORMBLOG
FRIDAY 27 FEBRUARY

Why do you blog?
Because I've got things to say and I can say them without them being edited by someone else.

What has been your best blogging experience?
Probably the reaction to a blog post I did after I spoke at my godmother's funeral. There was nothing political about it, it was

an intensely personal blog post, but the response to it showed the blogosphere community at its best.

What has been your worst blogging experience?
The so-called blog war with a blogger who shall remain nameless. I felt as if I was being stalked and didn't enjoy it at all. But in the end, if you put your head above the parapet you will get shot at.

What are your favourite blogs?
Tom Harris MP, Guido Fawkes, Dizzy Thinks.

What are you reading at the moment?
The autobiography of Jimmy Armfield and Richard Evans's history of the Third Reich. He taught me Austrian history at university.

What is the best novel you've ever read?
The Aachen Memorandum by Andrew Roberts.

What is your favourite movie?
Airplane. I like weird humour.

What is your favourite song?
'Miss You Nights' by Cliff Richard. (!)

Can you name a major moral, political or intellectual issue on which you've ever changed your mind?
Devolution. I'm now a vocal supporter of an English Parliament.

What philosophical thesis do you think it most important to disseminate?
The economics of Adam Smith.

What philosophical thesis do you think it most important to combat?
Marxism.

Can you name a work of non-fiction which has had a major and lasting influence on how you think about the world?
A book called *In the Arena* by Richard Nixon. Nixon is a great writer and this book had an effect on me largely because it crystallised

what being in politics is all about. In order to make a difference you have to be in the arena – not just on the sidelines mouthing off.

Who are your political heroes?
Margaret Thatcher, Ronald Reagan, Konrad Adenauer.

If you could effect one major policy change in the governing of your country, what would it be?
To halve the size of the state.

What would you do with the UN?
Move it to Switzerland, halve its size and budget, reform its voting structures and change the terms of engagement for UN peacekeepers.

What do you consider to be the main threat to the future peace and security of the world?
Islamic fundamentalism.

What personal fault do you most dislike?
Selfishness.

In what circumstances would you be willing to lie?
To save someone's life.

What commonly enjoyed activities do you regard as a waste of time?
Fishing where you put the fish back.

What, if anything, do you worry about?
My weight.

If you were to relive your life to this point, is there anything you'd do differently?
Where do I start? I wouldn't have stood in North Norfolk at the last election if I had known what the result would be, I suppose, even though I enjoyed it immensely.

What would you call your autobiography?
End of Part One.

Who would play you in the movie about your life?
Patrick Duffy.

Where would you most like to live (other than where you do)?
Washington DC.

What is your most treasured possession?
My Jack Russell, Gio.

Who is your favourite comedian or humorist?
Frankie Howerd.

Who are your sporting heroes?
Paolo di Canio, Trevor Brooking, Ian Botham.

Which English Premiership football team do you support?
West Ham.

If you could have any three guests, past or present, to dinner, who would they be?
Richard Nixon, Otto von Bismarck and Cliff Richard.

What animal would you most like to be?
My Jack Russell, Gio.

ARE YOU A SHOUTER OR A SIMMERER?
MONDAY 2 MARCH

One of the subjects we discussed on *Woman's Hour* this morning was whether having a temper can be a good thing. Apparently some new study from Harvard says that showing your anger at work can help further your career.

I reckon you can divide people into door slammers and sulkers. I am very much in the first category. I know I have a tendency to lose my temper volcanically, but within thirty seconds I am back to normal. Experience shows me that many people have difficulty coping with this. If they have a row about something with someone, most people harbour a grudge until at least the next day. I rarely do. For me it's over quickly, done and dusted, let's move on.

Anger at work is, in my view, more destructive than constructive. However, there's a delicate balance to be struck between showing emotion and being intimidating. Few people get it right.

Election campaigns bring out the worst in people and I defy any candidate or agent to get through a campaign without toys being thrown out of prams. The key is never to let it show with campaign volunteers.

PRINTING MONEY IS THE ECONOMICS OF ROBERT MUGABE
THURSDAY 5 MARCH

Nothing, and I mean nothing, will ever convince me that printing money is the solution to our problems. There is absolutely no guarantee that the £75 billion quantitative easing will improve liquidity in the economy, and the big danger is that in the long term it could lead to an inflationary problem. No one has ever shown, to my knowledge, any instance where printing money has led to anything but a worsening economic situation. You can bet your bottom Deutschmark that the Germans will do all they can to prevent the European Central Bank from following suit. And they have very good reason.

What we are experiencing is Mugabanomics. And it can only end in tears.

The way to get confidence back into our economy is not to print money, but to encourage the return of sound money. This move has delayed that by a very long time. I'm horrified that Conservative politicians haven't spoken out against this potentially disastrous move. In fact, no one has. It's about time someone did.

Update: A political friend of mine rang me this morning and defined quantitative easing as 'what Nicholas Soames does at 7 a.m. each morning'. Best not to think about it too much.

A DAY IN NORWICH, A FINE CITY
SATURDAY 14 MARCH

I spent the whole of yesterday in Norwich. It made me realise how much I miss the place. For those who don't know, I spent four very happy years at the University of East Anglia studying

German in the early 1980s, then spent two years working for the then Norwich North MP, Patrick Thompson. I then went back to Norfolk in 2003 to stand for the Conservatives in North Norfolk and I write a fortnightly column for the Norwich-based *Eastern Daily Press*. Norfolk is a county which it is impossible to escape from. Even though I am from Essex, I still regard Norfolk as a second home.

Yesterday I went to see my old lecturer from UEA, Gordon Turner, who I hadn't seen for many years. He was one of those people in my life who went the extra mile to help me. One of those special people who enhance every life they touch. I wondered if he had changed, but I needn't have worried. It was as if there hadn't been two intervening decades since I graduated.

I then went to the university campus to speak to 120 politics students, alongside Steve Richards from *The Independent*, about how blogs are affecting the mainstream media. The session only lasted an hour but I really got the feeling that the students got a lot from it. There were some excellent questions. Afterwards I went for a drink with a couple of the students. Wandering around the campus and student union building was very odd. It was as if the intervening twenty-four years hadn't happened. Do other people feel like this when they visit their old school or university? I felt like a ghost, invisible to everyone else, yet somehow back where I spent four extremely happy years.

Leaving Norwich I kept thinking how much I missed the place. I wonder if I will return one day, and this time for good.

WHY IS TOM HARRIS PROUD OF HIS VOTING RECORD?
FRIDAY 27 MARCH

Something's been troubling me. Gnawing away. On Tuesday, Tom Harris wrote a blog post about intending to vote against his party on a three-line whip for the first time ever. It was over the issue of gay hatred. As it happens, I agree with his stance. However, his argument is not the reason for my disquiet. It was his opening paragraph:

> Since being elected in 2001, I have never, until today, voted against my party on a three-line whip. That is something I'm extremely proud of.

Just think about that. He's saying 'my party, right or wrong'. And for the first time in eight years, he's decided to break with that belief. Why he should be proud of behaving in a robot-like fashion for nearly four years is something I find difficult to comprehend. A party system inevitably requires whipping, and I make no bones about that – and politicians must recognise that they are elected under a party label – but for an MP to be proud of never having voted against the party line is something to be remarked upon. It is even more bizarre when I know Tom to be someone who does indeed have a mind of his own.

So why is he proud of this? I have to say that if I had been an MP for nearly eight years and had only ever voted for the party line, I wouldn't feel proud. I'd feel slightly ashamed.

AN EMAIL TO DAMIAN MCBRIDE

I have just sent an email to Damian McBride, the Prime Minister's head of strategy. On the *Daily Politics* yesterday, Guido Fawkes made an allegation that McBride had given Derek Draper his marching orders on how to trash my reputation as a blogger, and in particular how he should smear me over the Carol Thatcher golliwog remarks. This wasn't the first time I had heard the allegation made.

I intend now to submit a Freedom of Information request on this subject as I regard it as a hugely serious breach of McBride's role as a civil servant – paid for by the taxpayer – if indeed it is true. Several people have warned me off doing this. 'Let it lie,' they say. One lobby correspondent advised me: 'Don't get on the wrong side of McBride.'

I'm afraid they 'misunderestimate' me.

But I will say this. I hope Guido's allegations are wrong and that Damian McBride can truthfully tell me that he gave no such advice to Draper either by email or verbally. But if these emails do exist, they will come to light through an FOI request. Someone else said to me that they will just delete the emails, if they exist. I reminded that person that to do so would constitute a criminal offence. It's the kind of thing a certain Richard Nixon got into rather a lot of trouble for.

WHY THE EXPENSES ISSUE NEEDS TO BE ADDRESSED NOW

I was going to write this post twenty minutes ago, but thought I had better calm down. I have just spent nearly an hour doing a phone-in programme with BBC Radio Wales. I have never experienced an angrier group of people in any programme I have taken part in. Every single caller thought politicians were thieving, lying scum, and there was nothing I or anyone could say which would have persuaded them otherwise. I chuntered on about there being bad apples in any profession, but they all thought that every single politician had their snouts in the trough.

The other London-based pundit was Sean O'Grady, economics editor of *The Independent*. He played to the audience and essentially agreed that they were all at it, and they all enjoyed twenty weeks' holiday a year and hardly worked the rest of the time. I'm afraid I lost my temper. O'Grady used to work for the Liberal Democrats. He knows full well that the overwhelming majority of MPs put the hours in and when Parliament isn't sitting, they're to be found doing constituency work. He even seemed to suggest that they shouldn't be allowed to employ their own staff or have any second home allowance at all.

In all the interviews I have done over the last twenty-four hours on this, I have tried to be balanced and non-partisan. This is not a party political issue, but it strikes at the very core of why many good people just won't go into politics nowadays. They just don't want to be tarred with the same brush of contempt which was so apparent in this phone-in.

I almost feel as if I should be paid danger money for having the temerity to defend politics as a profession. It's a pretty thankless task at the moment – and it isn't made any easier by journalists like Sean O'Grady playing to the crowds. It happened last night too, when I had to correct Stephen Nolan on 5 Live, who had blithely stated as a matter of fact that MPs don't have to pay capital gains tax on their second homes. 'They're exempt', he said. When I challenged him on it he had the good grace to apologise.

But the trouble is, everyone believes this kind of thing, because they think it is entirely plausible that MPs are indeed exempt (I hope to God I was right!).

Politicians need to wake up and understand the level of contempt felt for them out there beyond London. Some of the younger politicians understand this very well. And they know that urgent reform is needed. This reform cannot wait until after the election. It needs to be discussed and introduced almost immediately. But the trouble is, while we have the existing Speaker and the existing roadblocks to reform in the House of Commons administration system, it just won't happen. Gordon Brown has neatly finessed the expenses issue by asking the Committee on Standards in Public Life to combine a report on expenses with one on second jobs. Because of work underway, the inquiry won't even start until the autumn, and, guess what, it won't report until after the election. That is simply not on. Don't the 200 new MPs who may be elected in 2010 deserve to know what their terms of employment will be in advance?

Someone needs to grab this issue by the throat. If Gordon Brown won't do it, perhaps David Cameron and Nick Clegg ought to have that long-awaited conversation and come up with a joint solution.

And one final thing. Several producers of the programmes I have been on have been shocked at the reluctance of MPs to go on the air and defend their profession, or give their views on the system of expenses. 'My colleagues would lynch me,' one Labour MP told 5 Live. Doesn't that just about say it all?

HSBC: THE LISTENING BANK?

I got a call from HSBC this morning. This is how the conversation went:

HSBC: I just need to check your postcode.

Me: No, you don't.

HSBC: It's for security.

Me: I don't have an account with you.

HSBC: Well, it's for security, sir.

Me: But I don't have an account with you. Why would you need to speak to me unless you are trying to sell me something?

HSBC: It's for security, sir.

Me: Can I have your postcode please?

HSBC: We don't give out that information.

Me: [Bangs head on desk] Exactly.

HSBC: I need your postcode, sir.

Me: Are you completely deranged?

HSBC: If you'd just give me your postcode, sir.

Me: Do you play the robot in *Star Wars 4*? Listen to this very carefully. I am not giving you my postcode. Why don't you do something innovative, and if you want to tell me something, write me a letter.

HSBC: Well, I need your postcode, sir.

Me: [Click.]

OBAMA SAW MY SISTER'S BEAVER
TUESDAY 31 MARCH

My sister lives near Saffron Walden, on the Stansted flight path. Seeing as I have nothing better to do (being stranded at Leicester station), I thought I would share with you a text message I received from her this afternoon: 'AIR FORCE ONE JUST FLEW OVER MY BEAVER'.

I should perhaps explain that her house is called Beaver Lodge... And she comes from Essex. Isn't it a good job she made no mention of Bush?

I'll just get my coat.

DUPLICITY AND LOVE
SUNDAY 5 APRIL

I seem to have developed a worrying habit of going to the cinema to see the wrong film. Some years ago I went to see *Lord of the Rings*, thinking I was going to watch a remake of the *Lord of the Flies*. Last night, in Cardiff, I went to see *Duplicity*, a film starring Clive Owen and Julia Roberts. I had remembered seeing a trailer with Clive Owen in it. The only trouble, it turns out the trailer had been for *The International*. *Duplicity* is a poor man's *Hustle*, with an incredibly ropey and belaboured plot and wooden dialogue. But there was one line, which I remember, which rather hit home. It concerned a definition of love. It went something like this: 'She knows who I am, what I'm like. But she loves me anyway.'

Are your cockles warmed?

MY PART IN THE DOWNFALL OF THE DOCK LABOUR SCHEME
FRIDAY 10 APRIL

In September 1987, I was on holiday in Michigan when I decided to buy a copy of *The Times*. I had just finished a two-year stint as a researcher in the House of Commons and needed to find a new job. Quick. I saw an advert for the position as Public Affairs Manager for the British Ports Association and National Association of Port Employers. In those days, lobbying was in its infancy and, to be honest, I wasn't sure what the job would really entail. Anyway, I spent an hour in the University of Michigan library in Ann Arbor (which remains one of my favourite towns in the world) touching up my CV and constructing a letter of application. A month later, I had beaten 200 other applicants for the job and started work in a rather dingy office in New Oxford Street. While preparing for interviews, virtually everyone I spoke to said, 'Ah, you'll be trying to persuade the government to get rid of the Dock Labour Scheme.' Dock Labour Scheme? What the hell was that? It certainly didn't sound very exciting. I started researching it and was horrified by what I found. It was a piece of employment legislation which gave registered dock workers privileges far and above those enjoyed by other workers. They had a guaranteed job for life, it was impossible to sack them, when they retired their jobs automatically passed to their sons and they were paid at rates other workers (and indeed dock workers in non-scheme ports) could only dream of. Spanish practices were rife, and if a port closed down dockers were transferred to the nearest port, even if it was run by a different company and there was no need for them.

How on earth could this scheme exist after eight years of a Thatcher government, I asked myself. I wasn't the only one. But Margaret Thatcher was frightened of the dockers. Nigel Lawson writes in his memoirs:

> Margaret displayed cold feet to a quite remarkable degree. She suggested [at a meeting in 1985], first, that it would be more sensible to do nothing and let the Scheme wither on the vine. She then expressed acute anxiety about the effect of a dock strike on the balance of payments and sterling. I replied that if anyone should be worried about that, it would be me, and I was not... But Margaret was adamant. She concluded that there was no prospect in abolishing

the Dock Labour Scheme this side of an election – then still some
two years off. A disappointed Nick Ridley [Transport Secretary]
accepted her verdict and that was that.

So my task was to launch a campaign to persuade Margaret
Thatcher to do the necessary and get rid of this piece of iniquitous
employment legislation. It soon became clear that one of the reasons
the port employers had recruited me was because I had previously
worked for a Tory MP who had been a PPS at the Department of
Transport. They thought I knew my way around that department.
I didn't like to tell them I had never set foot in it, let alone met a
single civil servant from the DoT!

Together with my boss, Nick Finney, I launched a hearts-and-
minds campaign aimed at politicians and the media. Barely a week
seemed to go by without someone writing an op-ed calling for the
scheme to go, or for a tabloid news report to appear about Spanish
practices in the industry. Tory MP Jacques Arnold put down an
Early Day Motion, which rapidly attracted more than 200 signatures – more than any other that session. He and his colleague Nick
Bennett kept up the parliamentary pressure, with debates, questions and meetings. It was then that I got a call from an MP I had
never heard of, David Davis. 'I think you need to change strategy,'
he said bluntly. We met and I was impressed by what he had to
say. He proceeded to write a pamphlet for the Centre for Policy
Studies titled *Clear the Decks*, and took a grip of the campaign
in Parliament, gently (or not so gently) elbowing aside Arnold
and Bennett. David Davis's advice and actions turned out to be of
crucial importance, and it was then that I marked him out as 'one
to watch'. We also met with Michael Meacher and John Prescott
(Labour's Employment and Transport spokesmen), who made it
clear that they couldn't publicly support us, but they knew the
scheme was an anachronism and although they would go through
the motions of having to make sceptical remarks about our stand,
they wouldn't lift a finger to support the unions.

We were clearly knocking at an open door throughout the
Conservative Party. But the door at No. 10 remained firmly shut. We
quickly realised that a campaign purely based on the iniquities of
the Dock Labour Scheme wasn't going to persuade she who needed
to be persuaded. So we decided to commission a report from some
economic consultants, WEFA. Their report was given the remit of

outlining the economic benefits of repeal. They concluded that up to 48,000 new jobs would be created. Their reasoning was easy to understand, for in the sixty-three DLS ports (which included London, Southampton, Bristol, Cardiff, Liverpool, Clyde, Forth, Tees, Hull and Immingham – but not Dover and Felixstowe) the port authorities were prevented by law from allowing any non-port-related activity within their boundaries. If the scheme didn't exist they could utilise their land however they wished.

Secondly, we needed to show that a national dock strike would not be as calamitous as the Prime Minister feared. Traditionally, the port employers and shipping lines had been regarded as soft touches by the unions. We knew the ship owners wouldn't change, and we knew that the chairman of P&O had Mrs T's ear. So we had to demonstrate that the port employers would be completely robust and not buckle under union pressure. So we produced a guide for the employers on how to deal with a strike in the event of repeal.

We decided to hold a one-day conference for the employers on the subject, and scheduled it for 6 April 1989. A few days before the conference, one of the civil servants phoned and told us to prepare for an announcement that the scheme was about to be repealed. 'When's the announcement?' we asked tentatively. 'I haven't told you this, but it will be on 6 April,' he said. Oh. My. God. The day of our 'Preparing for a Strike' conference. We knew no one would believe this to be complete coincidence, but that is exactly what it was. We debated whether to call it off, but decided the downsides of that were worse than people thinking we were in collusion with the government.

Mobile phones had only just been invented, and I remember spending half that day with a massive Vodafone handset glued to my ear. The employers themselves hadn't got a clue what was about to hit them. Finally, at 3.30, Norman Fowler, the Employment Secretary, stood up in the Commons and made the announcement. 'Thunderbirds are go,' said my informant. We then made the announcement to the employers, who received the news in stunned silence. They thought it was a joke, or prelude to some sort of role-play exercise. But it wasn't. It was for real.

Immediately, many dockers walked out in a series of wildcat strikes. The T&G union under Ron Todd was caught totally on the hop. They never really thought this day would come.

A couple of days later, disaster struck. Our entire strategy document had been leaked to *The Independent*. We never found out who had done it, but Nick Finney and I initially thought that the game was up. Quite the reverse turned out to be true. The contents of the document scared the unions half to death. They couldn't believe the level of pre-planning which had been happening. We had identified which ports were likely to strike and which would remain open for business. We had identified small wharves all over the country which could take shipments if the major ports were shut. We had even laid plans to fly in foreign dock workers if necessary. The leak actually proved to be a masterstroke, as it transformed the port employers' reputation both in the eyes of the unions and the government.

The unions announced plans for a national ballot of dockers, which we knew would vote in favour of strike action. But we had prepared for that and had carefully laid out plans to take them to court. When we did, the union won. We appealed to the High Court and I remember attending the hearing on a Saturday afternoon. We thought we had little hope of the verdict going in our direction – but it did. I remember looking over to the BBC's industrial correspondent, John Fryer, and we both shook our heads in a state of bemusement. It was a grievous blow to the T&G who were having a very difficult time keeping their more militant members in check. There was violence on the picket lines and violence by striking dockers towards those who returned to work. Employers were threatened with violence and worse. I regularly received threatening phone calls and mail.

While all this was going on the Dock Labour Scheme (Abolition) Bill slowly made its way through Parliament and eventually received Royal Assent on 6 July. By that time, strike action was dying out and was very sporadic. Court action, the return to work by many dockers, and the ability of importers and exporters to find other ports to get their goods in and out meant that the unions knew that the game was up.

I remember being at my parents' house one Saturday afternoon in July 1989 and being told that dockers at Southampton and Tilbury had just voted to go back to work. Indeed, that gave rise to one of the best headlines I have ever read in the *Sunday Sport* the next day:

HORSE FART SIGNALS END OF DOCK STRIKE

Apparently, at the Tilbury mass meeting, which was held in an open field, a horse had wandered up to the assembled dockers while they were being addressed by a union official. Just as he encouraged them all to return to work, the horse broke wind in a very loud manner. I was quoted in the *Sunday Sport* story saying, 'That just about sums up the whole strike.'

That signalled the end of a three months' stint where I was working 6 a.m. to midnight every day and appearing on news bulletins and radio stations almost non-stop. Our hearts-and-minds campaign had been a great success, even if one industrial reporter dubbed me 'master of the trite press release'. But the feeling of complete let-down at the end of it was terrible. The phone stopped ringing. I hadn't got a job any longer, really. Even though we had scored a tremendous success, I had the same feeling after the general election campaign finished in 2005. There was nothing to make the adrenalin flow any longer.

During those two years I made contacts in the media and in politics who would feature a lot in my life over the next two decades. I've already mentioned David Davis. Kevin Maguire was a young industry reporter on the *Daily Telegraph*. Paul Routledge was Labour editor on *The Observer* and could be guaranteed to ask the one question I wouldn't want to answer. But perhaps my clearest memory of that whole time was being rung up during the strike by another industrial correspondent saying his editor needed a front-page story and he needed me to give it to him. He was clearly the worse for drink, so I ended up dictating a story to him, which ran word for word in next day's paper. Those were the days.

I remember saying to someone around that time that if I never achieved anything else in my life, I would look back on the past two years and know that I had done something which would benefit the country hugely over the coming decades. And so it proved. The sixty-three former scheme ports could now at last complete with non-scheme ports like Felixstowe and Dover on a level playing field. No longer would they be held to ransom by trade unions, who could previously bring them to a standstill with no warning. They could now develop their land banks and attract new businesses into port areas. In short, the abolition of the DLS has created tens of thousands of new jobs, just as we predicted. It has enabled Britain's ports to compete with their European neighbours, and it enabled the government then to privatise many of them during the 1990s. But that's another story.

DAMIAN MCBRIDE SCANDAL: FATAL FLAWS OF THE PM'S PITBULL
SUNDAY 12 APRIL

Thanks to Damian McBride and Derek Draper, whom I like to think of as the Dick Dastardly and Muttley of British politics, I have had to abort my Easter plans. You see, I was their first victim. Before I explain how, let's rewind a few months.

Last October, I met Draper for lunch. I really should have known it would end in tears, but he held a strange fascination for me. I remember writing him a short note after his fall from grace over the Lobbygate scandal in 1998. I didn't know him well, but I am a sucker for someone on their uppers and wanted to wish him well. Ten years on, he wanted to pick my blogging brain as he intended to launch an internet blog. Over lunch, I explained to him patiently the pitfalls of the internet. Indeed, I had to be very patient indeed as his knowledge of online matters was only slightly superior to that of my 78-year-old mother, who has never touched a computer in her life.

Three months later he launched LabourList to much media fanfare. At last, so the pundits wrote, there would be some competition for right-of-centre blogs such as Guido Fawkes, ConservativeHome and my own. But then it all went wrong for Draper. He ignored every bit of well-intentioned advice he was given. His blog authors all came from his contacts book. The site contained few articles that could not have been written in Labour Party HQ, and there was precious little grassroots input. He was accused of censoring comments and using the site as a vehicle for his own giant-sized ego.

As LabourList started to tank, he looked for help elsewhere. And he set his sights on Damian McBride, the Prime Minister's director of strategy.

McBride was Gordon Brown's licensed pitbull. Like most Labour spin merchants, he liked nothing more than sinking his fangs into Conservatives; he relished confrontation. He was to Brown what Alastair Campbell was to Blair, and he seemed not to care whom he offended in the process. Talk to any Westminster journalist and they will have a gory tale about the man they call 'McPoison'.

McBride revelled in making enemies, conveniently forgetting the maxim that all those who you offend on the way up are unlikely to come to your aid on the way down. He didn't just brief against Conservatives, he would slag off anyone he felt wasn't totally loyal to Gordon Brown – and that meant anyone who could reasonably be described as a Blairite. Many a minister felt his wrath – not directly, but through the pages of a national newspaper.

Health minister Ivan Lewis, who spoke out injudiciously, suddenly found text messages to a woman who was not his wife plastered all over a Sunday tabloid. Transport minister Tom Harris, who committed the cardinal sin of being a Blairite and an entertaining blogger, found himself despatched to the back benches after being overheard at the Labour Party conference by McBride and his Downing Street acolyte Tom Watson saying something less than flattering about the Dear Leader.

No second chances, you see. It explains why former Home Secretary Charles Clarke was so willing to put the boot in on Saturday and demand McBride's scalp.

Over the past two days, it has been said that McBride should have had better things to do than indulge in political assassination. There's an economy to save, after all. But political assassination is exactly what he did. He was not a foreign affairs or economy adviser. He was a political boot-boy whose function was to work on the PM's behalf, which is why it is a bit rich for Brown now to pretend he is shocked to discover what McBride got up to. Brown wrote McBride's job description and left him to get on with it. As ye sow, so ye shall reap.

In early February, I appeared on the *Today* programme to talk about Carol Thatcher's use of the word 'golliwog'. I wasn't there to defend it and I didn't. But I tried to explain how a 55-year-old woman with her background would use the word without necessarily thinking it would cause offence.

My reward? To be branded a racist sympathiser by Draper on his blog. My first reaction was to laugh. But as it went round and round in my head, I got angry. And so started a minor blog war, which drove many extra readers to Draper's site.

A few weeks later, I was told that the whole thing had been dreamt up in Downing Street as a way to 'get Dale' and destroy my reputation as one of Britain's leading bloggers. I was told that McBride had sent an email to Derek Draper giving him his

marching orders on how to smear me. Indeed, it has been suggested
that McBride wrote the poisonous blog post himself.

I then bumped into Draper towards the end of March, following an unedifying appearance he had just made on the BBC *Daily
Politics* programme alongside my fellow blogger Guido Fawkes. He
wanted to let bygones be bygones.

'What about these emails?' I asked.

'They don't exist,' he lied.

'I can't have personal or business relationships with anyone who
calls me a racist and thinks they can get away with it,' I said, and
walked off.

It was then that I decided to put in a Freedom of Information
request into the Cabinet Office to try to get a copy of the email. Out
of courtesy, I emailed McBride and copied in Draper to tell them
what I was doing. That request is still being processed.

Some may see this as a schoolboy spat between two bloggers with
egos the size of mountains. Maybe. But my experience is important
as it demonstrates how the No. 10 lie machine will target anyone
whose reputation it wishes to damage. I'm in a position to fight
back, but what about the dozens of journalists who have to accept
the bullying for fear of being ostracised and never getting another
story? Or the dozens of MPs and ministers who know that to speak
out is to invite career disaster?

Perhaps this sort of affair is symptomatic of something more
deep-rooted at the heart of government. All administrations flag
after a while. They become gaffe-prone. People go off-message
more frequently. A sense of malaise is almost palpable. It's what
happens when empires crumble. A bunker mentality sets in and the
leader encourages the wagons to circle. It took eleven years for it to
happen to Margaret Thatcher, but with Gordon Brown it has taken
less than two.

When you're a leader in trouble, you turn to those whose undy-
ing loyalty you know you can count on. That's why Brown was
reluctant to let McBride go last September after he had been found
briefing against Ruth Kelly. Instead of firing him, he moved him
sideways and out of direct contact with the media. But at the same
time he brought back his old ally Charlie Whelan.

Whelan is now political officer for the giant Unite union, and
he funds Draper's website. It was he who persuaded Geoffrey
Robinson, the co-proprietor of the *New Statesman*, to dispense.

with the services of the magazine's award-winning political editor Martin Bright, who was considered not on-side with Brown. Whelan was also copied in on McBride's emails to Draper as he had agreed to fund the new Red Rag blog, which was to play host to the smears about Tory politicians. I suspect there is far more about to emerge about Whelan's pivotal role at the heart of the Brown empire.

If Gordon Brown really wants to bring about a new era at Downing Street, he can do several things – take away Alastair Campbell's pass which gives him free access to the building; reshuffle Tom Watson out of No. 10; but, most significantly of all, tell Derek Draper his services as editor of LabourList are no longer required.

The trouble is, our Prime Minister is wedded to the notion that seeking political conflict and dividing lines is the be-all and end-all. And he's incapable of changing.

TWENTY FIRSTS MEME
FRIDAY 24 APRIL

First job
Mucking out my dad's pigs on a Saturday morning for 10p an hour.

First real job
Researcher to Patrick Thompson MP 1985–7.

First role in politics
Chairman of UEA Conservatives in 1981.

First car
An orange Ford Cortina Mk III, lovingly nicknamed the Big Jaffa. I wrote it off on my twentieth birthday.

First record
'Long-Haired Lover from Liverpool' by Jimmy Osmond. The shame lives with me still.

First football match
Cambridge Utd v. West Ham in a 1974 testimonial at the Abbey Stadium.

First concert
Darts at a free concert in Harlow in 1977.

First country visited
France, on a day trip to Boulogne at the age of seven.

First TV appearance
Multi-Coloured Swap Shop in 1978.

First political speech
April 1982 during a debate on the Falklands at my university. It all
started there...

First girlfriend/boyfriend
Rachel Elliott at Ashdon County Primary School. She had a runny
nose.

First encounter with a famous person
Cyril Fletcher from *That's Life* at a pantomime in the Arts Theatre
Cambridge c. 1973.

First brush with death
Hitting a Transit van head on at 50 mph in the days before seatbelts. The long bonnet of my Cortina Mk III saved me – and my
two sisters.

First house/flat owned
70 Howard Road, Walthamstow, in July 1988 – probably the worst
time ever to buy a flat.

First film seen at a cinema
The Sound of Music at Saffron Walden Cinema, which is sadly no
longer there.

First time on the radio
On the Radio 1 *Breakfast Show* with Mike Read in 1981 on 'Beat
the Jock'. I didn't.

First politician I met
Shirley Williams, who spoke at my school in 1977.

First book I remember reading
The Secret of Spiggy Holes by Enid Blyton.

First visit to the London Palladium
1978, to see the reunion of Cliff and the Shadows!

First election
1985 Norfolk County Council election, Catton Grove Ward. My finals were the next day. Had to be postponed after I suffered from shock having knocked a motorcyclist off his bike on polling day and breaking his leg. He was a Labour voter...

A SHOUTING MATCH LIVE ON AIR WITH GEORGE GALLOWAY
SATURDAY 2 MAY

I have never shouted at a radio presenter before, but I have just had the mother of all rows with George Galloway on TalkSport. Quite incredible. I had been invited on to talk about the thirtieth anniversary of Margaret Thatcher's 1979 election victory.

He started off by introducing me as an 'apologist for Margaret Thatcher'. I explained that 'apologist' is a pejorative word which I object to. I then started talking about what the country was like in 1979 and how it had been brought to its knees by the trade unions. He interrupted me and went on a two-minute monologue about how awfully she had treated the steel industry. I tried to interject on several occasions but it soon became clear that my mic had been cut off. When eventually he finished his monologue I complained bitterly that he was trying to silence me, and it developed into a very ugly spat in which I accused him of propagandising and not understanding the role of a talk-show host. We were both shouting at each other, which I am sure was very unedifying to listen to. I debated whether just to put the phone down, but in the end decided to continue. In fact, even during the on-air row he closed the microphone so a lot of my ranting wasn't heard.

I am still fizzing.

WHAT DO WIDDECOMBE AND CURRIE HAVE IN COMMON?
TUESDAY 5 MAY

What should I make of the fact that I get emails today from Ann Widdecombe and Edwina Currie announcing they both have new email addresses? Just askin'...

Reminds me of a wonderful afternoon at the Tory party conference in 2002, just after Edwina had published her diaries. Ann was doing a signing on the Politico's stand and was doing her best East End barrow-boy selling act. 'Get your *Clematis Tree* here. Very clean novel. No sex, no violence, no swearing. Buy it for Granny for Christmas.' At just that point we had a delivery of 500 copies of Edwina's book. I covertly placed a big pile of them on the desk next to Ann. Eventually she cottoned on and pulled a face. Her sales patter changed somewhat. 'Very clean novel,' she shrieked, pointing to her book. She then pointed with a disdainful look on her face to Edwina's book. 'Very dirty diaries!'

It must have worked. During the course of the week we sold 500 Widdecombe novels, but only fourteen of Edwina's diaries. Actually, her book was an excellent read and was about far more than just the affair with John Major. If you haven't read it, you should.

REFLECTING ON MY RADIO PRESENTING DEBUT
SATURDAY 9 MAY

Last night I made my debut as a radio presenter on PlayRadioUK.

I have to say I enjoyed myself tremendously. We had some great calls and the lines were flashing for the whole programme. It's quite disconcerting when you see all the lines flashing at once because your immediate reaction is to finish a call and move onto the next one so you can get everyone in. But I tried not to do that too much so everyone could have their say. Much of the programme was taken up with MPs' expenses, but we did cover other subjects as well. It was great to receive calls from all over the country and from the US and Canada too.

Tom Harris phoned in, which was nice of him, and several blog regulars also joined in. Molesworth1 gets the accolade as caller of the night. John Hirst (Jailhouselawyer) rang too to talk about his pet issue of votes for prisoners. I hope he thought I gave him a fair crack.

I was supposed to play quite a bit of music, but we had so many calls I ended up playing only one song, 'Apologize' by Timbaland, which I dedicated to the Prime Minister.

Did anything go wrong? Apart from me fluffing the name of the radio station at the top of the programme and Skype freezing at one stage due to the volume of calls, not too much. I got a bit mixed up with the faders from time to time but generally it all went very smoothly. I deliberately didn't have a script so I could move from subject to subject at will. What I found most difficult was keeping on top of all the different methods people were using to communicate with me in the studio. I think I concentrated too much on the phone calls and didn't use Skype enough, or read out enough emails – and I forgot about Twitter completely.

The producers told me afterwards that the audience had been several times what they were expecting and the level of phone calls was huge for a first show.

SEVEN POINTLESS THINGS ABOUT MOI
SUNDAY 17 MAY

1. My German oral for my final exams at university had to be postponed because the previous day a motorcyclist broke his leg when he hit my car as I was taking three old ladies to vote. It's a long story.
2. I taught tap dancing to Libyan schoolchildren as a summer job in 1984.
3. I was once chased by a Hungarian prostitute (female!) and had to flee the country. It's an even longer story.
4. I had all my wisdom teeth removed in one go and felt absolutely no pain.
5. I can't whistle.
6. I have great difficulty in tying anything, especially shoelaces and ties. If you ever want a good laugh, watch me try to tie shoelaces. I get there in the end, but in a very roundabout way.
7. I got the slipper at primary school for looking up my teacher's skirt. The psychoanalysts among you can make of that what you will.

WHY DO I DO IT?

My partner thinks I am mad. 'What on earth are you doing, going to North Wales to speak to sixty people who've never heard of you?' he asked on Thursday night. 'Are they paying you?' It was an interesting question. I find it very difficult to explain to people outside politics why I do what I do. Most sane people would think my partner has a point. Why would I drive 300 miles there and 300 miles back for absolutely no reward?

But all I am doing is what scores of politicians of all political persuasions do each weekend. OK, I am not a politician, but Michael Dobbs does it, Matthew Parris does it, Michael Brown does it. We do it because it's one way we can help local parties raise much-needed funds to fight their campaigns. We do it because our lives do not allow us the time we used to devote to doorstep campaigning and we feel a little guilty about that. So I have a rule of accepting two speaking engagements every month to help raise money for the Tory Party. My partner still thinks I am mad, but there you go. I'll show him this email which I got earlier today from one of the dinner guests on Friday night in Aberconwy:

> It was a pleasure both to meet you and to hear you speak. You asked why so many would want to pay money to come and listen to a person they had never met. Let me tell you, there are sixty people in North Wales who would be delighted to hear you again, should you ever return!

And that is why I do it. Because invariably they are thoroughly nice people.

THE HATE MEME
SUNDAY 24 MAY

Things have become too serious of late on this blog. Time for an amusing meme! Tory Politico has tagged me with the 18 Most Hated Meme. I don't do 'hate' very well, so not sure how good this will be...

1. Most hated food:
   Avocado or prawns – foods of the devil
2. Most hated person:
   Neil Warnock
3. Most hated job:
   Mucking out my dad's pigs for 10p an hour
4. Most hated city:
   Sheffield
5. Most hated band/song:
   U2
6. Most hated website:
   Guess
7. Most hated TV programme:
   Heartbeat, which I am forced to sit through every Sunday night
8. Most hated British politician:
   Iris Robinson
9. Most hated artist:
   Any modern artist: I'll say Tracey Emin purely because she's the only one I can name
10. Most hated book:
    Das Kapital: it's done more damage to the world than any other
11. Most hated shop:
    Harrods, because of who owns it
12. Most hated organisation:
    The BNP
13. Most hated historical event:
    Fall of Lady T
14. Most hated sport:
    Horse racing and synchronised swimming, if you can call it a sport
15. Most hated technology:
    Apple Macs – waste of space
16. Most hated annual event:
    One of the big four winning the Premier League
17. Most hated daily task:
    Getting up
18. Most hated comedian:
    Jimmy Carr, just because he isn't funny

SHOULD I HAVE QUESTIONED THE PM'S STATE OF MIND?
SATURDAY 6 JUNE

Last night I took part in a very bad-tempered half-hour paper review on Sky News alongside Eve Pollard and Michael White of *The Guardian*. White was not in a good mood, as we were doing it on the Sky News platform opposite the House of Lords rather than in a nice warm studio.

Why did it get bad tempered? Because White started being sexist and I questioned Gordon Brown's mental state. He accused Caroline Flint of having a 'hissy fit'. 'Don't be so sexist,' I said. Eve Pollard nodded in agreement. 'I'm not, and don't try that one with me.' 'You'd never use that expression about a man,' I said. He was furious.

It went downhill from there. I've thought long and hard about whether I was right to question the Prime Minister's state of mind on live television. What I said was that anyone watching Gordon Brown's press conference would have come away with the impression that he was having some sort of breakdown on live television. I said it because that's how it appeared to me. The weird hand movements, the stutter, the repetition of various phrases – 'I am not arrogant' – the declaration that he was 'honest' seconds before he lied to Tom Bradby about never having considered sacking Alistair Darling, his odd facial expressions ... I could go on. As it turned out, I said little that Nick Robinson didn't say on the midnight BBC TV news bulletin. Anyone who saw that press conference would have come away with the same impression.

But it enraged Michael White. 'Don't say that,' he hissed. 'I'll say what I like if I believe it,' I replied. 'Not with me, sonny,' he responded. 'Don't try and tell me what to say, you're not going to bully me,' I hit back. It got even worse when I accused Brown of lying over Alistair Darling. This is Denverthen's account...

> Iain Dale, covering the front pages with Sir Michael White and Eve Pollard, became very animated when White began to put his usual moronic, self-satisfied Labourist spin on Brown's humiliation. Dale, after ripping White a new one for his extra-terrestrial nonsense, pointed out that Brown lied through his teeth in his press conference earlier today when he claimed he had never wanted to sack Alistair Darling. White sort of protested, but Dale nailed him by saying that White had known about it all along.

In the commercial break Michael had another go at me, but I robustly defended myself. I've appeared on TV with him often enough to know that he will defend the indefensible where Labour is concerned, and anyone who saw his defence of Brown – who, he reckoned, had had a good day! – would have laughed, just as I did. He blustered that it was completely wrong to have said that Brown was mad, which is not what I did at all. Suggesting that someone is at the end of their tether or having a breakdown is not the same as saying they are mad.

But did he have a point? Even if I believed it could be true (and I do) was it right to question the Prime Minister's state of mind on live television?

TRAVEL WOES
THURSDAY 11 JUNE

Today did not get off to a good start. I'm off to Florida for five days to attend a conference on 'America and Europe: The Ties That Bind'. I got up at 5.30 under the misapprehension that my flight left at 8.55. It doesn't. It's at 10.35. And, furthermore, it turned out that the ticket had been booked for tomorrow instead of today. I daren't even tell you how much it cost to change the ticket.

And on top of that I left my Blackberry on the back seat of the car that delivered me to Terminal 3. Luckily I eventually managed to retrieve it. Can you imagine the pain of five days without a Blackberry?

I don't know what it is about me, but I seem incapable of going on a foreign journey without some incident or other.

KILLING SPEED
THURSDAY 13 AUGUST

This morning I attended a two-and-a-half-hour-long speed aware-ness course, having been caught doing 37 mph in a 30 limit in Brixton at 3 a.m. one morning in early June. I will admit to being slightly sceptical of what it would entail, but I have to say I found the whole thing very useful. I wouldn't say it was enjoyable – that would be going too far – but it held everyone's attention and people approached it with an open mind.

Twenty of us gathered in a rather odd building next to Bromley station. We were encouraged to arrive by train due to 'limited parking'. That was of course a complete lie, as there was free parking about fifty yards away. As I was buzzed through the door, six or seven others were waiting to be let through another door in an anteroom. 'It feels like queuing up to be processed in a prison,' I blurted out, causing a small titter from the others. 'Not that I would know,' I added quickly.

What surprised me was the social make-up of the twenty people present. Twelve were women and virtually everyone was over forty. There wasn't a boy racer in sight.

We all had to do a computer test to start with, which proved to be an interesting experience for the two female pensioners who thought a mouse was something to be frightened of. It included some videos where you had to click when you thought you were the right distance away from the car in front, or when you spotted a hazard which could cause an accident. Most of the questions were designed to see what kind of driver you are. It won't surprise you to know that when I got the results, I was rated as driving 'very much faster than average', even though I hadn't had a speeding ticket within the last three years and haven't had an accident either. I also drive further away from the vehicle in front than average. I have a faster than average reaction to potential hazards, which will come as a shock to my partner, who specialises in trying to brake even when he is a passenger in a car with me as he thinks my reactions are very slow! I have a slightly higher than average 'emotional reaction' while driving and can become easily distracted. I have an 'extreme tendency to sleepiness'. So the lesson is, if I offer you a lift home after doing a late-night paper review, say no.

The main point of the course was to highlight the difference between driving at 30 mph and 40 mph, and from that point of view it was highly successful. OK, it stands to reason that the faster you drive, if you hit someone, the more likely they are to die. But when you are told that at 30 mph the person has a 90 per cent chance of surviving, while at 40 mph they have only a 10 per cent chance of surviving, it does make you think. Everyone on the course had been caught doing between 30 mph and 40 mph.

We were all asked why we had been caught. In my case, I hadn't realised I was over the limit. One person said she was rushing someone to hospital. The course leader said that 15 per cent of people who drive too fast to get someone to hospital, end up there themselves through having an accident.

Perhaps the most shocking statistic was that if you break down on the motorway and decide to sit in your car on the hard shoulder, your life expectancy is reduced to twelve minutes – twelve minutes!

Here's something else I didn't know. We were asked what percentage of collisions occur on urban roads, rural roads and motorways. I guessed 50–30–20. The true statistics are 71 per cent on urban roads, 25 per cent on rural roads and a mere 4 per cent on motorways. In terms of deaths, 40 per cent occur on urban roads, 54 per cent on rural roads and 6 per cent on motorways. It's because if you have a serious crash on an urban road or motorway you are likely to be taken to hospital within an hour, whereas on a rural road it may be hours before someone even finds you.

How many speed cameras are there inside the M25, do you think? Most people thought between 2,000 and 5,000. The number is actually 651, with another 187 at traffic lights. Each one costs £40,000. The course leader was at great pains to point out that they were only erected in places where there had been four accidents causing serious injury or death. I still find this assertion difficult to believe, thinking of the location of some that I know. I questioned whether it would not be better to spend the £40k on eight of the flashing speed signs, which I have to say have a much better effect on my driving than speed cameras do.

So, in short, I am glad I attended. The course held our attention throughout, even if at times people felt they were being spoken to as if they were naughty children. But it never felt as if we were being lectured at. Perhaps the least credible part of the course was when the course leader asserted that she never, ever speeds. No one believed her. Until she told us that five years ago her thirteen-year-old daughter had been hit by a motorist doing 37 mph in a 30 limit. She survived but is still receiving treatment for the injuries she suffered.

We all stared at our feet. As well we might.

A thought occurs to me. Why don't we make everyone who takes a driving test take one of these courses before they can drive on the roads? Charge them the going rate so there's no cost to the taxpayer. Wouldn't it be better to get them young, rather than wait till they have transgressed?

TODAY IN YEREVAN
SUNDAY 6 SEPTEMBER

It's twenty past one in the morning here in Yerevan, Armenia. I never like arriving somewhere new in the dark as it is difficult to know what to make of the place, but from what I have seen so far the Armenians certainly like their monuments. The hotel is excellent (my criterion is good WiFi!) and the Blackberry works. Hurrah. I am here as an ambassador for the John Smith Memorial Trust, and one of the tasks over the next two days is to talk to Armenian journalists and politicians about the use of the internet in politics, as well as to recruit Fellows for the Trust's 2010 programme in the UK. The Trust funds training programmes for aspiring leaders from the former Soviet Union countries. I gave a lecture to one of them back in June.

My only knowledge of this country, and indeed the only reason I had heard of Yerevan, was because West Ham played them in the 1976 European Cup Winners' Cup. But I have done a lot of boning up and am now an expert on Armenian history. Sort of. I have to do several TV interviews over the next two days and I suspect that will test my knowledge or ability to talk sensibly on a subject I have no idea about. No change there then...

MEETING THE ARMENIAN MARGARET THATCHER
MONDAY 7 SEPTEMBER

Having had only four hours' sleep, today took a bit of getting through. Eyelids were drooping at one stage. This morning was spent in meetings with the British Council here in Yerevan and then with the British ambassador to Armenia, Charles Lonsdale, at the embassy. We had lunch in a French restaurant where we were serenaded by some very loud French music. Watching my travel companion Aisling from the John Smith Memorial Trust eat her salmon steak to the strains of 'Je t'aime' was a delight indeed. During the afternoon we made our presentation to thirty or forty possible candidates for a JSMT fellowship, encouraging them to apply to come to Britain next summer for five weeks.

This evening we attended a reception at the ambassador's

residence, related to the EU Skills initiative. It turned into a highly entertaining evening, firstly because the ambassador took a shine to my tie – clearly a man of taste.

I then had the pleasure of having an uproarious chat with the Armenian Deputy Foreign Minister, a lady called Karine Ghazinyan. She's only been in the job six months, having previously been Armenian ambassador to Romania and Germany. Armenian ministers are not politicians – they are appointees of the Prime Minister. She was the most untypical diplomat I have ever met – a real Margaret Thatcher in the making if ever I saw one. She also had a good line in jokes from the Soviet era:

> Both the American and Soviet constitutions guaranteed freedom of speech. The difference was that the American constitution guaranteed freedom after the speech.

Boom boom.

BEDKEE YERTAM HIMA ARMENIA
TUESDAY 8 SEPTEMBER

Today has been a whirlwind. Three very different TV interviews in Yerevan, a visit to the genocide museum and memorial, a trip outside the capital to see a first-century AD pagan temple and a monastery, a meeting with a dozen Armenian political bloggers, drinks with an organisation called Britain Connect and finally dinner with alumni of the John Smith Memorial Trust Fellowship programme.

Everyone here keeps asking if I am going to blog about today. To be honest I am so knackered I'd rather go to bed, but I guess I had better do my duty. The other thing people are very keen to find out is what I think of Armenia. I have to be honest and say it is one of the friendliest countries I have ever been to, even if the drivers are absolute lunatics! It's also a country with a tremendous sense of national identity and pride. There's a real can-do attitude and a desire to learn how to do things better, which is why the JSMT programme is so well received here. I really think I will try to come back here for a proper visit – two days is just ridiculous.

The TV interviews were mainly about the JSMT and internet politics. However, I was asked one curveball question by an interviewer who is also writing next year's Armenian Eurovision entry (he hasn't got a hard act to follow). He asked where I thought Armenia would have moved to in five to ten years. I was tempted to say that I suspected it would still be bordering Turkey and Iran, but thought better of it. Instead I managed to compose a vaguely sensible answer about building better relations with Turkey and other neighbours. People recognise the value of restoring relations with Turkey, but Azerbaijan is a different kettle of fish. Travel between the two countries is almost impossible and there is a latent antipathy. For a landlocked country like Armenia, it is not good news to be at loggerheads with two such powerful neighbours. I understand the reasons, and they are perfectly valid, but bridges clearly need to be built.

One great thing about Armenia is that they cannot abide John Prescott. Apparently he came here as an election observer and achieved the unique distinction of annoying both the government and the opposition.

The genocide museum is located on top of one of the hills which surround Yerevan. Its position is superb. While it hasn't got the same emotional tugs as other genocide and holocaust memorials I have been to in Israel and Rwanda, its understatement is to its credit. It's not a large place and doesn't take very long to go round, but it does what it intends to. You emerge wondering how on earth it was allowed to happen. And you wonder at your own ignorance of the details. More than 1.1 million Armenians died. And finally you think to yourself, if only the world had acted to stop it, might the ensuing Nazi Holocaust have been prevented? When asked about his plans for the 'Final Solution', Hitler is reputed to have retorted, 'And who remembers the Armenians?' Well, I remembered them today.

The trip to Garni, about forty minutes outside Yerevan, was the highlight of the whole visit. There hadn't been time for sightseeing, but last night the British ambassador urged our British Council visit planner Mariam (who, incidentally, is brilliant at her job) to find a gap in the schedule to take me to Garni. She did so and we headed off there mid-morning in a BMW four-wheel-drive jeep driven by an absolute lunatic. Armenian roads and Armenian drivers are second only to Rwandans in the unique brand of danger which they jointly present. Three times I thought we were a dead cert for a head-on collision. No matter, we got there. And back. The monastery at Geghard was worth the whole trip. Unspoilt by tourists (so far), it dates back to the first century AD. The pagan temple at Garni was similarly impressive and dates back to the same era.

I head back to England tomorrow morning feeling that the trip has been worthwhile, both from the point of view of its purpose of promoting the John Smith Memorial Trust and also because I learnt a lot about a new country. One of the TV interviewers asked me my views of Armenia and if I liked it. At the end of my reply I said: 'And in the words of Arnold Schwarzenegger, "I will be back."' I meant it. Unfortunately the translator had never heard of Arnie and didn't bother translating it!

IT ALL COMES DOWN TO TRUST
FRIDAY 11 SEPTEMBER

From time to time I am invited to give talks in schools about politics. If I understand it correctly, if I am to continue doing this in the future I will have to register on a new government anti-paedophile database, so that people can be reassured I am not likely to interfere with the children while I am there. Even parents who drive their neighbour's kids to school will have to register.

I can accept that people who work in schools should be CRB checked, but this scheme goes too far. The whole thing is a dramatic overreaction to the Ian Huntley case. Huntley was a one-off. It was probably never possible to prevent what happened to Holly and Jessica, and I doubt whether this scheme will give children 100 per cent protection. It seems to me to be Big Brother writ large, bureaucracy gone mad and a dramatic extension of the power of the state.

Presumably this scheme will also mean that politicians will have to sign up to it. Local councillors too. Well, I for one won't be signing up to it. I don't need to prove my innocence to anyone. Some of you might rejoice in the fact that it may mean I won't be able to impart my words of wisdom to school kids any longer. Fair enough. But what about the local historian, what about the local bank manager or careers adviser who decides that they are not going to subject themselves to this? In the end it is the kids themselves who will lose out.

But there is a far more important point to this, and it is about trust. What message does it send out to kids if none of us can be trusted to do the right thing, to behave responsibly when around children? What are they supposed to think? Surely we should be encouraging a culture of trust rather than appearing to want to destroy it. It is just this sort of measure which is eating away at the very foundations of our society, and it is why Anthony Seldon has written an excellent new book on the subject, which will be published this month.

AN EVENING WITH SIR LES AND DAME EDNA
THURSDAY 17 SEPTEMBER

Last night I went to see Sir Les Patterson and Dame Edna Everage at the Royal Albert Hall. What a disappointment. I last saw them on stage about fifteen years ago. I remember leaving the theatre with my cheekbones hurting because I had laughed so much. It was rather different last night. It started well, with Les Patterson delivering fifteen minutes of the kind of filth we have grown to love him for – but then it all went wrong. He proceeded to deliver a rambling monologue, accompanied by a full orchestra, about the story of 'Peter and the Shark'. It wasn't funny, it wasn't memorable. In fact, it wasn't anything. Few people could work out the point of it, apart from filling twenty-five minutes.

Then Dame Edna came on and did her usual stuff, all of which was amusing and well received. She then brought out this huge file and spent thirty minutes giving us a musical history of Australia, again accompanied by an orchestra and also a full choir. There were moments of humour, but for the most part it was dreadful. The only bits of light relief came when she missed her cues completely.

OK, I suppose the Albert Hall isn't the ideal venue for comedy, but I think most people just wanted pure, unadulterated Dame Edna and Sir Les. And what they got was something very different. I'd estimate that a sixth of the audience left before the end. I have to admit I was very tempted to join them.

BEHIND THE SCENES AT LBC
THURSDAY 24 SEPTEMBER

When you get a call saying 'Can you present our evening show tonight?' from a nationally renowned broadcaster, it kind of throws your schedule.

A few weeks ago I did a try-out for LBC to present a show with Yasmin Alibhai-Brown. We spent forty minutes in a tiny studio doing a mock show. To be honest I wasn't sure that it went very well. Anyway, something must have sparked.

I had an important meeting this afternoon to decide on which new titles to commission for Biteback Publishing, and I didn't get to LBC until just after 5.00, so there were only two hours to prepare. We decided on the subjects and then I had to record a couple of trailers and do a live taster on James Max's drivetime show. Having not eaten since breakfast, I popped out into Leicester Square to get something to keep my energy levels up – not good for the diet!

And before I knew it, it was time to go into the studio. One-and-a-half minutes to get my papers sorted out and off we went. No script. Talk about being thrown in at the deep end. We spent the first forty-five minutes discussing the Lib Dems and asking listeners: 'What's the point of the Lib Dems?' Mike Smithson from PoliticalBetting. com came on and was fairly scathing about the conference and Lib Dem strategy against the Tories, as was virtually every caller with the exception of the ever-loyal Mark Thompson who called in having just got home from Bournemouth. People really don't like Vince Cable's mansion tax.

In the second hour we did the regular Wednesday night panel with guests Will Straw, Baroness Ludford MEP and James Brokenshire MP. We had a lot of callers and talked about Baroness Scotland, Gordon Brown and climate change. That hour went by very quickly indeed.

In the final hour we talked about assisted suicide, following today's clarification of existing law by the DPP. I hope people felt I treated it with the sensitivity it merited. I interviewed Debbie Purdy, the MS sufferer who had forced the law to be clarified. She was a brilliant interviewee and rather inspirational, I felt. I then spoke with Nadine Dorries, who thinks the law should remain as it is. She pointed out the dangers of the state condoning assisted suicide. We had quite an abrasive interview although she remained very calm. I think she felt I had given her a bit of a hard ride.

The last part of the show was the stickiest as there was a problem with the phones, so I had to extemporise like mad. But I think I just about pulled it off.

And, before I knew it, it was all over. I have to say I thoroughly enjoyed it. To be honest I felt totally at home. A professional radio presenter friend of mine tweeted me afterwards and said: 'That was the most laidback debut I've ever heard. You're a natural.'

That meant a lot. But it was the text from the LBC MD which I was dreading. I needn't have. It ended with the words: 'Consider yourself part of the LBC team.'

Job done!

WHY I'D LIKE TO BE MP FOR BRACKNELL
TUESDAY 29 SEPTEMBER

Some of you may have seen on various sites over the last two days that I am in the final round of the parliamentary selection for Bracknell. I didn't want to say anything here until the shortlist was officially announced by the local party.

There are seven of us in the final of the open primary, which takes place on 17 October. The others are Rory Stewart, Margaret Doyle, Katy Lindsay, Philip Lee, Julia Manning and Ryan Robson.

As regular readers will know, I haven't applied for a seat for nearly two years. I decided that the launch of my new business, Total Politics, wasn't compatible with being a candidate due to time pressures, but that I would review the situation after eighteen months. Now that the business is up and running, and going well, I felt now was the time to plunge in.

To be honest, earlier this year I had almost decided to give up any parliamentary ambitions, but it was the expenses scandal which got me fired up again. And however much people tell me I would have more influence doing what I do now, rather than being an MP, I cannot agree with that. If you want to effect change you've got to get 'in the arena'. Douglas Carswell has proved that you really can achieve things as a backbencher.

At the end of August, CCHQ advertised eight constituencies for selection, including Bracknell. I didn't apply for any of the others.

I'm a great believer that you shouldn't have a scatter-gun approach and that you need an affinity with a constituency you wish to represent. I'm certainly not going to pretend I am a local expert yet, but it's an area I know quite well.

I was delighted to be shortlisted from more than 200 applicants, and last Friday the seven of us addressed the local Association's Executive. On Saturday, I joined some local activists to campaign in a council by-election, and over the next three weeks we are all going to be out and about in the constituency, meeting voters, learning, listening and encouraging people to attend the open primary on 17 October.

I think it is a great shortlist, packed with people who have real life experience outside politics. Having met the other six on Friday, I think any one of us would make a great MP for the area.

THE HATEFUL *DAILY MAIL*
THURSDAY 1 OCTOBER

Just by writing this blog post, I will probably damage my chances in Bracknell. Some will say, 'If you can't take the heat...' But I am damned if I am going to stay silent when I see a national newspaper indulge in a homophobic attack on me. A year ago, the Richard Kay column in the *Daily Mail* printed a fairly vile column about my civil partnership – full of innuendo and just plain nastiness. Today, the Ephraim Hardcastle column goes one better. Here's what they had to say about Bracknell...

> Overtly gay Tory blogger Iain Dale has reached the final stage of parliamentary selection for Bracknell, telling PinkNews: 'I hope any PinkNews readers who live in Bracknell will come to the open primary on 17 October to select their new candidate. You don't even have to be a Conservative to attend.'
>
> Isn't it charming how homosexuals rally like-minded chaps to their cause?

Overtly gay. Nice. Anyone who has ever met me will have a good laugh at that one. I wonder if Peter McKay, the editor of Ephraim Hardcastle, ever describes himself as 'overtly straight'. Just imagine if I was Jewish and the same words had been used:

Overtly Jewish Tory blogger Iain Dale ... Isn't it charming how Jews rally like-minded chaps to their cause?

Get my drift? And of course the pay-off line is something out of the Nick Griffin handbook. As Stephen Glenn points out, I do not rally anyone to my cause. I don't even ask for support – I just encourage people to attend. Normally I would think it's just not worth bothering with, and accept that in politics you have to take the rough with the smooth. But I'm afraid I have had it with the *Daily Mail* and their particular brand of hate. In my view, this breaches section 12 of the Press Complaints Commission code of conduct. So I have sent in a formal complaint. Perhaps readers might like to do the same.

> I wish to complain about an article about me in the Ephraim Hardcastle column of the *Daily Mail* today. I believe it breaches section 12 of the PCC code.
>
> The story refers to my application for the Conservative candidacy for the parliamentary seat of Bracknell and in my opinion breaches section 12 of the code of practice on discrimination, which states that 'i) The press must avoid prejudicial or pejorative reference to an individual's race, colour, religion, gender, sexual orientation or to any physical or mental illness or disability.'
>
> The paragraph in the Ephraim Hardcastle diary column rests specifically on the fact that I am gay. It describes me as 'overtly gay', which to anyone that knows me is ridiculous. It is designed to be pejorative. The article concludes: 'Isn't it charming how homosexuals rally like-minded chaps to their cause?' This is clearly pejorative, snide, unkind and sneering – and in breach of the code of practice. It is designed to hurt, and designed to make readers of the column think less of me as a political candidate. My sexual orientation is irrelevant to my decision to stand as a candidate in Bracknell.
>
> I hope you will investigate and ask the *Mail* to apologise.

I'm not holding my breath, but if I just ignore it, it will encourage the *Mail* to think that they can print it and get away with it. I really thought that we had got away from this sort of thing and it's very sad that we haven't. Attack me for my beliefs and actions, by all means, but for this? The only thing which will make the *Mail* sit up and think twice before it does it again is for there to be a backlash.

If by standing up to the *Daily Mail* and drawing attention to this issue, it hijacks me in Bracknell, then that will be a bitter blow to have to take, but if I sat back and just accepted this sort of thing, what sort of person would that make me? And, worst of all, if I did say nothing, it would just encourage them to do it again to someone else in the future. I simply cannot do that.

I will live in hope that the local media in Bracknell will approach the issue of a candidate's sexuality in a mature and adult way, and give it a massive shrug of the shoulders.

QUOTE OF THE DAY: STEPHEN NOLAN
SUNDAY 4 OCTOBER

> Something I never thought I'd ask on national radio...
> ...but what does Iain Dale taste like?
> – Stephen Nolan on Radio 5 Live

I'd better explain. Stephen was talking to a man who has a condition which means that he tastes words. When he heard my name, he said he tasted lamb. Sadly, I wasn't quick enough on the uptake to mention Norman...[†]

TELEGRAPH COLUMN: WHO'D WANT TO BE AN MP?
WEDNESDAY 14 OCTOBER

Admitting that you want to be an MP in the present climate marks you out as either a social misfit or someone suffering from delusions. I have almost got to the stage of feeling I should attend a meeting of Politicians Anonymous to bare my soul. My name is Iain and I want to be an MP. There. I've said it.

My family and friends think I am mad. Why would I want to subject myself to a life of constant public scrutiny over everything I say or do? Well, I take the view that if those of us who aspire to public service allow ourselves to be put off by the current breakdown in trust between voters and politicians, we are heading for a very slippery slope indeed.

---

† Iain's opponent in the 2005 general election, Norman Lamb.

The present situation over MPs' expenses is very serious, and the disconnect with voters is worse than it has ever been, but let's not kid ourselves that there was ever a golden age in relations between voters and MPs. Voters have always been suspicious of politicians and their motives, and that is a perfectly healthy state of affairs.

What has changed is that people now believe that all politicians have their snouts in the trough. We've gone back to the days of eighteenth-century rotten boroughs. All that's missing is Hogarth to capture the scene.

Last Saturday, I spent the morning talking to shoppers in Bracknell, where I am competing to become the Conservative candidate. Expenses came up in conversation several times, and I found myself having to try to prove that I wasn't an expenses criminal in the making. I showed my ten-point Pledge of Integrity, in which I promise, among other things, to live in the constituency, but not at the cost of the taxpayer. I promise not to claim for food or furniture. I promise not to promise what I cannot deliver and to tell constituents my real views at all times. And much more.

But the point is, I shouldn't have to spell this out. People should be able to take it for granted that their elected representatives will act with honour and candour at all times. Five years ago, as the Conservative candidate in North Norfolk, I issued a similar pledge as I could see which way the wind was blowing. This initiative did not go down well with several Tory MPs, nor with my fellow candidates. 'Imagine where this might lead,' said one. Indeed. Just imagine.

It is not often that I am five years ahead of my time, but now almost every Tory candidate is issuing a variation of the same pledge. Chloe Smith, the party's newest MP, made it a key feature of her by-election campaign in Norwich North.

Why do we have to issue a pledge of integrity? Because people think politicians don't know the difference between right and wrong. And nor does the system of scrutiny by which they are governed. It is tragi-comical to think that several MPs who have done nothing wrong will have to pay back money for offences they didn't commit, while a former Home Secretary who wrongly claimed £116,000 in second-home expenses gets off without paying anything. No wonder voters think politicians have the morals of an alley cat.

It would never occur to me to claim £400 a month for food I

would have consumed anyway, let alone to charge the taxpayer for a television or garden furniture. My mother said to me recently, 'Thank God you lost at the last election. You might have got caught up in all of this.' I'd like to think I wouldn't have, but when the party whips tell you to make sure you claim for this, that or the other and that you should view it as a salary increase, you can see why some members did what they did.

For the new intake of MPs who will be elected in 2010, things must be different. Their levels of personal morality and probity will have to be beyond reproach. It is down to them to make the change, ensure things are done differently and to rebuild trust with the electorate.

I can't pretend I am not daunted by the challenge that lies ahead. But if David Cameron and George Osborne can face the economic thunderclouds that stand in their way, the rest of the troops must look to their own challenges, in particular the way they conduct themselves in Parliament and their constituencies.

Cameron recognises that the world has changed: 24-hour news, blogs and Twitter mean that the old command-and-control methods deployed so successfully by Alastair Campbell and Peter Mandelson are now utterly redundant. In an age of increased individualism and easy communication, such attempts to control the message jar with the public's expectation of how politicians and political parties should operate. As effective as command-and-control may have been in the past, today it simply serves to weaken public confidence.

Nor will the next tranche of MPs be particularly easy to boss. The Tories know that after the next election there will be at least 150 new Members on their benches in Parliament and maybe many more. Half of the Conservative Parliamentary Party won't be used to the ways of the whips. Their test will be this: will they succumb to the old ways of doing things and behave like sheep, or will they act as a group and insist on doing things differently?

In the past, it was easy for whips to threaten an MP who was intending to rebel. 'We had thought of you as ministerial material, but if you vote this way, you'll end up on Standing Committee B on European Statutory Instruments.' That was usually enough to divert the cowering member into the correct division lobby. But not everyone goes into politics determined to climb what Disraeli called the 'greasy pole'. Not everyone wants to be Prime Minister.

Douglas Carswell, the Tory MP for Clacton, has proved that you really can change things, even from the backbenches. It was he who got rid of Speaker Martin. Many of his ideas, in particular about devolving power from central government, have now been adopted as Conservative Party policy, but he steadfastly resists the allure of front bench office.

Those bent on career advancement will always be vulnerable to control by the party machine. Yet the rise of political primaries in selecting parliamentary candidates, the public appetite for direct debates between party leaders and the emergence of political blogging all point to a new age of politics in which individualism and independence are rewarded. David Cameron has recognised the public's desire for change by promising to curb the powers of the whips, enhance the role of select committees and give more time to backbenchers in debates.

The rise of political blogs is provocative to a political hierarchy determined to exercise control. My own blog provides me with tremendous reach and arguably gives me influence far beyond that enjoyed by the majority of current backbenchers.

I understand, therefore, the pressures that will be put upon me to stop blogging if I am selected as a parliamentary candidate. But my blog's success lies, at least in part, in the fact that I am not restricted by the party line and that I can say what I think on given issues without reference to the desires of party whips. To misquote William Hague, I am in the Conservative Party, but not run by the Conservative Party.

Unsurprisingly, that's not something that sits easily with aspirations for advancement within the party. Indeed, at the most senior levels of government such individualism stands opposed to the principle of Cabinet collective responsibility.

If I am to look at myself in the mirror each morning, though, I must do it on my own terms, while recognising that there will always be limits beyond which I cannot venture. Can I successfully tread that tightrope? Time will tell. But if a party demonstrates a lack of trust in its own candidates' good judgement, the public will want to know why they should trust those candidates to exercise good judgement on their behalf.

REFLECTING ON BRACKNELL AND MOVING ON
SUNDAY 18 OCTOBER

First of all, I have been overwhelmed over the last twenty-four hours by all the emails, texts, tweets and blog comments people have left. Ninety-eight per cent of them have been very nice and almost made me feel like I am reading my own obituary!

Yesterday was a very good one for Bracknell Conservatives. At the end of the day the open primary has to be judged a success. I told the selection that I believe any one of the seven candidates would be a good MP and I stick by that. It was a very strong shortlist.

I arrived at the venue at 1 p.m. and dished out my leaflets on each chair in the auditorium. BBC South were there and wanted to do an interview, but I was reluctant to do one unless the others did too. At 1.30 the room started to fill up with constituents, many of whom were very keen to have a chat before the proceedings got underway. I wasn't sure if this was really allowed, so after a short time retreated to the rather spartan room which had been set aside for the candidates. Just before 2 p.m. we were called down to draw lots in front of the audience. I drew number seven, meaning that I was last on. I didn't know whether to be pleased or not. Would they all be so punch-drunk by the time I appeared that they would just want it over with? Or would it be an advantage? The others seemed to believe I had struck lucky. But it meant that I had three-and-a-half hours to sit there, with no contact with the outside world, until I was on.

Obviously we didn't listen to each other's performances, so I can't tell you exactly what was said. As we were waiting, most of the others were boning up on some local issue or other or rewriting bits of their speeches. I am afraid I take the view that if you don't know it by now, you never will. So I just sat there mentally rehearsing a few lines in my head. Some went into a separate room to practise their speeches out loud. I kept thinking, 'Should I be doing this too?' But in the end, you have to do it your way.

We all had to do a three-minute introduction, then answer questions for twenty minutes and then do a three-minute wind-up. The questions had all been submitted in advance and were put to each candidate. There were no spontaneous questions from the floor.

Eventually, at about 5.20 p.m., my turn came. I was really pleased with my opening statement. I decided to address the issue of trust and the reason we were all there. I was told afterwards that I was the only one who had addressed the expenses issue head-on. Was this a mistake? Surely not.

We then moved on to questions. I know at the executive round that I was far too loquacious in my answers so I was determined to be more succinct. We covered a huge range of issues including nuclear power, working with the local councils, Europe, Heathrow, how we would split our time between Westminster and the constituency, Trident, the euro, our personal priorities and the NHS. I am sure there were others which I can't recall now.

I got a couple of rounds of applause when I mentioned I was in favour of an English Parliament and against the government's plans for a so-called paedophile register, and I also made them laugh a few times.

I was really pleased at how the question session went and felt that I had given very robust and honest answers to every question. Perhaps things were going too well...

I then made a mistake. I didn't use my full three minutes at the end. I thought that the audience had probably had enough, as they had been sitting there for more than four hours. So I reiterated the point that it was up to a new MP to restore trust and expressed the hope that they would allow me to be given the chance to do that. I was told afterwards that several people had voiced the opinion that I should have used the full three minutes. But, apart from that, I genuinely think that I performed well.

We then trooped off back to the candidates' room to await the verdict. Time after time, the Association chairman, Lesley Philpot, knocked on the door to deliver the terrible news to one of the candidates.

I knew my best chance was to win on the first or second ballot. When it went to four ballots and it was down to Rory Stewart, Phillip Lee and myself, I had an inkling that the game was up. Why? Because I reckon I am a bit of a Marmite candidate. You either love me or you hate me. I don't do well on second preferences! I always knew that when the supporters of the other candidates had to vote again, I might not do as well. We weren't told the figures, but I wouldn't be at all surprised if I had been ahead on round one or two, but gradually slipped back. I guess I'll never know.

So when Lesley came into the room for the final time and told me I was out, I wasn't in the least surprised. I'm normally quite emotional in these circumstances, but on this occasion remained completely calm. One or two of the other candidates were clearly devastated. For some reason I wasn't – not because I didn't care, or didn't want it badly enough: I did. But somehow I just knew Phillip was destined to get it. I had told quite a few people right from the start that if I didn't win, I hoped he would, and I genuinely meant it. I didn't know him well, but I knew enough to believe he'd be a good choice. So when Lesley came back and told him he had won I was delighted to shake his hand and wish him well. Rory took it very well. He had clearly made a huge impression and I have no doubt he will soon be selected elsewhere – maybe Penrith next weekend.

There have been a lot of comments about whether open primaries are working. Personally, I have absolutely no complaints about the system used in this selection. It was conducted fairly and transparently. The Association Agent, Mary Ballin, did a terrific job and I'd like to thank all the members and councillors I have met over the last three weeks for their unfailing courtesy and helpfulness.

My only doubt about the whole process would be the fact that there were seven of us in the final. It was too many and made the event far too long-winded. It would be better in future to allow Associations to reduce the shortlist of six to four at an executive round. I know this issue has caused some angst in other constituencies.

So what now? Obviously I wanted to win Bracknell – I think I made that fairly clear. But anyone who expects to apply for one seat and then win it is either delusional or very lucky. Michael Howard applied for forty-four before he got one. Bracknell was the first seat I had applied for in two years.

Will I apply for others, having fallen at this hurdle? You bet I will.

I didn't apply for Devizes, Gosport, Esher or Central Suffolk as the deadline was last Monday and I wanted to concentrate on Bracknell, but I'll certainly now apply for other seats as they become available. But I won't use a scatter-gun approach and apply for everything. It has to be the right constituency.

ALBUM REVIEW: MANGO GROOVE – *BANG THE DRUM*
SUNDAY 1 NOVEMBER

You know the feeling. You've waited years for one of your favourite bands to release a new album, and then it arrives in the post. That special tingle down your spine. The sense of anticipation. The fear in the back of your mind that you are going to be disappointed. The exhilaration of playing the first track and realising it's as good as you hoped it would be. All of that happened to me yesterday when I received a copy of *Bang the Drum*, the first all-new Mango Groove album in fourteen years. But this was no ordinary copy – it was a signed copy sent to me personally by Claire Johnston, the group's lead singer, who I have developed an email friendship with ever since I first wrote about my love for her band on the blog last year.

Mango Groove, for those who don't know, are one of South Africa's most successful bands. They play a crossover of African pop, big band and pennywhistle music.

This album is vintage Mango Groove and they have lost nothing of their original style over the years. The whole album is a happy-go-lucky mix of boppable, danceable melodies sprinkled with the odd ballad. Claire Johnston has done a couple of promo interviews about the band's comeback and the new album, which are eminently watchable for the way in which she and other band members switch between English and Afrikaans at the flick of a switch in mid-sentence. Bizarrely, you can understand most of what they say even when they speak in Afrikaans.

There are very few bands I would pay a lot of money to see, but Mango Groove is one of them. I first heard their music in a coffee bar in St Martin's Lane in the mid-1990s and I have been captivated ever since. I've never been to South Africa, but if they plan a concert tour next year, I shall be off there like a shot.

WE MUSTN'T BE AFRAID OF RISK
SATURDAY 7 NOVEMBER

If you were a teacher, would you seriously think about taking pupils on a school trip? With all the 'elf and safety' provisions that now exist you'd have to be either brave or stupid to take kids on the kind of foreign trips and geography field trips I went on in the 1970s.

Surely part of growing up is forming the ability to make your own risk assessment. I know I did that most weeks of my childhood, growing up on a farm. You can never protect children from all danger. The trouble is that whenever there is an isolated incident of a child being hurt, or even killed, the papers go mad and demand immediate action from lawmakers in order to ensure that 'it can't happen again'. The politicians have to be seen to be doing something and acting quickly. They invariably overreact and go too far in creating new laws, which are then gold-plated by overzealous civil servants. That's the ridiculous system we have collectively created and now tolerate.

I feel really strongly about this for this reason: school trips are a fantastic thing. They allow children to broaden their horizons, experience new things and to learn things they could never hope to learn in a classroom.

Allow me to personalise it. In the late 1970s, I went on two school exchange visits to Germany. I was crap at German before this, but due to the two trips I came to excel in the subject and went on to do a degree in it. I went to UEA in Norwich to do my degree, where I became involved in active politics. I know I wouldn't be where I am today without having gone on those two school trips. So thank you, David Lewis. Thank you for having the courage to take sixty unruly kids on a ferry to the Hook of Holland, then on a train to Cologne, and then on another train to Bad Wildungen.

I know many school exchanges still take place. But I am damn sure there are many that don't. After all, what if the foreign partner parents are paedophiles? No CRB checks in Germany, you know.

I wonder whether Mr Lewis would have taken us to Germany under the current system. Knowing him, he probably would. But I know there are many others who would think the risk of being sued was just not worth the candle.

If I were ever to become an MP I would make it my business to try to start dismantling this system of regulation which has led to us becoming a totally risk-averse society. And then maybe thousands of kids can enjoy the same kind of opportunities I had.

YOUR IDEAL POLITICAL DINNER PARTY

I was talking to someone the other day about the demise of the dinner party. And it set me thinking. If I held a dinner party for twelve people in politics who I know, who would I invite to guarantee the sparkiest conversation? Anyway, this is the list I came up with...

Christine Hamilton
Yasmin Alibhai-Brown
Gyles Brandreth
Professor Peter Hennessy
Jeremy Paxman
Michael Cockerell
Ann Widdecombe
Emily Maitlis
Shirley Williams
Tony Benn
Professor Mary Beard

The thing is, would I get a word in edgeways? Probably not, but for once in my life I think I would enjoy just listening!

LETTER TO MY SIXTEEN-YEAR-OLD SELF
SATURDAY 19 DECEMBER

Dear Iain,

This could turn into a 100-page epistle, if I am not careful. As you know, you have had a perfect childhood – brought up by two loving parents in a wonderful rural environment. I know you know how lucky you have been. Life isn't always this perfect, as you are about to find out, as you enter adulthood.

My first bit of advice will not come as a surprise. You need to develop a harder edge. You can't be liked by everyone, no matter how hard you try. There are people out there who will want to do you down and slag you off. You cannot win everyone over and there's no point in trying. You know that throughout your school days you have been bullied by various people and yet you've never stood up to them. Now's the time to start. Do it once and it becomes very easy the next time. You know you give the impression of being an extrovert, the life and soul of the party and willing to speak up in a meeting. Yet you and I both know that you have an innate shyness which you constantly seek to repress. Few people know the real you. Keep it that way. Those who want to dig beneath the surface will do so. Those who are only interested in you for what they can get out of you won't bother. There will come a time when everyone seems to want to know you. To want a bit of you. Beware of those people. They're easy to spot. They're the ones who look over your shoulder at a party to see if there's anyone more important there. What I am saying is that you should be very careful of loving the spotlight a little too much. Fight your natural disposition for your head to get that little bit too big. It's a fight you will probably never win, though!

My second piece of advice is about your future career. You and I both know that you knew you didn't want to be a farmer from about the age of eight, even though everyone in your wider family expects you to take over the farm. We also know how difficult it has been to carry on the pretence that you would be going to agricultural college. But getting ungraded in Physics O Level and grade D in Biology was a pretty good indication to everyone that this is not a direction in which you are headed. You feel you are letting your parents down, but you're not. They want what's best for you and will support you in whatever you do. You know that deep down. At the moment, because you've suddenly found out that German is the only subject you excel at, you intend to be a German teacher. Fine, you think that now, but don't put all your eggs in that basket. Your career is likely to take a very different direction. You recently joined the Liberal Party and have discovered an interest in politics. If I told you now that Margaret Thatcher would have a huge influence on your future life and that you would write books about her, you'd probably laugh.

Throughout your career you'll come across people you feel inferior to or that in some way they are better than you. You will envy the self-assurance and confidence of those who have been to public school and Oxbridge. Fight it. You know deep down they are no better than you, but it is true that you will always have to fight that bit harder than they do to get where you want to be.

You know as well as I do that you are, and will be, under tremendous pressure to conform – not just to what is expected of you career-wise, but also in your personal life. People will expect you to get a girlfriend – indeed, a succession of them – and get married and live happily ever after. Just like most of your friends and cousins (except most of them end up divorced!). Life ain't like that, as you are already coming to realise. You don't have to pretend to me. I know the inner feelings you've had since the age of eight, and so do you. You know that society in 1978 demands you should feel ashamed. But you don't. And you're right not to. So far so good.

The Britain of 2010 is very different from that of 1978. You won't believe me now, but one day you will somehow summon up the courage to be open about exactly who – and what – you are. The path won't be smooth and one or two people will be hurt along the way, and it may well mean that you don't achieve what you want to in your career, but you will have no regrets. No one you care about will shun you, you just need the courage to say 'Accept me for who I am or do the other thing.'

You're scared. That's natural. You won't make the first move. You carry on the pretence for some time, and break a number of female hearts along the way. You're not playing them along – you genuinely care about them, but deep down you know that there's something not quite right, that you need more. So you get to a certain stage and won't go further. One day – and it's some time off – everything will fall into place. I promise you that one day you'll find what you're looking for. And you'll be happy.

You have a wonderful life to look forward to, one which most people would envy. It's not all smooth sailing – it would be boring if it was, wouldn't it? But if it's any consolation, you'd probably settle for it now.

Bonne chance,

Iain

P.S. And if you ever think about applying to be Conservative candidate for North Norfolk: Don't.

2010

THAT EFFING GORDON BROWN
WEDNESDAY 6 JANUARY

My sister rang this evening to tell me about an 82-year-old auntie of a friend of hers. She sadly had a stroke on Boxing Day and was admitted to hospital in Brighton. The doctors suspected she might have dementia so they embarked on a series of tests. Eventually, the doctor turned to Auntie and asked her who the Prime Minister is, to which her response was 'that fucking bastard Gordon Brown'!

True story. Honest.

IAIN 1 YASMIN 1
SUNDAY 17 JANUARY

I know how you all love it when I mention Yasmin Alibhai-Brown, so here goes. On the BBC News channel paper review last night she talked about Jenni Russell's article in the *Sunday Times* on class. Here's how the exchange went...

> YAB: We had a funny kind of statement from the Communities minister (John Denham) that race didn't matter but class did...
> Iain: Well that puts you out of a job then...

Any smugness I might have been feeling evaporated a minute later when she started talking about the 'privileged few in the Tory Party – people like him...' as she gestured to me. Unfortunately, before I could reply Clive Myrie called time.

Score draw!

WHEN MO MOWLAM GRABBED MY BUM
THURSDAY 21 JANUARY

I wonder if the new drama about Mo Mowlam will feature the touching photo she had taken with me and my partner at the Labour conference in Brighton in 2000. She stood in between us and placed her right hand firmly on my right buttock and her left hand on John's left buttock. She then proceeded to give each of us a butt-cheek massage while a photographer took the pictures.

Or maybe they will include the moment when she walked out of Politico's, paused in the doorway, burped and then farted.

I truly think her brain tumour had eaten away at that part of the brain which controls embarrassment thresholds.

SAM GYIMAH WINS EAST SURREY
SATURDAY 13 FEBRUARY

Sam Gyimah won the East Surrey selection today. I think it went to four or five ballots. I am afraid I totally underperformed in my speech, although I thought the questions went well. Sam is a fantastic guy who will be a superb parliamentarian. I hope this puts to bed any remaining suspicion that local Conservative parties are racist. He won it on merit. I think that's curtains for me now in elected politics.

A DAY AT AUSCHWITZ-BIRKENAU
WEDNESDAY 3 MARCH

Back in 1984, I visited Dachau. I took my mother and sister. And it was true what they said: the birds really didn't sing there. It was a profoundly moving experience. My mother couldn't wait to leave and hated it. In 1990, just after the reunification of Germany, I drove to Buchenwald in the former East Germany. It was a very different experience. I was on my own and wasn't sure what to expect. While Dachau had been a bit of a tourist trap, with many of the buildings and ovens rebuilt, Buchenwald was more of a clearing in a forest. There was indeed a building with an exhibition, but the only sign of what had once been there were the foundations of each of the huts. I remember seeing a commemorative stone to the British men who had died there and finding it all very emotional. Walking around on my own I found myself trying to imagine what had occurred there a mere fifty years previously.

My first knowledge of anything to do with the Holocaust came back in 1978 when I watched an American TV mini-series called *Holocaust*. It followed the travails of various members of the Weiss family. I remember it being very schmaltzy, but it sparked a desire in me to learn more about what happened during those terrible years. I make no pretence of being an expert, but I have read reasonably widely on the subject. I even published a Holocaust memoir called *The Children's House of Belsen*.

So when I got an invitation from the Holocaust Educational Trust to accompany them on a student trip to Auschwitz I accepted with thanks. They receive government funding to take British sixth-formers to Auschwitz to educate them about what happened. On this trip they took 220 students from Norfolk. I assume they invited me because of my *Eastern Daily Press* column, and they invited Chloe Smith to go too.

So we all arrived at Stansted Airport this morning at 5 a.m. for the flight to Krakow a couple of hours later. We immediately headed to the local Jewish cemetery in Auschwitz, or Oswiecim, as it is called in Polish. It's very unkempt. Why? Because there is not a single Jew left here. Before the war, 58 per cent of the town's population was Jewish. A few remained after the war. But, by 2000, only one Jew remained, and in that year he died. Why did he stay? As an act of defiance? No one really knows, but Shimon Kruger's grave is one which all visitors pay their respects to.

At midday we arrived at Auschwitz 1 and were immediately greeted by the famous 'Arbeit Macht Frei' sign. We spent a couple of hours touring the place, looking at the different barracks, learning about what exactly went on there and having the opportunity to view many of the belongings left behind by those who were murdered. Perhaps the most disturbing point was when we were led into the underground gas chamber and looked up at the holes in the ceiling where the Zyklon B was poured in. Standing on the spot where thousands of innocent people breathed their last breath took some contemplation. But frankly, there was little time to take it in as there were so many other people there that we had to move on far too quickly. Indeed, the proximity of housing, shops, car

parks and traffic made it all very difficult to really 'get' the atmosphere of the place. We were all provided with headphones to listen
to the guide. To me it seemed less like a concentration camp than a
theme park.

Having become quite emotional at Dachau and Buchenwald, I
fully expected to repeat the experience here. But I didn't. Was it the
fact that modern-day life was intruding, or is it that I am twenty
years older and harder in outlook? I'd like to think it is the former,
as one or two others said they felt the same.

At 2.30 we moved onto Auschwitz-Birkenau, which is where
the majority of the killings happened. I had imagined it to be
in the middle of nowhere, with a long train track leading up to it.
But again, modern housing has intruded. Yes, the famous guard
tower is still there, and we were able to view the whole site from
it. But again, other groups wanted to have a look too, so we were
shushed out of the guard tower after what seemed like only a few
seconds. Viewing the wooden barracks was quite harrowing. It was
almost impossible to imagine how 1,000 or more people lived in
such surroundings, especially in winter. It came as little surprise to
learn that inmates had a life expectancy of only a couple of months.
We moved on to see the point where new arrivals disembarked the
trains, and then ended up viewing the ruins of the ovens and gas
chambers which saw more than 1 million people meet their deaths.

One thing I had been warned about was that if we encountered
Israelis during the visit, we shouldn't be shocked at their behaviour.
But I was. They went around brandishing Israeli flags and chanting
and cheering, almost as if they were trying to say, 'Look, we're still
here.' It was most odd. We all trudged round maintaining a respectful silence, but the Israelis approached it all in a very different way.
It made me feel very uncomfortable.

Throughout all of this we enjoyed the services of a Polish guide,
and a representative from the HET put everything in context for the
students from Norfolk. At the end, a rabbi, who had accompanied
us from London, conducted a short commemorative service, which
included five readings from the students. We were all then invited
to light a candle and place it on the railway track.

The HET clearly does an excellent job. It gets £1.5 million from
the government to fund trips like this, and they clearly have a deep
effect on the students. As we went round the camp it was great to
listen in on the conversations they were having about the issues

raised. I remember especially one seventeen-year-old speculating what he would have done if he had been a German soldier operating in one of the camps. He had clearly given it a great deal of thought.

My only complaint, and it is more of a suggestion than complaint I suppose, is that I would like to have heard more about the non-Jewish victims of the Holocaust. The fact that the disabled, trade unionists, homosexuals and gypsies were also victims in their hundreds of thousands rated hardly a mention. Of course everyone knows that the overwhelming majority of those killed in the Holocaust were Jewish (90 per cent of those killed at Auschwitz were Jews), but that shouldn't hide the fact that thousands of others were killed in Auschwitz and the other extermination camps. I raised this with one of the HET people, who maintained that the word 'Holocaust' referred exclusively to Jewish victims. I was surprised at this interpretation, as it has certainly never been mine. If you look up the word 'Holocaust' on Wikipedia you can interpret it both ways. And I would like to think that if taxpayers' money is being used to fund these trips (something I agree with), they could be rather more all-encompassing and make more of an effort to explain why other minorities were also targeted by the Nazis. But perhaps that is a minor quibble compared to the undoubted excellence of the service provided by the HET. I hope this is taken as constructive criticism, as it is meant to be.

It was a very tiring day for everyone, and one which ended with a range of emotions coming to the fore. Horror about what had happened only seventy years ago on the very ground we had trodden; sadness at how human beings could ever inflict such suffering; and a slight sense of disappointment that neither I nor, from what I could see, any of my travelling companions was openly emotionally affected by what we saw.

Eyes didn't moisten, no tears were shed. I still find that hard to explain.

A TRIBUTE TO MICHAEL FOOT

Michael Foot has died at the ripe old age of ninety-six. Whatever one's politics, he was a true political great. The first time I ever really heard of him was when my grandmother gave me some well-meant political advice when I was about thirteen years old. She told me, 'Just remember, all Labour governments spend more than they can afford, and Michael Foot's a Communist.' Well, she was half right.

A few years later, during the 1983 election, I and a few Conservative student friends went along to St Andrew's Hall to hear Michael Foot rally the Labour troops. It was packed out, with a good 1,500–2,000 people there. I played an inadvertent part in helping in him make a very good speech when I decided to indulge in a little light heckling. He loved it and sprang to life. I seem to recall he said something about Norman Tebbit, I shouted out something and off he went. It was done in very good humour, which is why we were allowed to escape the meeting without being lynched!

He also used to come to book launches at Politico's and would sit and hold court to an admiring coterie. I was privileged to publish a book of Michael Foot's essays to coincide with his ninetieth birthday and I also recorded an hour-long interview with him which was then released on CD. By that stage he tired very easily, and we had to record the interview over a three-hour period to allow him to have some rest. I recently donated several hundred copies of the CD to *Tribune* magazine. He was probably *Tribune*'s most famous editor and I thought they could make better use of them than I could.

There's no doubt that Michael Foot, over a fifty-year period, had a huge effect on the Labour Party and socialist political thought. I may not have agreed with him on much, if anything, but no one can deny his lasting political and literary influence. He may have been a disastrous leader of the Labour Party, but he was a man of principle and conviction. I don't have to agree with him on much to admit that politics needs more like him.

IN PRAISE OF VODAFONE
FRIDAY 5 MARCH

Last month my mobile phone bill was £2,500, and it turned out the month before's was even more. I tweeted about it and was contacted by Vodafone's web relations team. To cut a long story short, they have spent the last month trying to get to the bottom of it. No one is totally sure, but it appears that UberTwitter caused it.

Last night I had a phone call from Vodafone to tell me that they have waived the £5,400 charges. You can imagine the sigh of relief!

I'm the first one to jump on big companies when I have a bad customer service experience, so let me congratulate Vodafone's web relations team for the way they have handled this. They have phoned me each week to let me know they hadn't forgotten, and that they were still investigating.

I draw two lessons from this. Honesty is always the best policy in these situations, and if you are polite and non-aggressive, a positive outcome is more likely.

And while we were at it they reckoned I was on the wrong tariff and are changing me to a better one for the same cost.

Result! Thank you, Vodafone.

THE POPE'S APOLOGY ISN'T ENOUGH
SUNDAY 21 MARCH

The news that Pope Benedict has written a letter to Cardinal Sean Brady apologising for the Catholic Church's role in the Irish child abuse scandal is, of course, a welcome development. But it does not go far enough. The Pope makes no apology for the cover up, and he seems quite content for those who perpetrated these terrible misdemeanours to remain in office.

No one in the Irish Catholic Church seems to be willing to stand up and accept culpability for what went on. Wouldn't it be nice for Cardinal Brady to accept that someone's head has to roll, and it should be his? Instead, he stands by while men of the cloth, under his rule, give interviews to radio stations saying that they would not report paedophiles to the police because of the 'need for confidentiality'.

I spoke about this on last night's *Stephen Nolan Show*. Stephen had interviewed a man called Monsignor Maurice Dooley on his show the night before. I was listening at the time and felt almost physically sick at what I was hearing. He made clear that his church's rules were more important than the physical safety of vulnerable children. Would he report a paedophile priest who he knew was abusing kids? No, he said, he most certainly would not.

And this 'man of God' has no doubt preached his sermon today, somewhere in Ireland. The Catholic Church has 'distanced itself' from Monsignor Dooley. Not sacked him. They have distanced themselves. And it shows that the Catholic Church of Ireland has a long way to go before a line can be drawn under this terrible period in its history.

HANGING UP
MONDAY 22 MARCH

I don't normally go on BBC Radio London, and my experience just now reminds me why.

I've always been taught that, as a radio presenter, if a guest hangs up on you it reflects very badly on you. You've clearly failed to control the interview.

I was invited on to Eddy Nestor's programme to talk about the BA strike and strikes in general. I was told it would be just after 11.30 p.m. By 11.55 p.m., I had been kept hanging on for twenty minutes and had just been told there would be another guest. Normally if I do an interview I like to know who I am going to be on with so at least I can check their backgrounds if I have never heard of them.

Anyway, Mr Nestor proceed to speak to the other chap (I never did get his name), who was a trade union academic and had written two books on strike law. Just before he came to me Nestor explained that he only really understood about strikes when he went to Nottinghamshire during the miners' strike. When he came to me he immediately displayed antagonism and it seemed to me he was itching for a fight. He even got my name wrong and kept calling me Lain (as in Lane), but I've been called worse!

In situations where the interviewer gives the appearance of being antagonistic I usually reckon that attack is the best form of defence, so I outlined the BA position, calmly but firmly. Nestor proceeded to assert that the union had been the voice of sweet reason and that the employers were looking for a war. That, I said, was the union's position – it was they who were talking in a warlike manner. And it then went on like this...

EN: You're being very antagonistic.
ID: No, I think you are.
EN: Well, if you want to take me on, we can go there [with a sneer in his voice].

ID: When you have a guest on your programme, you might at least treat them with some respect.

EN: It's you who's not showing me respect.

ID: We can end it here if you like.

EN: OK...

ID: Bye then.

Now I can accept that might not show me in a good light either, but when you go on a late-night programme and you're not even being paid for it, the least you expect is that the interviewer show you a little bit of respect. He did not, and was clearly not used to someone standing up to him. Stephen Nolan he ain't.

Just because you host a radio show, it does not give you the right to treat guests who you disagree with, with contempt.

THINGS YOU LEARN FROM *PROSPECT*: NO. 94
FRIDAY 26 MARCH

It's amazing the things you learn from *Prospect* magazine. In a recent issue, their 'In Fact' section informs us:

> The entrance of the vagina has specialised nerve endings called Merkel receptors.

There has to be a joke there somewhere.

THE PERILS OF SAYING SOMETHING NICE
FRIDAY 2 APRIL

Last night I was in Oakham, Rutland to chair an election hustings organised by the Federation of Small Businesses, and a very lively event it was too. The panel consisted of local MP Alan Duncan, his Labour and Lib Dem opponents and two local businesspeople. The evening started on a controversial note when the UKIP candidate complained he had not been invited onto the panel. As soon as he opened his mouth, it became clear why. If I had allowed him on he would have sent the 100-strong audience to sleep within minutes.

Anyway, that's not the point of this post. The point is this. After the evening had ended, I tweeted that I had found the Lib Dem candidate, Grahame Hudson, very impressive but the Labour candidate less so. In fact, not at all. Immediately, I was bombarded by Lib Dems who presumed that I would therefore support Hudson over Alan Duncan (as if) and by one or two Conservatives who felt it was terrible of me to say anything nice about a political opponent.

Doesn't this just illustrate what's wrong with politics? In the hustings, both Alan and Grahame often agreed with each other. Indeed, to be fair the Labour guy, John Morgan, agreed with the other two very occasionally.

And there's nothing wrong with that. It doesn't mean anyone's about to defect. It doesn't mean you're betraying your own party when you find common cause with others. Just because you can admit to finding an opponent impressive, does not mean you are encouraging others to vote for them.

TWENTY PIECES OF ADVICE TO ELECTION CANDIDATES

I've just been re-reading my blog posts from the last election campaign in 2005. The experience brought back lots of memories – not all of them bad! But it did make me think about the pitfalls of being a candidate and how to get through an election campaign intact. For what it's worth, here's my advice to first-time candidates...

1. You can't do everything yourself. Let others take the strain. You are the leader of the campaign. Act like it.
2. Keep your cool. There will be moments in the campaign when you want to scream your head off. Resist the temptation. Count to ten. Then count to twenty.
3. Your campaign workers are volunteers. They don't have to turn out to help you. They do it because they want to. Motivate them. Treat them well.
4. Make sure all your literature is proofread. Three times. And not by you.
5. If you have a campaign blog, never write a spontaneous blog post. Always run it by someone else first. Be incredibly careful what you tweet. Imagine your name in bold print in the

Daily Mirror. If you hesitate before pressing SEND, it probably means you shouldn't.

6. Make sure you keep to your normal sleep patterns. You may think you are Superman/Superwoman, but you're not. You need your sleep. Make sure you get it.

7. You don't need to hold a long campaign meeting every morning. Three times a week is usually enough. Make sure that the only people who attend are those who really should. Restrict meetings to half an hour.

8. Posters do not gain extra votes. But they make your local party feel good and give your campaign the appearance of momentum. Do not put them up too early. And do not put them up all at once. And if they get ripped down, make sure your campaign team has a strategy for replacing them within twenty-four hours.

9. Personalise your 'Sorry You Were Out' cards. Include your ten campaign pledges on them. And include an apparently handwritten message and signature.

10. Do not drive anywhere yourself. Especially do not drive your campaign vehicle. Appoint a PA who will drive you everywhere and cater for your every whim. Tell them to make sure you eat properly, and regularly. McCoys, Coke and Mars bars do not a healthy diet make.

11. If Party HQ offer you the chance of a visit from a politician whom even you have barely heard of, turn them down. Even if you have heard of them, consider turning them down. Visits from national politicians use up too many resources and rarely attract a single extra vote.

12. Don't canvas before 10 a.m. or after 8.30 p.m. It looks desperate and annoys people. And be very careful about canvassing on Sundays. People don't like it. Use Sundays to catch up on deliveries in areas with no deliverers.

13. Resist the temptation to strangle the next person who asks, 'How's it going?' or, 'Are you going to win?' They're only being polite.

14. If you're in a high-profile marginal seat which the media find interesting, avoid spending half your day giving them interviews. Your only media focus is local. Ignore Michael Crick. He's not there to help you.

15. Avoid the natural desire to believe what voters tell you on the

doorstep. Most of them will tell you what you want to hear in order to get you off the doorstep. If they say 'I'll see how I feel on the day' you can safely put them down as a Liberal Democrat.

16. Your 'Get out the Vote' operation is more important than anything else you do during the campaign. Satisfy yourself that your agent and campaign managers have it in hand and they know what they are doing.

17. Ignore those who tell you not to appear at your count until it is well underway. It's your moment. Relish it. Prepare your speech. If you lose unexpectedly, you will be remembered for how you react. Act graciously towards your opponents during the counting and in your speech.

18. If you lose, you will be tempted to blame someone. Your party leader. Your local party. Anyone but yourself. Don't. Whatever your personal thoughts, no one likes a bad loser. Be dignified and take it on the chin.

19. If you win, hubris may take over. It really wasn't all down to you, you know. And make sure others know you know that.

20. Make sure you write a personal thank-you letter – and I mean write, not type – to all those who helped on your campaign. Do it within a week of polling day. You really could not have done it without them.

WOULD YOU LIKE A FREE SPERM KEYRING?
SATURDAY 3 APRIL

A friend of ours has come to stay the weekend, and has very thoughtfully brought us a gift. She works for the Learning and Skills Council, helping youngsters get into employment. The government is now apparently encouraging the LSC to get into the business of sex education and giving out free condoms. Nothing wrong with that. Indeed, it may be quite a good idea. Part of the sex education is to educate young men that there are different sizes of condom and that they should make sure they buy the right size in order to avoid unfortunate splits. They are taught that condoms come in extra large, large, medium and, er, 'trim' sizes! And to aid them, they are given a piece of card called 'Size and Shape'. This is to inform them that it's not length that matters but, er, girth. (Please note how I am trying to keep this tasteful.) However, they are then told not to put their, ahem, 'appendages' through the holes in case they get paper cuts! You really couldn't make this up.

I'm assuming the LSC doesn't pay anything for these items, as they are plastered with adverts for Pasante condoms – from 'trim' to king-size.

As well as these handy cards, participants are also given a keyring ... with a plastic sperm hanging off the end. Apparently they get a free keyring if they agree to have a chlamydia test... I'd be intrigued to find out how much these keyrings are costing the LSC – or should I say the taxpayer. They contain no message and I cannot think what purpose they serve.

WHY I HAVE TO DISAGREE WITH CHRIS GRAYLING

Fasten your seatbelts. Just before I went down to the studio to talk about Labour posters on the *Stephen Nolan Show*, I saw the breaking story about Chris Grayling. Tomorrow's *Observer* has a recording of him saying that he felt that the rights of bed-and-breakfast owners to refuse admission to gay couples should be respected. He differentiated between B&Bs and hotels, which he thought had no right 'in this day and age' to refuse admission to gay couples. It turns out that he voted for the legislation in 2007 which prohibits B&B owners from doing this, and he says he would not wish to turn the clock back.

I fundamentally disagree with him on the main issue. This is not about property rights. If you open your house to paying guests, it is no longer just your house. You are running a business, just the same as anyone else, and you should be subject to the same laws as anyone else. If you do not wish gay people, black people, Jews or anyone else in your house, don't open it to the public. Simple as that. No one would accept a shop owner refusing to serve a particular type of person, would they?

We all know the reaction of any right-thinking person to any B&B owner who refused an Asian couple accommodation, so I see no reason why it should be different just because of your sexuality. If my partner and I booked into a B&B and were refused at the door we'd probably feel an inch tall. So what, some may say.

Get over it. I disagree. Discrimination is wrong in whatever form it takes. Period.

So on the radio I made clear my disagreement with Grayling. Of course, that wasn't good enough for some. Should he apologise, I was asked? I said that he should only apologise if he meant it. Too often we demand apologies out of political correctness. My opponent in the discussion was ex-*Mirror* editor David Banks, who is normally quite pleasant. This time he went totally over the top and accused the Tories of wanting to go back to sexual apartheid and apartheid by race. That rather lost him the argument.

The trouble is, this will feed those like Ben Bradshaw and Chris Bryant who pick up on any apparently anti-gay comment in the Conservative Party as a sign that the party as a whole hasn't changed and would secretly like to bring back Section 28. It's rubbish of course. I know it, you know it, they know it, but it suits their agenda within the so-called gay community to feed fears and worries. It's what they do best. And of course they have already been at it tonight.

Do I believe Chris Grayling is homophobic? No, I do not. Do I believe that his views, as expressed, will be damaging. Yes, I do. He has just issued the following statement:

> Any suggestion that I am against gay rights is wholly wrong – it is a matter of record that I voted for civil partnerships. I also voted in favour of the legislation that prohibited bed-and-breakfast owners from discriminating against gay people. However, this is a difficult area and on Wednesday I made comments which reflected my view that we must be sensitive to the genuinely held principles of faith groups in this country. But the law is now clear on this issue, I am happy with it and would not wish to see it changed.

All fine words, but I have to say I still disagree. I do not think we must be sensitive to faith groups who promote discrimination and bigotry. We wouldn't be sensitive to groups who provoke racial discrimination, so why should we be sensitive to those who appear to condone sexual discrimination? As someone just said on my Facebook thread...

> I know why he said it – Christian rights etc. And I don't suppose I'd want to stay at their B&B but you can't back gay civil partnerships

with tax credits and then let those same gay couples be refused a roof over their head for the night cos someone doesn't like what they do in bed. B&Bs are not churches. They are a business 'service'.

Exactly. However, let's not go overboard about this. Grayling voted for the current position and said on the recording, I believe, that he is content with it and would not change it. He expressed a personal opinion, which, however much I might disagree with it, he has every right to do. But he is shadow Home Secretary and will have to defend himself. Because I am afraid I can't.

AND SO IT BEGINS...
MONDAY 5 APRIL

After what seems years of waiting, it's finally happening. The election is on. As I sit here tonight, two thoughts come to mind. I think of all the candidates up and down the country, many of whom have been campaigning in their patches for up to four years. The next four weeks will determine their fate. Some will experience the elation of victory, and their work will have been worthwhile, while others will suffer the pain of defeat – and believe me, I know what that pain feels like.

The other thought I have concerns those who in four weeks' time may be given the chance to govern this great country. They wouldn't be human if they didn't feel some sense of foreboding. Even the most self-confident politicians have some element of self doubt, however hidden it might appear to be.

I'll be quite honest, I am gutted not to be fighting this election as a candidate. I'm going to spend a bit of time helping my friends Tracey Crouch in nearby Chatham & Aylesford and Simon Jones in Dagenham & Rainham, and I'll also be putting my LBC election night programme together.

DROWNED OUT BY MANDELSON'S CRISPS
TUESDAY 6 APRIL

I suppose my chief memory of today has to be the moment I was drowned out on national radio ... by a packet of crisps. It wasn't any old packet of crisps. It was a packet being consumed, nay, chomped on by no less a personage than the First Secretary of State himself. Peter Mandelson, for it was he, had finished giving his answer to 5 Live's Peter Allen so decided to tuck in while I responded to a quizzing from 5 Live's silver fox. Halfway through my answer I was interrupted by the programme's presenter, Colin Murray, who asked the Dark Lord if he would mind stopping stuffing his face as his mastication was drowning out my answer. Naturally everyone collapsed laughing. The incident provoked a number of tweets to the programme and my own feed, the best of which was that 'Lord Mandelson is the kind of politician who slides uphill.'

He then proceeded to assert that the NIC increase could actually create jobs (no, really) on the basis that when they did it last time in 2002, employment went up the following year. I was having none of that and pointed out to Lord M that we weren't in a recession then, and that as the only one with a mic on who actually runs a business, if my cost base was added to in this manner it was more likely to encourage me to shed staff than employ new ones. He didn't have an answer to that.

Mandelson exuded total confidence in a display of languidness, the like of which you don't often see. He dismissed Sarah Teather as if she didn't exist. Indeed, he pretended he didn't know who she was at first.

What was noticeable today was that College Green was crawling with Labour politicians plus Vince Cable, Chris Huhne and Ming Campbell. The only shadow Cabinet members I saw in the two hours or so I was there were Messers Gove and Hague. I got a lot of airtime because there didn't seem to be many Tory politicians for the broadcasters to choose from. To be honest I wasn't comfortable with Teather and Mandelson as I felt an obligation to appear as if I were the official Tory spokesman. Fine, I can carry that off, but I'm far happier speaking for myself. Perhaps it's just as well that I'm not a candidate. If I keep telling myself that, one day I may even come to believe it!

MEETING TOBY ZIEGLER
THURSDAY 15 APRIL

Like most of you, I suspect, I am a massive fan of *The West Wing*, so to be on the same programme as Richard Schiff today was a huge honour. We were both on the *Daily Politics*. Sometimes when you meet actors it is a real let-down. Without a script they appear monosyllabic. Not Richard Schiff. After the programme we had a good fifteen-minute chinwag about the state of the election campaign and how Barack Obama was doing in America. He was particularly interested in what might happen in the event of a hung parliament and wasn't very impressed with the Lib Dems' website which he had been looking at earlier this morning. He was amused they used the word 'different' six times in the main article, and thought their policy proposals seemed very dumbed down. Who am I to disagree?

BIRD LIFE (AND DEATH)
SATURDAY 17 APRIL

Driving to Swaffham last night I came across a very touching sight. Those of you who have never lived in the countryside will no doubt snigger at what I am about to write, but who cares.

By the side of the road lay a dead hen pheasant, which had clearly been hit by a car. But, by its side, was a cock pheasant pushing at it with its head, trying to revive it, clearly distressed by the loss of its partner.

I had never really thought about birds having emotions. I wouldn't have thought their brains were big enough. But when I drove back later that evening the cock pheasant was still there, apparently grieving.

THESE SHAMEFUL ATTACKS ON CLEGG WILL BACKFIRE
THURSDAY 22 APRIL

What a terrible indictment of the British press we see this morning. The *Mail* runs a spurious story about Nick Clegg making a supposed Nazi slur against Britain. The *Express* reckons he wants us to be overrun by immigrants. The *Telegraph* accuses him of, well, properly declaring donations made to him to employ a member of staff. I haven't seen *The Sun* yet but, judging by their tirades against him over the last few days, he will probably be accused of fathering Kerry Katona's latest child and then paying her to get rid of it.

What a disgrace. And they say blogs are biased. On Sunday, I
wrote:

> Personal attacks on Nick Clegg will not work. They will backfire
> on those who make them and rightly so. Everyone who knows Nick
> Clegg likes him. He's a transparently likeable individual. Anyone
> trying to make out that he's anything else will come a cropper.

I don't want Nick Clegg to win. I don't want him to be Prime
Minister. But he is not the devil incarnate. He's a nice guy, doing
a fair job of leading his party. I do not agree with many of his
policies. I think many of them are misguided. But I am happy
to accept that he believes they will be best for the country. I
am happy to debate them with him or any other Lib Dem and
that's what politics and this election should be about. It should
be about debating ideas, arguing about policy. It shouldn't be
about this sudden urge to denigrate Nick Clegg as a person. It
will backfire on those who promulgate these attacks, because
most people can see with their own eyes that he is a transparently
decent individual.

Of course politicians should be scrutinised and questioned. But
not like this.

It's this kind of story which my mother will tell me proves
her right in her delight that I was never selected as a candidate.
She thought I was mad to want to get into parliament because she
thought I would be subjected to personal attacks like this,
or worse.

And who's to say she wouldn't have been right? And there you
have it. An explanation of why so many good people don't even
bother to apply to be candidates any longer. Why would they put
themselves through what Nick Clegg is going through?

I predict that these vicious attacks on Clegg will only serve to
increase his popularity and position in the polls. If that happens,
it will be a sure sign that the power of the press to influence an
election is on the wane. And that would be about the only good
thing to come out of this sorry state of affairs. Because in those
circumstances, we would definitely be in hung parliament territory.
And that would not be good. Not good at all.

TEN THINGS YOU WON'T HEAR DAVID DIMBLEBY SAY ON ELECTION NIGHT...
MONDAY 3 MAY

1. It's 10 p.m. and our exit polls show David Cameron heading for a clear majority.
2. And here's Jeremy Vine in his cowboy uniform.
3. That was Nick Clegg paying tribute to the two old parties.
4. If you click the red button you can see Emily Maitlis naked.
5. And now over to Iain Dale in the LBC studios...
6. Please don't text or tweet us. We really can't be arsed to read them out.
7. We hear that Gordon Brown is paying a last-minute visit to Rochdale.
8. For the very best in political analysis, read Adam Boulton's blog...
9. In Morley & Outwood, Ed Balls doubles his majority.
10. And that's the end of the programme. I'll be back at 10 p.m. to see the new Prime Minister enter Downing Street. Mr Clegg has had quite a night.

ARE THE BBC/ITN/SKY ABOUT TO HAVE EGG ON THEIR FACES?
THURSDAY 6 MAY

So the exit poll shows the Tories on 307 seats, nineteen short of an overall majority. Don't panic, chaps and chapesses. My view is that by 4 a.m. this poll will have been shown to be wrong. It seems too incredible to be true that the Lib Dems are only predicted to get fifty-nine seats. I'll run naked down Whitehall if that turns out to be true.

In 1992 the BBC exit poll predicted a hung Parliament. We got a Tory majority of twenty-one. Will history repeat itself? I wouldn't bet against it.

A FEW THOUGHTS
FRIDAY 7 MAY

An astonishing night. As predicted there was no such thing as a national swing. Seats the Tories should have won, they didn't, and others no one predicted they would win, they did. What no one predicted was the disastrous night the Lib Dems have experienced. Not only will they end up with fewer seats, but their vote share may even be less than in 2005.

For Conservatives, there are many good things to take out of tonight. They gained more seats than at any election since 1931. But there were many more they should have taken and didn't. What on earth happened in Edgbaston, for instance?

The Lib Dem performance was all over the place. They lost many more seats to the Conservatives than anyone thought, but still managed to gain several seats too – Wells, Eastbourne and Solihull being three. They won several Labour seats like Redcar and Norwich South. They have also lost a lot of seats in the south west to the Conservatives. Bizarre. I just hope they don't end up on fifty-nine seats, as the exit poll predicted, otherwise I might have a rather unpleasant duty to perform (see above).

Congratulations to Caroline Lucas for making a breakthrough for the Greens. I'm sorry for Charlotte Vere, who would have made a brilliant MP. I half considered applying for this seat when it came up again, but I'm afraid I could see the writing on the wall and didn't think I could turn it round.

So where does this leave us? The constitution gives Gordon Brown the right to try to form a government. It is unlikely he would be able to do so, even in a formal coalition with the Lib Dems, as they still wouldn't have a majority. But let's face it, as David Blunkett has admitted, Brown has lost the election. He hasn't got a mandate.

Can Cameron form a government with 310 seats? I'd say yes. And he can do it without begging the Lib Dems for support. However, he may think that we need a stable long-term government and that it would be a good idea to form a coalition. If I were him, I would seriously think about that. It could be argued to be in the national interest.

One other thing before I have to get some sleep. The conduct of this election has been the most unprofessional ever. If the chairwoman of the Electoral Commission had anything about her she would resign, as would the chairman of the Association of Returning Officers. They have failed the country and need to be held to account for it.

I've seen many friends elected tonight and I congratulate them all warmly. Several other friends didn't quite make it. There's one man I want to pay tribute to tonight, and that is my friend Simon Jones, who pushed Jon Cruddas very close in Dagenham & Rainham. He will be gutted tonight as his campaign deserved a win.

I had a great time presenting LBC's election night coverage and I hope those of you who tuned in liked it too. Perhaps the highlight was upsetting Esther Rantzen by congratulating her on her ability to get a Labour MP elected. She was very upset when I asked her if her entire campaign wasn't just one giant ego trip. She then had the cheek to accuse me of having an ego by asking an elderly lady such a question. As if.

WHAT NEXT?

Many things remain unclear, but let's stick to what we know. We know that David Cameron has said he believes there should be a 'strong government in the national interest'. We also know that Nick Clegg has said that he would talk first to the party which has most seats and most votes. So that would be the Conservative Party.

So quite how Gordon Brown, who must be licking his wounds and opening tubes of superglue in his Downing Street lair, imagines he will be able to open negotiations with a party that doesn't want to speak to him is anyone's guess.

If the Tories have 306 seats and can entice the DUP into some sort of agreement, they could realistically govern without a coalition with the Lib Dems. I'd be quite happy for them to have a go at that, but it is clear that a second election would have to follow within a very short time.

These are the likely power blocks, which demonstrate that whichever way you cut it, Labour cannot form a majority coalition. There's no way the SNP and Plaid would be part of it.

The only way the Conservatives could do so is through a formal coalition with the Liberal Democrats. Many Conservatives would recoil at that. I am not one of them. If it has to be, it has to be. Our economy cannot stand the uncertainty of a minority government in the long term.

I believe David Cameron and Nick Clegg have enough in common to be able to come to an agreement on many policy areas.

I don't see electoral reform as an insuperable barrier. I also don't see Europe as the barrier which many Lib Dems probably imagine it to be, although I accept there are potential difficulties there.

But a formal coalition is only worth the candle if it is for the long term – four or five years. The Lib Dems need to be bound in.

If I were David Cameron I wouldn't rush into anything. He doesn't need to. He knows he holds the whip hand and so does Gordon Brown. I doubt anything will be resolved today.

The elephant in the room with regard to a second election is the fact that neither the Lib Dems nor Labour can afford one. Indeed, I doubt the Conservative coffers are very full either. So realpolitik may well play a role here as well as the practical consequences of the parliamentary arithmetic.

A FULL COALITION CAN WORK

Hilarious. I have just been dropped from a *Newsnight* discussion on a potential Tory–Lib Dem coalition because I am seen as too pro Lib Dem. I never thought those would be words I would ever write. But I know what they mean.

I have spent most of the day explaining on the media why I believe a full coalition could work – not just a supply and confidence agreement, but a full coalition, with Lib Dem ministers and a formal four-year-long coalition agreement along the lines of what they do in Germany. This is the only way a lasting, stable government can be brought about. The early discussions need to centre on the areas of agreement rather than disagreement. The difficult bits can come later. If there is goodwill on both sides agreement can be reached.

There will be red lines on both sides. That's clear. But I truly believe the Lib Dems are far more likely to come to an agreement with the Conservatives than with Brown. Brown can only carry on if he creates what the Germans would call an *Ampelkoalition*, whereby all the Irish and nationalist parties are included too. Even then he could barely get a majority. And there's no guarantee that his own MPs would vote in favour of electoral reform.

It is widely thought that electoral reform will be the sticking point between the Lib Dems and the Tories. It doesn't have to be. Cameron's opening gambit of a Commission on Electoral Reform won't be good enough for the Lib Dems. They've been there, done that with Tony Blair.

I'd offer them a free vote in Parliament on whether there should be a referendum on electoral reform. And my final position, if that failed, would be to offer them a referendum but then campaign in favour of FPTP in that referendum campaign. I could also envisage PR being offered for the House of Lords and local elections.

I think Lib Dems have been slightly taken aback by Cameron's offer. They want to be reassured he really means it. Nick Clegg's task must now be to convince a sceptical party that this is a road they should go down. As I have repeatedly said, the Lib Dems presumably came into politics to change things. They now have their first real opportunity in a century to wield real power and do just that.

The question is, will they take it?

THE CHANGE COALITION IS COMING
SUNDAY 9 MAY

I've noted with wry amusement that ever since I came out as an enthusiast for the Change Coalition, the media invites have dried up. Believe me, after Friday's marathon I am hardly complaining. I can do with the rest, but note how the news channels are concentrating on using Tory pundits (e.g. Fraser Nelson and Tim Montgomerie) who could at best be described as sceptical about a coalition, if not downright hostile. That's hardly surprising. News channels and programmes always like to invite on Tory guests who may disagree with the line the party is promulgating. What a pity they don't do this as often with Labour pundits. They can't get enough of Brown enthusiasts like Charlie Whelan or Kevin Maguire.

I'm making the supreme sacrifice and abandoning my plans to go to Upton Park to see West Ham's last game of the season, in favour of following what's unfolding in Westminster.

I am really confident that by the end of the day we will have good news, and that the Change Coalition is forging ahead. We may not have quite reached the endgame, but my sixth sense tells me that we're nearing it.

This is a time when Conservative activists need to invest some trust in the party's leadership. Norman Tebbit's efforts to undermine

Cameron's position are nothing new. He's been doing it for the last five years. I wonder what he'd have thought of someone who had tried to do that to Margaret Thatcher in the mid-1980s. I know. He'd have had them neutered. Of course there will be people in the Conservative Party who don't want to do a deal with the Lib Dems. In normal circumstances I would be one of them. But we are not in normal circumstances and we have to do what is best for the country. It's no good following Norman Tebbit's logic and sticking your head in the ground like an ostrich and ignoring the realpolitik of the situation. You have to deal with the cards you are dealt, and that's what David Cameron and his colleagues are doing now.

JOKE OF THE DAY
MONDAY 10 MAY

Knock, knock.
Who's there?
Gordon.
Gordon who?
That's politics…

A NEW DAWN HAS BROKEN, HAS IT NOT?
TUESDAY 11 MAY

Well, it's finally happened. Labour has bowed to the inevitable and called off talks with the Lib Dems. Gordon Brown will apparently resign the office of Prime Minister tonight and David Cameron will travel up the Mall tomorrow morning (or perhaps even tonight) to kiss hands with the Queen.

At last.

That is, barring any unforeseen problems with ratification of the coalition deal by Lib Dem MPs or their Federal Executive. I think both bodies will realise that if they play silly buggers, the electorate would take a long time to forgive them.

The negotiations have been tortuous, but maybe that was inevitable. The Conservatives have conceded a huge amount to get this far. The Lib Dems never expected them to offer a referendum on AV.

The rumour going round College Green is that the Lib Dems will get six Cabinet seats, which is two more than I would have thought they would be entitled to. There is no word on what they will be, but my tip about Nick Clegg being Deputy Prime Minister looks a good bet.

There will be several disappointed Conservatives tomorrow, who had expected to get Cabinet jobs, but won't. Chris Grayling will be devastated if he is dropped, but I'm afraid he may well be. Hot rumour is that a return from David Davis may be on the cards, assuming Nick Clegg doesn't take the job himself. Alternatively, Michael Gove or Theresa May could be in the running.

The best thing about today is that it means that we finally get to see the back of Mandelson and Campbell. Yesterday they attempted to launch a pseudo-coup. Thank God it failed. Labour people were too sensible to be dragged along with it and credit is due to John Reid, David Blunkett and others for pointing out that it couldn't work.

I feel very excited by what is happening. And I don't mind admitting to being slightly wistful that I am not part of it. Except, I suppose I am, but in a different way to that which I had intended. However, being outside the tent may be even more interesting than being inside it. At least, that's what I keep telling myself.

THE TRAVAILS OF DAVID LAWS
SUNDAY 31 MAY

Until yesterday, David Laws was barely known outside Westminster. But the revelation that he claimed £40,000 over eight years to rent a room from his gay lover soon put paid to that.

David Laws is hardly the only gay in the Westminster Village. But he is perhaps the only one who thought his relationship could escape the glare of media scrutiny.

This rather quaint belief might have been reasonable had he not been thrust into the public limelight as a Cabinet minister. After all, a backbench Lib Dem MP in a gay relationship is almost considered par for the course.

But through his stellar performance as Chief Secretary to the Treasury during the first three weeks of the coalition, Laws made himself a target.

Firstly, he made public the private note left on his desk by his predecessor, Liam Byrne, which said: 'I'm afraid to tell you there's no money left.'

And secondly, he pulled out of *Question Time* last week after Labour refused to withdraw Alastair Campbell as its spokesman on the programme.

This accusation may be way off beam, but it wouldn't at all surprise me if somebody's tricks department had tipped off the *Daily Telegraph* about the nature of his relationship with James Lundie and it was that which provoked them to trawl through their expenses files again.

It is a sad fact that without the 'gay' element, this story would not be so big. It just shows that if you go into politics nowadays and you are not open about your private life, it may come back to haunt you in a big way.

It's healthy to be open and completely transparent, and I am sure that now David Laws has taken that massive step to 'out' himself, he will wonder why he didn't do it years ago.

But we need to understand why he didn't before we rush to judge him. Intensely private people – and yes, some politicians are just that – recoil from talking about their sexual proclivities.

There are some things you just don't do. We're not Americans. We don't like baring our souls. And, most of all, we don't like hurting our families. I know. I have been there.

I have wanted to be an MP all my adult life. But the thing that stopped me going for it was my own homosexuality. I grew up in a small village, among a community with very conservative views.

Despite attending a left-wing university in the early 1980s, I did nothing to act on my 'inner gay'. I went through most of my twenties not acknowledging my own sexuality to anyone but myself, let alone my family.

In the mid-1990s I started a relationship with my now civil partner, John. He would often visit my parents' home and they all got on like a house on fire.

To my family he was my 'friend'. Nothing more. But when I reached the age of forty and decided I wanted a political career, I knew I would have to be open. I certainly didn't want anyone to 'have' anything on me.

Everyone told me that my parents would already know. But they didn't. It proved to be one of the most difficult conversations of my life. I then told several long-standing friends, all of whom I felt I had let down by not having said anything before.

No one who hasn't been through that experience can comprehend the trauma I went through. The same trauma David Laws is going through this weekend.

So I understand his wish to remain private and not have to tell his family. But in this age of transparency, openness, blogs and Twitter, it is simply not possible to maintain that veil of secrecy over such an intensely personal part of your life.

It's all very well for people to assert that times have changed and there is a greater acceptance of different lifestyles in society. Of course that is true, but it doesn't make it any easier for family members with devout religious beliefs to accept a lifestyle they have been taught is both wrong and will result in eternal damnation. And that's the same whether you're a gay politician, gay welder or a gay chairman of a FTSE 500 company. Just saying that 'times have changed' is overly simplistic and ignores personal realities.

By all accounts, David Laws was a broken man yesterday. I suspect he wanted to resign there and then. I believe David Cameron was right to try to dissuade him. After all, what exactly is he accused of? Claiming up to £950 a month for renting a room in a flat in Kennington. I'd say that was very good value for the taxpayer. I tried to do the same thing last year and couldn't find anything for less than £1,200.

What his critics are saying is that in 2006 he should have moved out of the flat he shared with his partner when the parliamentary rules changed to ban financial relationships between spouses or civil partners.

Laws and Lundie weren't and aren't spouses or civil partners, so why should Laws have moved out? If he had, it would have cost the taxpayer more money.

If Laws had been seeking to maximise his expenses, he would have surely made his constituency home in Somerset his second home and claimed mortgage interest on that, or he would have bought a flat in London himself.

David Laws has said that he and James Lundie do not consider themselves partners in the conventional sense. They do not share bank accounts and have different social circles.

They clearly don't entertain together or go out in public together.

What legally constitutes a 'partnership' is an area fraught with legal difficulties.

For instance – and I hesitate to even venture here – it is perfectly possible that despite what John Humphrys asserted on the *Today* programme yesterday, they do not even share a bed. Some people don't. Would that mean that under the law they are not 'partners'?

I don't envy the Standards Commissioner in some of the questions he is going to have to ask.

But even if David Laws has transgressed the rules in a minor way, are we really saying that one of the most talented members of the Cabinet should have been sacrificed?

Are we really insisting that if all our politicians aren't whiter than white, they should quit? It's a very strange logic. If that rule had applied in the twentieth century we would certainly have been deprived of the services of both Lloyd George and Churchill.

We must beware of moving to a situation where only single, white, rich, straight, blameless males can go into politics because, believe me, that's where we're heading.

Yesterday morning, I thought the tremendous goodwill in the country towards the coalition could have saved David Laws's career. His resignation last night meant I was not correct.

When I was presenting LBC's *Breakfast Show*, I detected no appetite for a 'scalp' from the listeners, and even my blog readers – a fairly judgemental bunch – seem to be split fifty-fifty on whether he should resign.

In the end, the whole sorry farrago comes down to this: Did David Laws defraud the taxpayer, or did he intend to? The answer to both questions is no. But in the end, for his personal reasons, he could not tough it out and decided to quit.

HECKLED IN CHELMSFORD
WEDNESDAY 9 JUNE

Ann Widdecombe and I have done around fifty or sixty of our theatre shows up and down the country, but never has a member of the audience got up, shouted to us to 'F*** off' and stormed out of the theatre. Until last night in Chelmsford, that is.

It was near the end of the second half when an Agnetha Faltskog looky-likey asked Ann about equality laws. Ann explained why she had voted against most of them and then started talking about the Chris Grayling episode and how it's supposedy impossible to express Christian viewpoints, especially on gay issues. Normally in these evenings I regard my role as a prompt rather than an aggressive interviewer because, after all, people have come to see her rather than hear from me. But once or twice I like to have a bit of a row with her onstage, as the audience seem to like it. So I then ripped into her but, as you would expect, she gave back as good as she got.

At this point a young guy in the audience, who had already heckled during an earlier question on the coalition, got up and shouted, 'F*** off' and started to walk out. He then turned again, gave us the finger and shouted 'F*** off, you homophobes' before flouncing out, followed by his very embarrassed friend. Nice.

The only heckling we have ever had before was a couple of years ago when a woman in a box turned out to be blind drunk.

On both occasions, it was the audience who turned on the heckler. As compère, I didn't really have to do anything.

At the end of the show a man came up to Ann and said, 'I'm a Christian and I'm gay and I agree with what you said.' There's always one!

A CANDIDATE NO LONGER
THURSDAY 17 JUNE

Last night I attended a reception at No. 10 and had a brief chat with David Cameron. He said he hoped I would try for a seat at the next election. I explained that that wouldn't be happening and that I had made a decision well before the last election not to try again if I didn't get a seat then.

I also said that I felt that at fifty-two (which I will be if this parliament lasts five years) it was unlikely that I would be selected anyway. I've made my views known before about the virtues of selecting older candidates, with real-life experience, but politics in this country is becoming youth obsessed and I doubt whether I would be able to stem that particular tide. Of course older candidates do get selected, but they are very much the exception rather than the rule – exactly the opposite of how it should be.

Anyway, there are things I'd rather do over the next few years rather than flog what I consider to be a dead horse. I've always wanted to be a parliamentarian, but I'm not obsessive about it – perhaps that is where I have gone wrong!

So, to formally bring this part of my life to an end I have emailed Sayeeda Warsi, the new chairman of the party, to ask her to remove my name from the party's list of approved candidates.

I feel strangely liberated...

TORY MP RECOVERS FROM 'SUICIDE ATTEMPT'
SATURDAY 19 JUNE

During the initial stages of the expenses scandal, Nadine Dorries warned that she thought it entirely conceivable that an MP might attempt suicide. A political hailstorm rained down on her, with bloggers and fellow politicians calling her remarks 'over the top' and far worse. Indeed, the party leadership briefed against her, describing her as 'wacky'.

Sadly, today it has been reported that her prediction apparently came true on Thursday, when Conservative MP David Ruffley allegedly threw himself in front of the Gatwick Express. Thankfully he survived with only minor injuries. Perhaps we will never know the whole reason which led him to do this – and depression usually relates to more than a single thing – but it has been an open secret among his colleagues that he was very badly affected by the expenses saga and the *Telegraph*'s accusations against him. The fact that he was cleared of doing anything wrong would not have changed the way he felt.

Depression is a terrible thing. Whatever you think of Alastair Campbell, you should read the part of the interview I did with him where he talks candidly about how it affected him. Those of us who have never suffered from it cannot begin to understand it. The temptation to tell someone to 'snap out of it' is always there. But snapping out of it is easier said than done.

David Ruffley, or Ruffers as he is known to his friends, has received a lot of support from colleagues and the party but in the end it's not possible to stop someone from going down a particular path if that is what they are determined to do. Now he has reached the absolute nadir, everyone around him can provide the love and support he will need to recover from this awful episode.

ANYONE FOR TENNIS?
FRIDAY 25 JUNE

There was a time, in the late '70s and early '80s, when I would go to Wimbledon every year, but my interest in tennis waned in the 1990s as the main players just resorted to bashing the ball from base line to base line. Seeing a player come to the net was as rare as a British tennis victory. Today I am going to Wimbledon for the first time in at least fifteen years.

Strangely, in World Cup week my interest in tennis has been reawakened after Wimbledon has been hit by the same disease of 'underdogitis' which has affected the World Cup. Even the sainted Roger Federer came as close as you can get to losing in the first round. And then there was the match which ended 70–68 in the final set. This match has been lauded as the greatest in modern tennis history, and a tribute to the fitness of the two players. The latter is certainly true, but in some ways it displayed all that is wrong with modern tennis. During the match a record 212 aces were served. Aces certainly have their place in the game, but most people go to tennis matches to see exciting rallies, rather than ace after boring ace.

I used to be able to name all the top players. I would have at least heard of most of the Top 100 players in the world. I marvelled at the skills of the likes of Jimmy Connors, McEnroe, Lendl and Nastase. But today I couldn't name more than the top five in the world. And, apart from the Williams sisters, the leading women players are a mystery to me. But then women's tennis always has been the Vauxhall Conference of tennis – slow, plodding and full of grunting. There have been some great women in the game – Chris Evert, Billie Jean King, Martina Navratilova and Steffi Graf – but be honest, apart from Venus and Serena Williams, there are very few who you would pay good money to go and see.

MILIBANDS INTO THE SUNSET?
WEDNESDAY 28 JULY

Last night I did a ten-minute interview with David Miliband on LBC. He was on good form and we had a good joust about the leadership contest. He admitted it hadn't been the 'rumble in the jungle' some in the media had hoped for.

At the end I asked him this: 'I warn you now, this is the most difficult question you will be asked this week. If Nick Clegg and David Cameron are *Brokeback Mountain*, which film are you and your brother Ed?'

He roared with laughter. I suggested *Last Man Standing* which he thought was 'very cruel'. He then said, 'Let's hope it's not *Two Brothers into the Sunset*'.

Incidentally, we had a cracking programme last night, with interviews with Kitty Ussher, Philip Blond, Nigel Farage and David Miliband. Perhaps the highlight was the medical hour when a GP comes into the studio to dispense medical advice to listeners. The first caller related his problem with anal fissures. You've got to admire someone who's willing to go on the radio to talk about that. We also had a guy who kept fainting in his sleep. My first thought was: how would he know?

DON'T TRY THIS AT HOME
SATURDAY 31 JULY

On Tuesday, I interviewed Matthew Parris. He lives in a riverside flat in Limehouse, so we sat outside on the balcony and chatted away for an hour and a half. As we sat down and I switched on my tape recorder he looked over to the other side of the river and said, 'Tomorrow night I'm going to swim across the Thames.' I looked at him incredulously. 'You're mad,' I said. 'People die doing that.' 'No, it'll be fine, I've worked it out. At 3 a.m., there won't be any tide.' 'I really think you ought to think about that again,' I urged. 'No, it'll be fine. There will be someone here holding a flashlight so I can see where to swim to.' I shook my head. 'I'm afraid it doesn't work like that. You'll end up halfway round the Isle of Dogs.'

I emailed Matthew on Thursday to ask how it had gone. 'Read my column on Saturday,' he replied. Well, at least he wasn't dead and I didn't have to torture myself with the thought that had I been more vehement in my warnings he might not have gone through with it!

THE JOYS OF LIVE PHONE-IN RADIO
WEDNESDAY 4 AUGUST

What I love about presenting a phone-in-based radio show is that you can never predict what's going to happen. And so it proved tonight.

In the first hour of the programme we covered the story about the Advertising Standards Authority ruling in favour of Channel 4's decision to screen adverts for the Marie Stopes pregnancy/abortion advisory clinics. First of all I talked to Nadine Dorries, who took the view that these adverts should not appear on TV, and then to Simon Blake from the Brook clinic. He supported their right to be shown. And then it was on to the calls. What I hadn't bargained for was the three women who phoned in, each with a different but equally heartbreaking story about how they had come to decide to have an abortion, and how it had affected their lives. Talking to any woman in private about their traumas would be awkward enough, but doing it on national radio was a real learning experience. I tried to let them talk with little interruption, partly because any real intervention from me would have been invidious, but also because they clearly wanted to tell LBC listeners how their own experience had impacted on their lives. One of the callers bitterly regretted her decision to have an abortion and described how she thinks about it every day, twenty years later. Carol from Harrow was the last caller and her story almost reduced me to tears. Indeed, she was clearly finding it difficult to hold it together herself. I hated having to cut her off as we had to go to the 8 o'clock news. We phoned her back to check she was OK and she asked my producer to tell me that she had no regrets about the abortion she had. It was the right thing to do at the time, but she now has two very healthy children and she wanted me to know she was very happy. Another lump-in-throat time.

Later on we talked about sentencing and whether life should really mean life. Towards the end of the slot I took a call from someone who said he had been in prison on several occasions. I asked him when the last time had been and he said he had got out in 2001. He had then got a job as a youth worker which had transformed his life. Asking him about why he had been to prison several times and how he had decided to 'go straight' was in some ways a rather humbling experience. When you ask someone on a live radio phone-in about very private things, you always worry that they might simply hang up or refuse to discuss the issue. OK, they have phoned in so they clearly want to say something, but talking about criminal records and very private health issues are not things that you are necessarily expecting to discuss with several hundred thousand people listening.

But, as I say, it is why you just can't beat live phone-in-based radio shows. Those of you who have been listening will no doubt have been able to tell how much I have been enjoying myself over the last ten days. And, strangely, it's often when I am discussing subjects way outside my comfort zone that I enjoy it most.

WHY GAP YEARS MATTER
SUNDAY 15 AUGUST

A *Sunday Telegraph* article which raised my ire this morning was the one about some university bod advising eighteen-year-olds not to go on gap years. Instead, she said that they should concentrate on getting work experience and extra training. Balls.

Going on a gap year was the best decision I have ever made – apart from hitching myself to Mr Simmons, of course. Oh, and getting Gio from Battersea, but I digress.

I spent my gap year in Germany, mainly because the following September I would start my German degree course at UEA. It seemed a good idea to gain a greater degree of fluency in the language before I started. By the time I came back I was virtually fluent and had a far better grasp of the language, which meant that I was able to sail through the first year.

But there was something more important than that. I grew up during that year. I became an adult. I no longer had my parents and family to rely on. I was on my own. Independent. I well remember the day my parents took me to Harwich to get the ferry to the Hook of Holland. I remember going up the escalator and losing sight of my mother, who was in floods of tears. To be honest so was

I. She told me a few years ago that at that moment she thought she genuinely wouldn't see me again.

I duly arrived in Bad Wildungen, a spa town in Hessen, close to the Edersee of *Dambusters* fame, to which I had been twice before on school exchanges. It took me several weeks to find a job.

I had gone out there with only about £100 (it was 1980, after all!) and was about to run out. But the Werner Wicker Klinik came to the rescue and I got a job as a nursing assistant in the swimming pool area. I had no lifeguard qualifications and certainly knew nothing about nursing. But it was a job. And it paid: DM 1,650 a month – a huge amount to me.

The next thing to do was to get my own room. Up to that point I had been staying with my penfriend's family. It was the first time I would live on my own. And I didn't like it at all. Although I had made quite a few friends, it was always soul destroying to spend an evening in a solitary room watching an old black and white TV. And, believe me, German TV was dreadful. Dubbed episodes of *Dallas* proved to be the highlight of the week. 'Sue Ellen, bist du schon wieder besoffen?' 'JR, ich hasse dich.' It wasn't quite the same, somehow.

But I lived above a bar in the Brunnenallee, so life was never particularly quiet. And the work was incredibly rewarding. I ended up doing a lot of physiotherapy and hydrotherapy on the patients, again with no training. Most had suffered spinal injuries in motorcycle accidents, or had spinal conditions associated with scoliosis. I spent the first few days wandering around in a bit of a daze, just feeling sorry for everyone. I can't remember who, but someone said the secret of being able to work in a hospital like that is to take the emotion out of it and never feel sorry for the patients. Once I had got my brain around that, it was fine.

It was in that year that I became a man. Now, that sounds an odd thing to say, but I would not have missed it for the world. And if eighteen-year-olds are now being discouraged by some bureaucrat from UCAS from having the same life-enhancing experience as I did, then things have reached a pretty pass.

So if you are a teenager reading this, ignore the woman from UCAS. Follow your instincts. If you think a gap year is what you need, move heaven and earth to make it happen. I've never regretted it for a minute.

WHEN YOUR MIND GOES BLANK
FRIDAY 20 AUGUST

Nicky Campbell has written the *Spectator* diary this week. In it, he tells how he is organising a memorial service for Allan Robb, the 5 Live presenter who died earlier this year. He recounts an anecdote which sent a knowing shiver down my spine...

> Allan told stories with great comic precision. One of his best was how, when interviewing John Major during the 1992 general election, his mind went blank. In a panic, he remembered the *Spitting Image* portrayal of the PM as a grey man obsessed with eating peas. 'And do you like peas?' asked Allan. Major didn't have the faintest notion what he was on about. 'I like a variety of vegetables but peas I am relatively neutral about,' he answered after a bewildered pause.

Your mind going blank is an interviewer's or presenter's worst nightmare. It happened to me once doing a Sky News paper review, about five years ago. I had worked out my next sentence, but when I came to speak it my mind went completely blank. I just looked at the presenter, mentally shouting 'Help!' At the end I profusely apologised but she reassured me it had happened to her the previous week when she was interviewing Jack Straw.

I had another episode last night on LBC. At the end of the second hour I started to explain that in the next hour we'd be discussing the Catholic Church and gay adoption. But the words just wouldn't come out in the right order. In the end I just said, 'This is a bit rubbish, isn't it?' I know people always say listeners or viewers love it when something goes wrong but, at the time, the presenter feels a sense of total humiliation. The key is to recover quickly and move on.

WHY LANGUAGES MATTER
WEDNESDAY 25 AUGUST

If I had become an MP, I had decided one of the causes I would take up in Parliament would be the teaching of languages in schools. Figures released today illustrate why I was right to be concerned.

The numbers taking French as a GCSE have halved over the

last eight years, with German showing a similar decline. The last government removed the compulsion for fourteen- to sixteen-year-olds to take a language several years ago, and we are now seeing the long-term effects. Many schools discourage kids from studying languages as they are considered 'difficult' subjects in which pupils are less likely to attain 'A' grades.

We have never been great linguists in this country, and many take the attitude that we don't need to learn a language because everyone abroad speaks English. That's an incredibly 'Little Englanderish' attitude and one which hampers people who do business abroad. The ability to converse with people in their own language can open many doors.

Perhaps, however, we are also guilty of being too conservative in our teaching of languages. Maybe instead of sticking to trusty old French and German we should be encouraging schools to offer more courses in Spanish, Arabic, Mandarin and Russian.

I studied German at university because I had intended to become a German teacher. With such a declining demand for German teachers, I'm beginning to think it's lucky my career took a rather different turn!

THE *ANY QUESTIONS* EXPERIENCE (2)
FRIDAY 27 AUGUST

Well, I'm in the BBC car driving the 300 miles back to Kent (no, there are no trains at this time of night, since you ask) reflecting on my second experience of *Any Questions*. And seeing as I won't get back to Tunbridge Wells until 3 a.m. I thought I'd write a little missive about appearing on the programme.

I suppose that given our hosts in Newcastle were the Workers' Education Association I shouldn't have been surprised to get a hostile audience, but it comes to something when you're booed before you even sit down! And, frankly, they didn't get any friendlier. By the end I reckoned I could have told the funniest joke in the history of joke telling and not got a laugh.

My fellow panellists were Deborah Mattinson (Brown's pollster), Matthew Taylor (Blair's head of policy) and Adrian Fawcett (CEO of the General Healthcare group).

The warm-up question was asked by a lady who wanted to know

if the coalition would still be in place by the time the Cameron baby starts nursery school. We all gave slightly formulaic answers and all agreed the coalition was probably there for the long term. At the end the questioner came up to me and thanked me for my eye contact. She didn't like the fact that none of the others looked at her.

And at 8.02 Eddie Mair welcomed the Radio 4 audience, and off we went. The first question (I think) was predictably about the IFS report. I made a slightly nervous start and I seem to remember being booed a couple of times when I defended the coalition's economic approach. But in the end I think the sparring got me into my stride.

Next came a question on health and how the system should be financed and structured. I thought this was probably my best answer and I seemed to make the audience think a little judging from their faces. I talked about how the NHS could never meet all the demands made on it and we had to get away from the 'public good, private bad' prevailing attitudes. I said it wasn't structures that were important, it was outcomes. I also questioned a system which spends £4 billion on gastric bands but can't provide much needed cancer drugs. As I hadn't had a boo yet, I then suggested some people who wanted gastric bands ought to eat less. Cue the boos!

We then had a question about the cat woman and who or what we'd like to put in a wheelie bin. Deborah Mattinson stole my answer. She said she would put Mrs Bale in it. Bugger, I thought, what do I say now? I said that I'd put Mrs Bale in the big cat enclosure at Whipsnade Zoo for fifteen hours as I am a believer in restorative justice. Not a titter. OK, not that great, but any other audience might have at least pretended to laugh. Not this one.

There then followed three questions which none of us could have predicted – on paternity leave, adult education and library cuts. I don't think any of us gave particularly insightful answers, although I did have a brief spat with La Mattinson when she professed to be deeply suspicious of the Big Society, implying that volunteering was bad if it meant taking over the functions of the state. Matthew Taylor talked a great deal of sense on this and deprecated the left's knee-jerk response to the Big Society.

We finished with a question about Twitter from someone who turned out to be one of my blog readers. Bless you, sir!

So all in all, I'd call the whole thing a bit of a score draw, with the audience possibly winning on points for the level of booing. I certainly didn't enjoy it as much as I did on my first appearance a year ago in Ottery St Mary, and I suspect the audience didn't either. Far too much agreement!

HOW DOES PC WORLD STAY IN BUSINESS?
SATURDAY 4 SEPTEMBER

There's a reason I hate going to PC World, and yet, like a dog returning to its sick, I continue to do so. Today's visit illustrates why I reckon it's the chain store with the worst customer service in Britain. It's staffed by acne-ridden, monosyllabic teenagers with barely a GCSE between them, few of whom know anything about the products they are supposed to be flogging. And its computer system seems to hail from the time of Noah's Ark. It makes BBC Basic look state of the art.

Anyway, why did I end up there today? Because Olly Grender, bless her heart, finally persuaded me to buy an iPad after she showed me all the things she did on hers. She has a lot to answer for. So, I've decided to go over to the dark side. I started to order one online from the Apple store, but then thought, bugger it, I want one and I want it now, so off I trolled down to PC World in Tunbridge Wells. Normally when I try to buy anything from there, there's some sort of problem. Usually they haven't got what I want in stock, but today I thought I had struck lucky, as yes, they had a 65GB 3G iPad in stock and also a Vodafone SIM to go with it. Excellent, I thought.

Then their computer system seized up. Five minutes later the assistant started asking me my marital status. I never quite know how to answer that one. They don't have a box for 'civil partnered'. So I said 'married'. He then asked how many credit cards I had. Er, none of your business, I said. In any case, I haven't a clue. Why do you need to know that, I asked. I should have known the answer. The computer says so, said the nerd-geek. He then told me all the other personal info they would require. This was all to set up a direct debit for Vodafone, nothing to do with PC World! I have never had to give any of that sort of info to Vodafone, so I am damned if I am going to give it to PC World, supposedly on their behalf.

I told them exactly where they could shove their iPad and have just come home and ordered it via the Apple store. Which, of course, I should have done in the first place. Lesson learnt.

How does PC World manage to stay in business? Because I am buggered if I know.

TRAVELLING TO ARNHEM
THURSDAY 16 SEPTEMBER

My dad turns eighty-one next month. He was nine when the Second World War broke out. For him, the war defined his whole life. He was fifteen when it ended. To this day he devours every programme he can watch about it. My parents' TV is permanently tuned to the History Channel or the Discovery Channel, much to my mother's chagrin.

Back in 1994, I took my father to visit the Normandy beaches, a couple of weeks before the fiftieth anniversary of D Day. My friend Daniel from Washington joined us with his father, together with a couple of family friends. We rented a cottage about twenty miles inland. It was one of the best holidays of my life – full of emotion, with some great banter with the French, who seemed to want to thank us personally for what our countrymen had done to liberate them in 1944. And it was great to spend five days with my dad, a man who normally hates holidays and hasn't got a lot of time for 'abroad'.

A few months ago my mother rang to say that my dad had got it into his head that he wanted to go on a battlefields tour to Arnhem, and would I go with him. He's got quite deaf and she didn't trust him on his own! So, to cut a long story short, in half an hour's time we leave for Dover to meet up with a coach full of people from all over the country. Tonight we're staying in Eindhoven and then we have three nights in Arnhem, where we'll be visiting various sites associated with Operation Market Garden, which took place sixty-six years ago this week, including the famous Bridge at Arnhem. We're also travelling over the German border to visit a cemetery of German war dead – something I never thought I'd ever see my father do. He still refers to them as 'Jerries'!

Meanwhile, wish me luck on the Channel ferry. I get terribly seasick. The first time I went across the Channel was in 1977 when I was on a school trip to Germany and we travelled from Harwich to the Hook of Holland in a force nine gale. Everyone, literally everyone on the ferry was puking their guts up. I remember deciding to lie on the floor underneath two seats. My next memory was someone puking up right next to my head. Luckily I only suffered a bit of splashback. And since then, I just have to look at a ferry and I get that queasy feeling in my stomach. The only way to avoid it is to blindfold myself. I kid you not. If I can't see, somehow it seems to keep my stomach settled. So, if you're on the 13.55 ferry to Calais and see someone with a blindfold, it's me.

FROM MONDAY, *THE IAIN DALE SHOW* ON LBC, EVERY WEEKNIGHT!
FRIDAY 17 SEPTEMBER

Over the last few months I have been a stand-in presenter for LBC in various time slots. Well, I'm delighted to tell you that I have been offered a permanent gig and I will be getting my own daily three-hour programme.

From Monday, I'll be taking over the 7–10 p.m. slot on LBC from Petrie Hosken, who is moving to the afternoon 1–4 p.m. slot.

I've only ever really had two ambitions in my life – to be a Member of Parliament and to have my own radio show. Well, at least now I can say I've had a 50 per cent success rate!

I have to admit I had thought this day was never likely to arrive. Having spent a decade doing punditry I reckoned that if it was going to happen, it would have done before now. But then Tommy Boyd came along.

Tommy was a name from my childhood. He made his reputation as the presenter of *Magpie*, a kids' programme on ITV, but then moved into Talk Radio, where he became a huge success. It was he who recruited me to do some programmes last year on the late lamented Play Radio. It was just me, a microphone and the listeners. I think I only did five or six programmes and a nine-hour local election night marathon, but it was enough for me to confirm in my own mind that I absolutely loved radio phone-ins and could hold my own as a presenter. Tommy was hugely encouraging and assured me when Play Radio went tits up that I had a big future in radio.

Last September, I went into LBC to do a short audition session, but to be honest I felt it was little short of a disaster and I never expected to hear from them again. But three weeks later I got a call around lunchtime to ask if I could present the show that evening.

Gulp. Talk about being thrown in at the deep end... But it seemed to go really well. Nothing happened then for some time as they were clearly waiting to see if I would get a seat. In February, I did a couple more shows, then I asked the LBC programme director Jonathan Richards if I could put some ideas to him for an election night programme. I did, he liked it and I hosted a six-hour programme which most regarded as a minor triumph.

Since then I have covered virtually every show in the schedule apart from the overnight slot. And in August I had four weeks sitting in for Petrie on the show I will now be taking over. I loved more or less every minute of it – except the one moment I got completely tongue-tied!

I guess you can tell what this means to me. I am hugely grateful for the confidence shown in me by Jonathan Richards and his production team. He and I both know that I am not yet the finished article as a radio presenter but his constant encouragement has instilled a belief in me that I can actually be really good at this. That's not meant to sound arrogant. Most things in my life I have had to learn. I've always had to work hard to keep up with others. That will be the same here, but for the first time in my life I am doing something I feel completely at home with. I sit in front of that microphone and think to myself, 'I know I can be good at this.'

The evening slot is a great one for me, as no one else is doing current affairs on the radio at that time. 5 Live and TalkSport do sport and Radio 4 is doing something artsy. Petrie has built up a very good audience over the last eighteen months and I hope to build on that. LBC calls itself London's Biggest Conversation, but we now get a lot of listeners all over the country thanks to DAB, digital TV and the thousands of people who now listen via the website, or their iPads or mobile phones. Excited? You bet I am.

But have no fear. I maintain my commitment to *Total Politics*, Biteback Publishing and indeed this blog. But perhaps you now realise why I have recruited an assistant. Because if I don't get some help organising my schedule and my life I'll probably end up in a funny farm. The one thing I am having to slowly come to terms with is that I won't be able to go out to dinner in the evenings, go to receptions or even slob out in front of the TV on a weekday evening for what will hopefully be some considerable time. Oh well, you can't have everything.

REMEMBERING ARNHEM SIXTY-SIX YEARS ON
SUNDAY 19 SEPTEMBER

I'm typing this before the commencement of the service at Oosterbeek military cemetery, near Arnhem. Sixty-six years ago this week, hundreds of British, American and Polish airmen and soldiers gave their lives in the cause of the liberation of Holland. And it is they whom we remember and honour today.

Sixty-six years seems a long time, yet in historical terms it is but the flicker of an eyelid.

My generation has been lucky never to have had to fight. For my dad's generation, the Second World War defined them and their world outlook. My dad was nine when the war broke out and fifteen when it ended, but it defines who he is today. He may not have fought himself, but he is determined that those who fought so he could live in freedom should never be forgotten. It's why we are here today, and it's part of the reason I love him. Not, of course, that I would ever tell him that to his face. We're British after all!

FOR US TO LIVE ALL THEIR TOMORROWS

I don't know how many of you have ever been to a Second World War cemetery, but it is a profoundly moving experience. I'm typing this looking out at rows of gravestones at a graveyard in Overloon. It's a comparatively small one with around 250 graves.

Earlier this afternoon we visited the Reichswald cemetery over the border in Germany. Buried there are more than 7,600 British, Commonwealth and Polish war dead. The grounds are simply beautiful. If anyone ever suggests cutting the funding of the Commonwealth War Graves Commission, I suspect it might not be good for their political health.

As you wander past grave after grave, your eyes are inevitably drawn towards the citations at the bottom of each one. As someone whose eyes tend to go moist during the first few seconds of a Lassie film, you can imagine what state I was in by the end of the visit. But it was this one which particularly moved me, as to me it summed up why we have come on this visit and why each year we remember those who died in conflict: 'He died to give us another dawn, for us to live all his tomorrows.'

Simply beautiful.

The grave marked the final resting place of Flying Officer D Hopkinson, died aged twenty-two, 17 May 1943.

HOW TO MAKE AN OLD MAN FEEL ... WELL, OLD
SATURDAY 2 OCTOBER

Has anyone said something that's ever made you feel really old? I mean, reeeeallly old? It happened to me on Thursday. My new assistant, Grant, suggested I should get tickets for an event at next week's Tory Party conference. 'Book 'em, Danno!' I said. He looked blankly at me. 'You know,' I said. '*Hawaii-5-0.*' He continued to look as if I was talking a language only heard on the planet Zarg. And then it dawned on me. Not only had he never heard the catch-phrase 'Book 'em, Danno', he had never heard of *Hawaii-5-0*. Not surprising really. The series finished in 1980, twelve years before Grant was born. I then went round the rest of the office and only one person had ever heard of it. I tell you, I felt ancient.

POOR GORDON
FRIDAY 15 OCTOBER

Last night as I was walking down the famous staircase in Downing Street, the one with the pictures of all former Prime Ministers, I wondered if they had already hung a picture of Gordon Brown. So I whizzed up the staircase again to have a look. As I got back to the top I saw one of the permanent Downing Street staff looking at me rather quizzically.

'I was just seeing if there was a picture of Gordon Brown,' I explained. 'No, he hasn't chosen his picture yet,' explained the staff member. 'Well, I expect that will take him at least two years,' I joked, thinking of his reputation for indecision. 'I hope he takes much longer than that,' came the instant reply.

I took that to indicate there wasn't a lot of love for Mr Brown among the permanent staff at No. 10. I almost felt sorry for him. Almost.

SITTING NEXT DOOR TO ALICE
SUNDAY 31 OCTOBER

Someone just texted me: 'What a bizarre sandwich to be the filling for...'

Indeed. I must admit, when they told me I would be doing a paper review on Andrew Marr with Alice Cooper, I did wonder how it would go. I was reassured that Helena Kennedy would be there too. She and I have done this before and I've always got on very well with her, partly because she's so transparently nice, and we share a similar outlook on civil liberties issues.

I arrived at TV Centre at 7.45 a.m. and slipped in behind Alice Cooper and his entourage of four. The BBC runner thought I was his bodyguard, I think. I chose my three stories – fire fighters, ginger rodents and Ann Widdecombe – while Alice was getting his make-up done. I don't think I am talking out of school to say that it took him considerably longer than it took me. The make-up woman said what all make-up artists say to me: 'Ooh, you've got a lovely colour, have you been on holiday?' Inwardly, I sigh. 'No, it's my natural colour,' I reply, wondering at the same time if that sounds awfully pretentious. I think I have some southern French blood in me somewhere. My mother's maiden name was French.

Anyway we had about twenty minutes to go before the programme started so we talked a bit about Alice Cooper's show at the Roundhouse tonight – and no, he didn't offer Helena and I free tickets, before anyone asks. He also told us about the time he thought he might be in the *Big Brother* house with Ann Widdecombe. 'You must tell that on air,' Helena and I chorused together. And so he did.

Just before 9.00 we were taken into the studio and sat on the famous sofa. I felt a little odd sitting in the middle, but before I had time to be nervous, off we went. I won't recount the conversation but I think of the four or five times I have done the Frost or Marr programme, this was the most enjoyable. Sometimes when there are three paper reviewers one gets a bit left out – and that happened to me the first time I appeared with David Frost back in 2003, when I was on with Polly Toynbee and the man who plays Trigger from *Only Fools and Horses*. And I have to admit, when I am on with two people who are far better known than me, I have a tendency to defer to them. But today, I felt we all got a fair crack of the whip and had a genuinely interesting conversation. At least, that's how it felt sitting on the sofa.

A TALE OF TWO LIVES
TUESDAY 9 NOVEMBER

I just phoned home and had the following exchange...

> Me: I've just been invited to meet Kylie Minogue and on the same day I'm having lunch with Karren Brady.
> John: How nice for you. I've just wiped Gio's bum.[†]
> Me: Er...

Not often that I am lost for words...

IS THERE A FUTURE FOR BOOKS?
SUNDAY 14 NOVEMBER

In *The Observer* today, Victoria Glendinning laments the lack of appetite among publishers for serious biography nowadays. In particular, she points out that publishers no longer pay the kind of advances on royalties that they used to. Indeed, and a good thing too. The level of advances had got ridiculous, with publishers seemingly only too willing to throw good money after bad in their desire to get one over on their competitors. In the end the house of cards had to come crashing down, and it certainly did.

Take the David Blunkett diaries, for instance. OK, not strictly biography, but the book was symptomatic of the malaise that had afflicted the industry. Bloomsbury had decided it wanted to get into the political biography market so it bid a ridiculous amount of money for a book which was never going to be a huge seller. The advance was somewhere in the region of £250,000 and that didn't include newspaper serialisation rights. Blunkett trousered close to £400,000 in all for a book which sold around 5,000 copies. Work out the finances on that for yourself.

Victoria Glendinning makes the point that for professional

[†] Gio is our Jack Russell, who is, er, having a few problems in the nether regions at the moment...

biographers it is difficult to eke out a living nowadays. She got an advance of £10,000 for her latest book, a biography of David Astor. In 1992 she got £50,000 for a similar book on Cyril Connolly.

In part this is also due to the amount of money being thrown at celebrity autobiographies by the big publishers. They do it because some of them can sell serious numbers. But for every celebrity autobiography which becomes a best-seller there are another dozen which flop and lose their publishers a huge amount of money – not just the advance, but the massive amount devoted to marketing.

All this means that the bigger publishers, like Macmillan, HarperCollins, Penguin, Random House and Simon & Schuster, have decided that the non-celebrity biography is one to steer clear of unless they are more or less 100 per cent confident that they can sell at least 10,000 copies in hardback.

But all this means that publishers like my company, Biteback, are now being offered books by authors and agents which even five years ago would have been way out of our range. But we are not changing our business approach to accommodate them. I'm simply not prepared to try to compete with big publishers on advances. Indeed, we don't pay any advances at all on the majority of books we take on. We can't and won't, because the business model for a publishing company like ours can't cope with advances beyond a few thousand pounds. And I mean a very few.

It's not that we are being mean-spirited. It's just that sales levels can't justify it. We'd all love to get that elusive best-seller, but in the real world we all live in we know that it's unlikely to happen. The world of bookselling is a very different beast to that which existed even eight years ago. Then, there were a multitude of bookshop chains – Waterstones, Dillons, Ottakers, John Smith, Blackwells, W. H. Smith and one or two other regionals. Now there is one – Waterstones. Even W. H. Smith has more or less reduced itself to the lowest common denominator.

The simple truth is that if Waterstones won't stock a book as core stock, and put it in each of its stores, you have virtually no chance of a book selling beyond a couple of thousand copies. Of course Amazon is crucial too, but the fact that it doesn't really have a serious online competitor gives it enormous buying power, leading to smaller publishers feeling as if they have been bulldozed.

In addition, small publishers are forced to accept deals which they know are fiercely uncompetitive. But if Waterstones, W. H.

Smith or Amazon demand 60 per cent discount, there's little scope for negotiation. And, in the case of the first two, they often demand a 'promotional' spend too, just to stock the book. For many publishers it has become the economics of the mad house.

So, we are all asking ourselves if e-books might be the saviour of the publishing industry. In theory they could cut out the middle man (i.e. the bookshop) and be sold directly to the public. But, in theory, that is also the same for physical books, and most publishers don't do much direct bookselling. At Biteback we are about to dip our toes into the e-book market. We've signed a deal with Amazon who appear to be about to become a monopoly supplier of e-books. But no one really knows the price level at which to pitch e-books. The consumer is canny enough to work out that if there aren't any print costs, the price should be lower, but some of the bigger UK publishers continue to stick their heads in the sand and try to charge the full retail price. The economics of e-books appear to stink. Say we charge £5 for a paperback whose bookshop price would be £10. Amazon will take 60 per cent of the £5, leaving £2 left, of which £1 goes to the author. That doesn't leave an awful lot for the publisher, does it? If sales levels of e-books are higher than that for physical books, then it might all work, but at the moment it is unclear if that will be the case, and how long it will take to get there.

All of this means that small to medium-sized publishers are having to become far more innovative in the way they market and sell their books. This ought to be a huge opportunity for independent bookshops to step up and fill the gap vacated by the big chains, who have all merged into one or gone out of business. But so far they show few signs of doing so.

This might all sound a bit downbeat and depressing. But for me it's not a threat, it's a real opportunity. We know there is a tremendous appetite for reading and for good, quality literature in this country. All we have to do is figure out how best to exploit it.

WOKE UP THIS MORNING...
SATURDAY 4 DECEMBER

I know it's wrong but this made me laugh. It's from the excellent Prisoner Ben Blog:

Sitting in the freezing cold yard under the yellow floodlights, two members of the musical fraternity begin jamming lyrics. It quickly descended into the default cynicism of Lifers:

> Woke up this morning,
> My baby was gone.
> F*****g social workers.

Well, it made me smile, anyway.

THE TIME HAS COME TO STOP BLOGGING (AND PARTY POLITICS)
TUESDAY 14 DECEMBER

Well, I am afraid this is the blog post where I tell you that I am giving up blogging. This decision has been coming for some time and was nearly made a month ago, but I couldn't quite bring myself to do it then. Well, today I can. There's no single reason, but let me try to explain as best I can why I can no longer blog in the way I have been doing over the last five years. First of all, let me say what it's *not* about. It's got nothing to do with the Conservatives being in power. There's this myth that blogging in government is less interesting than in opposition. I've never bought that argument. I think I have been quite open in making clear when I think the coalition has got things wrong, but I accept that is not the perception, and probably never will be.

The truth is, I no longer enjoy blogging and I think that this has been evident for a few months now to my readers. I hate the backbiting that goes along with it. I hate the character assassination that is permanently present. I no longer enjoy the pressure of feeling I have to churn out four or five pieces every day. I used to enjoy sitting in front of the TV at home in the evenings and writing blog posts at the same time. I can't do that any longer as I am on the radio every weekday evening. And when I am in the office during the day I have two companies to run. Something has to give.

And, if I am honest, I now feel that my blogging is having a negative effect on various aspects of my business and broadcasting life. For instance, yesterday I felt, for various reasons, I had to slightly caveat what I really wanted to say about Tom Baldwin's appointment. Another post in the last few days has caused an unfortunate situation too with a potential advertising client. My blog is indeed a personal plaything, independent of *Total Politics* or LBC, but the reality is that this is not how many in the outside world see it. And I now need to recognise that.

I'm working 9 a.m. to 10 p.m. five days a week. I enjoy it. I relish it. I thrive on it. I'm running a new publishing company which is, I believe, on the brink of great success. I've achieved a lifetime's ambition of having my own daily radio talk show. I am not about to put either of those things at risk. And, frankly, I'm not going to put my health at risk either. As I said above, something has to give in this life I am now leading, and I am afraid it is the blog.

I have also decided to give up all party political activities, as they too have hampered aspects of my business and broadcasting career in the past. I am, and will remain, a Conservative supporter, but that's as far as it goes.

Finally, I'd like to thank all my readers for sticking with me through good times and bad over the last five years. To the many enemies I have made along the way, I'll just say in a very Nixon-esque manner, just rejoice in the fact that you won't have me to kick around any longer. For the moment, anyway. For the most part, I have enjoyed the blogging experience and made a lot of friends through it.

Thank you, and au revoir.

• • •

I never actually said I wouldn't blog at all, ever again. I just couldn't do it five times a day. I still wanted to have a vehicle for my thoughts and so, from time to time, a new blog would go up on the site. And then, in July 2011, I started a group blog, Dale & Co.

2011

At 3.15 on Wednesday I heard some terrible news, which knocked the stuffing out of me for the rest of the day. Mark Hanson is a name few outside the world of new media and Labour politics will have heard of. But in his field he built up a great reputation for being an expert in the world of internet politics and PR, and being a thoroughly nice guy who never let his political allegiances. When I learnt of Mark's death yesterday, the world seemed to stand still. How could it have happened? I didn't know Mark well, but he was one of those people who you feel enriched by knowing. He was an enthusiast. Someone who, although a staunch Labour supporter, would happily put aside his tribal allegiances and engage with those on the other side of the political fence.

I first knew Mark when he was a regular contributor to the internet TV station, 18 Doughty Street. He brought humour and insight into any discussion and I always looked forward to his appearances. He had a certain northern bluntness, which translated well on TV and radio. He was the last person I'd have thought would suffer from depression, but it just shows, you never can tell.

Mental illness is still a taboo subject. Those who suffer from it are often embarrassed to discuss it even with close friends. It is a very lonely illness sometimes. I've never suffered from depression and often find it difficult to relate to those who do, or have. But I do know what a burden it can be. The burden was too much for Mark, something the friends and family members he leaves behind will struggle to comprehend for a long time to come.

Mark enriched the lives of all who knew him. To die at the terribly young age of thirty-four is nothing short of a tragedy. But it is a death which unites all his friends from left and right. It unites us in genuine grief.

AUSTRALIAN DIARY: THE FIRST WEEK
THURSDAY 2 JUNE

I last came to Australia twenty years ago, in September 1991. Last time Australia was in recession was in 1991. The week I arrive here the country goes into negative growth for the first time since 1991. Sorry, Australia, I seem to bring recessions with me. I didn't mean it. Honest.

There are very few countries in the world I could live in. Australia is one of them. When I came here twenty years ago, I had expected not to like it. I have no idea why I thought that, because I fell in love with the country. Unfortunately, on that trip I only had about two days' free time so had little opportunity to have a proper look round. We went to Sydney, Melbourne and Canberra, but spent all our time working. We were advising the Australian Liberal Party on reforming laws governing the employment of dock workers. On our first day in the country we were warned that if the dockers' unions found out we were here, our lives would be in danger. Nice. There was no such warning this time!

I never intended to wait twenty years to return, but time somehow just slipped by. So, why am I here? Well, those nice people at Microsoft invited me to do a week-long speaking tour and, frankly, who was I to refuse? I thought that it was rather idiotic just to spend one week here, so tagged on another week, and then had the bright idea of broadcasting my LBC show for a week from Sydney, and I will be doing that from 13 to 18 June. Unfortunately I miscalculated the time difference and I will actually be broadcasting my normal evening show from 4 a.m. to 7 a.m. in the morning.

I arrived in the country on Sunday morning and had a day and a half before my first speaking engagement.

On Monday afternoon I switched on the Australian version of Sky News (same graphics and music as the UK version, interestingly) to watch Question Time from the House of Representatives in Canberra. More of that later. Ahem. One thing though, I was rather captivated by the Australian Deputy Leader of the Opposition, Julie Bishop, who I had never encountered before. I tweeted:

> Loving the hairstyle of the Deputy Leader of the Opposition in Australia. I hear she was Krystal Carrington's stunt double in *Dynasty*.

I didn't realise I had so many Twitter followers here in Australia, as this appeared in most of the newspaper diary columns the next day. As you're about to see, I didn't learn my lesson...

My first speaking commitment was at the Sydney Institute on Monday evening, where I gave a talk on the world of political blogging and new media. It was a very engaged audience, who seemed well versed in British politics. Sajid Javid MP had been there the week before. Later that evening AMP hosted a dinner for me at the top of their harbourside office block. The night views over the Opera House and Harbour Bridge were stupendous. But it really was singing for my supper. There were about twenty guests and they grilled me between courses for a good couple of hours. Still, liking the sound of my own voice has never been a problem for me!

On Tuesday it was up early for the flight to Canberra. Very early. We got to the Hyatt in Canberra at about 10 a.m. I had two speeches to complete writing, but I was so tired I thought I'd have a quick zzzz before getting down to it. Quick zzzz. Hmmm. I woke up at 2 p.m. Bugger. But luckily just in time to watch Question Time again. In Australia, the House of Commons sits for only eighty days a year – an innovation we should copy – and on each day there is a ninety-minute Question Time session in which all government ministers partake. The behaviour in the chamber on this occasion was even worse than the day before. And that's saying something. I like adversarial politics. I would hate to have a sterile chamber like the US House of Representatives or the German Bundestag, but the Australians take adversarial politics to ridiculous levels. The pure hatred and loathing on the faces of the Prime Minister and Leader of the Opposition have to be seen to be believed. And the others take their lead from them. The Speaker, a gentle soul called Harry Jenkins, seems powerless to call order. Every few seconds he murmurs 'Order', but few take any notice. He names people. Still they take no notice. He can send people out of the chamber for an hour to cool down, and does. He can ban people. But they see no shame in being named or sin-binned. Indeed, it seems to be a badge of honour. The Speaker doesn't ever seem to stand. He just sits there and every twenty seconds or so, says 'Order'. To me, he is part of the problem. He's not an authority figure, and boy, does that chamber need an authority figure. Anyway, during Tuesday's session I tweeted this:

> The UK House of Commons is often accused of behaving like a playground. It has nothing on the Aussie House of Reps. Unbelievable behaviour.

This led to quite a strong reaction on Twitter and gained me about 200 extra followers. Remarkably, virtually everyone agreed. In retrospect I suppose I might have got a lot of tweets accusing me of being a whinging Pom, but there was only one blogger who really took issue with me and that was because of a bit of a misunderstanding. As a result of the tweet the BBC World Service rang and asked if I would expand on my view on their *World Update* programme with Dan Damon, which I duly did. Unfortunately they then posted a heavily edited transcript of my remarks, which they made out was an article by me. It wasn't.

And so it started. Radio interview after radio interview about what I had said. This afternoon I did a half-hour phone-in on Sydney's ABC 702AM station, which is their equivalent of LBC. Remarkably, every caller agreed with me.

Next morning, it was show time! I delivered the keynote speech at the Microsoft/Open Forum Politics and Technology Forum at Parliament House. My speech was to be on 'Openness and Transparency' and was scheduled to last forty minutes. I have to say I don't think I have ever given a forty-minute speech before. I reckon that unless you're Martin Luther King or Barack Obama, people tend to switch off after twenty minutes no matter how good you are. So I deliberately timed a vicious attack on Julian Assange for the 25-minute mark. It worked. I think.

I then took part in a ninety-minute-long panel with top Aussie blogger Stilgherrian (that's his real name; he doesn't have a second one), Gianpaolo Carrera from Microsoft, Professor Eric Clements from the US, Shadow Chancellor (or Treasurer as they say here) Joe Hockey and Senator Kate Lundy, PPS to the Prime Minister and Sarah Palin look-a-like (and I mean that in an admiring way, Kate!) and an expert in social media. It all seemed to go off well. I wasn't sure if my speech had worked, but all the Twitter reaction seemed positive.

Later on, over lunch, I delivered a second speech to the All-Party UK/Australia Friendship group of Senators and MPs. It was good to meet so many of them, especially the redoubtable Bronwyn Bishop, who I hit it off with – she's Australia's answer to Ann Widdecombe! I talked about the role of technology in the 2010 election.

Later in the afternoon we flew back to Sydney. I was due to have dinner with my old colleague from 18 Doughty Street days, Alice Wright, but I was so tired I put her off until Monday.

Today I had breakfast and lunch with Shane Stone. Shane is on the board of the holding company which owns Biteback, and he is the former Chief Minister of the Northern Territories and also a former Liberal Party President. Next week I am going to Darwin to stay with him. We're apparently going fishing in crocodile country, 300 km west of Darwin. Apparently the boats have to have reinforced floors to stop the crocs biting through. I shall try not to be a wuss.

I also went to the Microsoft offices to talk to thirty or forty of their staff. I did it all off the cuff today, which is my favoured method of speaking, and we had a really good Q&A. And that was the final part of the working bit of my trip.

I now have six days in Sydney to do as I please. I reckon I shall take a few day trips out of the city, maybe to the Blue Mountains one day and the Hunter Valley another. I also want to do a Sydney Harbour boat trip.

Just a final word about my first impressions of Australia on this visit. The one thing that has struck me so far is that it is an incredible, optimistic, cheerful nation. People actually smile at you. You don't get many smiles to the dozen in London, but here, it's as if people are enjoying life and are not letting problems get them down. Sydney is a very cosmopolitan city and on the outside at least has coped very well with integrating a huge number of migrants from fellow Asian countries. But the prices! My God, this is the most expensive place I have ever been in my life. It's far more expensive than Scandinavia and Switzerland. A Mars bar costs £2! A can of coke in the hotel is £5. I ordered a club sandwich, a cranberry juice and a cherry strudel dessert. The bill came to more than £55. Breakfast is £30. Madness. Luckily it's those nice people at Microsoft who are paying, but after Saturday I am on my own!

AUSTRALIAN DIARY: THE SECOND WEEK
MONDAY 13 JUNE

Sitting here basking in 32-degree heat, looking out over a balmy Darwin sunset in northern Australia I am wondering why anyone would ever leave this heavenly place. I've been in Australia for nearly two weeks and have loved every minute of it. It's a truly fabulous country and it's easy to see why so many Brits come here to live. It's a very optimistic country and you get a sense of the optimism just by looking into people's faces as you walk down the street. Strangers smile at you. They chat to you with ease. There are none of the scowls you get if you ever make eye contact with anyone on the streets of London. There's none of the scepticism so prevalent in our society in the UK. This is a can-do country with a positive attitude.

The political part of my trip ended a week ago – I was here to deliver a number of speeches for Microsoft Australia, two of which were in Parliament House in Canberra. So with that part of the trip over with, it was time to do a little relaxing and sightseeing.

On Monday I took a train ride up the coast to Newcastle, and very scenic it was too – the train ride, I mean, not Newcastle. I got to Sydney Central station early in the morning and bought my ticket, which was unbelievably cheap. Bearing in mind it was a 320 km round trip it only cost £8. I took comfort in the fact that it was about the only cheap thing I had encountered on my trip so far. I then asked how much a first class ticket would be. 'Sir, all our seats are first class.' That put me in my place.

The journey through the Hawkesbury River was stunning. The train never seemed to break more than about 50 mph and it took three hours before we arrived in Newcastle. I had been warned that it wasn't exactly a beautiful town, and so it proved. I wandered round the harbour area and up to Nobby's Beach (yes, honestly) before waiting to catch a trolley bus tour of the town at 1 p.m. The trolley bus duly arrived and I turned out to be the only customer. The driver said he couldn't take me on my own but would drop me at the town's new maritime museum. Which he did. And it was closed.

Buses in Newcastle are free, and all of them run virtually empty. There's a lesson there somewhere. I was amused to see that the buses were going to outlying town suburbs called Morpeth and Wallsend! So back to Sydney I went, and enjoyed the scenic railway for a second time.

In the evening I met Alice Wright for dinner in a wonderful Italian restaurant in Surry Hills. Alice was the floor manager at 18 Doughty Street and is now living in Sydney with her Aussie boyfriend. She is a speechwriter for the New South Wales minister for tourism. It was great to see her again and reminisce about all the programmes we made together.

It was another early start on Tuesday. I was picked up shortly after 7 a.m. from my city centre apartment by a tour company who were taking me on a trip to the Blue Mountains. James, the tour guide, immediately told me the bus would be very full. 'There are two of you,' he joked. And there were. Me and a Canadian girl called Angela. The advantages of travelling in the Australian winter. We started off by visiting an Aboriginal Cultural Centre and then headed up into the mountains. Stunning scenery and more than a little of the Grand Canyon about parts of it. We even saw some kangaroos. I know it's pathetic, but that was the highlight. 'Whatcha say, Skip? Grandma's fallen down a mineshaft?' Readers of a younger generation won't get that, but those of us who were brought up on *Skippy the Bush Kangaroo* will!

On Thursday I flew up to Darwin to spend the weekend with Shane Stone, a friend of mine who is a former Chief Minister of the Northern Territory. It's a four-hour flight from Sydney. To give you some geographical perspective, Darwin is further from Sydney than London is from Moscow. It's the dry season in Darwin at the moment and a very pleasant 30 degrees. We were joined by two of Shane's colleagues and were immediately driven to Crocosaurus Cove where we saw some very big crocodiles indeed! On Friday morning we headed out to Channel Point, which is a 140-mile drive, mainly on dirt roads. It's on the coast, opposite the Peron Islands, and is a compound of about twenty properties. It's totally isolated from anywhere. You walk along the beach and you feel as if you are about to star in an episode of *Lost*. I've never been fishing before, but that's what people do here. All the time. All day. Except that the wind was too strong, thereby preventing us from going out on the water. But we fished in a creek and laid crab traps. I eventually learnt how to cast a rod, but didn't end up catching anything. But I did catch crabs. There's a joke there somewhere.

We headed back to Darwin this morning. I had to laugh at the start of an article in the local Darwin newspaper today. 'Darwin is in the grip of winter. Temperatures descended to a chilly 25 degrees centigrade yesterday...'

We caught the afternoon flight back to Sydney. I'm now gearing myself up for the final week of my stay here, which will be dominated by broadcasting my LBC show every day from 4 a.m. to 7 a.m. from the Today FM studios.

And I am going to meet some long-lost relatives in Sydney, I never knew I had. More of that another time.

GIO – A TRIBUTE
FRIDAY 1 JULY

Gio Simmonsdale
1997–2011

Maybe it's somehow fitting that this will be the last ever blog post on this blog. It marks the end of two eras – the end of this blog, as in a few days time my new site, Dale & Co launches, and also the end of a life.

Five hours ago my beloved little Jack Russell, Gio, died. Those of you who have ever had the privilege of owning a dog will know what a devastating time this is for me and my family, who loved him with all our hearts. It is scant consolation to know that we gave him the best life a dog could possibly have, as a gaping hole has opened up in our lives, which can never, ever be filled.

Most Jack Russells are characters, and Gio was no exception. He was a cheeky little blighter and had us all wrapped around his little paws.

Gio was a Battersea dog. Back in early 1998 we went to Battersea, ostensibly to get a fully grown, house-trained dog. We emerged with a six-week-old Jack Russell puppy who was so small that I could hold him in the palm of my hand. People often ask why we called him Gio. I wanted to call him Rio, after Rio Ferdinand, but that was vetoed by he who must be obeyed. But I wear an aftershave called Aqua di Gio, and as I was shaving one morning I saw it on the shelf and thought to myself that Gio sounded enough like Rio, and it was just right for him. After that, my aftershave became known as Gio's piss...

When I grew up we had always had Jack Russells so I knew what wonderful dogs they could be, but I had no idea this little mite would give us so much pleasure and become such an integral part of our lives. He was a dog that everyone loved. And Gio loved them back. Well, almost everyone. He didn't care much for children, and let them know it in a typical Jack Russell kind of way – he would give them a nip. For some unfathomable reason he also didn't like people on bicycles. If he saw someone riding a bike he would literally go mental.

During the first few years of Gio's life, he would come to work with John and me at our Westminster bookshop, Politico's. We barred him in behind the counter, but on several occasions he escaped and delighted in running round the shop at full pelt, causing total havoc. The customers thought it was an absolute hoot.

In his early years Gio was a very fit and active dog. He loved going to the park and haring after a tennis ball I would throw. He never tired of it and would happily carry on for half an hour given half a chance. Sadly, this activity came to an end when one day he jumped off a sofa and damaged a knee ligament. Although we were still able to take him for walks, he wasn't allowed to run at all, which meant that over time he became a bit of a porker. This proved to be a real problem as Gio was a terrible food thief. You'd give him his meal and ten minutes later he'd give you a look which said, 'Daddy, why are you starving me? Give me some of your doughnut.' And believe me, he made you want to give in to his every demand. We didn't, but felt very guilty for refusing him anything.

My worst memory of Gio's life was when he was run over. And it was my fault. He was on an extendable lead and I was walking ahead of him when I suddenly became aware of an approaching car. It happened in slow motion. I heard a thud, and then Gio emerged from the side of the car and sat down on the pavement holding his paw up. I gathered him up, ran home bawling my eyes out, thinking he would die. We put him in blankets and rushed to the vet who diagnosed a sprained leg. It could have been so much worse.

Back in 2005, Gio spent a morning with me on the general election campaign trail in Cromer. We bought him a union jack coat. But sadly even Gio's charms couldn't rescue me from an inglorious defeat at the hands of Norman Lamb.

Gio was a dog that liked his routine. At 2 p.m. precisely he would sit by the dog-chew drawer. At 10 p.m. he would demand his nightly rich tea biscuit and slurp of cranberry juice. On his nightly walk he would go so far and no further. And, like all Jack Russells, a walk in his view was less about exercise and more about having a good old sniff.

But over the last year there had been a clear decline in the little scamp's health. He developed a slight heart problem and seemed to pant too much. We were warned by the vet that he might not be long for this world. But he was a doughty fighter and bounced back again. But just before I went to Australia it became clear that he was struggling. I dreaded going away for three weeks with the thought in the back of my mind that I might not see him again. My partner, John, and I chatted on Skype video twice a day and I made him show me Gio each time, just so that I could be reassured he was still alive. I know John dreaded having to tell me he had died while I was away.

Whenever I go away the one thing that keeps me going is the thought of the welcome Gio will give me when I get home. And that was my abiding thought as I flew back from Australia the Sunday before last. But instead of being delighted to see me when I walked through the door, and instead of giving my face a good licking, he just looked at me to say, 'Oh, you're back then.' And then he wandered into the kitchen. I was gutted. And I knew then that something was seriously wrong. He had also clearly lost a lot of weight. He'd come to my sofa for 'a love' – and just stared into my eyes, as if to say, 'Daddy, what's wrong with me? Please put it right.' That look never failed to bring a tear to my eye.

Anyway, the vet diagnosed diabetes. We were told he'd need an insulin injection every day. And then a minor miracle happened. An hour after the first injection he was back to his old self. He was eating properly, full of life, tail erect, being cheeky, keen to go on his walk, and everything seemed right with the world. But it wasn't to last.

I got home from my radio show on Friday night to find that a few minutes before I got there he had had what we thought was a hypoglycaemic attack. He had fitted. We got the vet out to see him, hoping beyond hope that he would be able to fix him. Instead he delivered the devastating news that Gio was unlikely to make it through the night. It appeared he had had a stroke. He wasn't in pain, but the sadness in his eyes told its own story. As the hours wore on, his breathing got gradually weaker, and at 5.30 a.m. he passed away.

Our lives will never be the same. He meant everything to John and me. He and John were devoted to each other. Gio knew that if he felt ill, it would be John that would make him better. He was the constant in Gio's life. John and I are very different. John is stoic and knows what to do if Gio is in pain. I collapse into an emotional jelly. And so it was last night. Gio spent most of his last few hours staring up at John and me. If he could have spoken, he would have said to John: 'Thank you, Daddy, thanks for being there for me. Thanks for giving me a wonderful life.'

If you haven't had a dog in your life you cannot comprehend the gaping void that can never, ever be filled. Someone said the best thing to do is get another dog immediately. I just couldn't. It would feel like betraying his memory.

As I complete this tribute to the best friend I am ever going to have, it provides little solace to know in my heart that we gave Gio the best life a dog could ever have. Maybe one day we'll feel ready to try to do the same for another rescue dog. But there will never be another Gio.

GIO: THE AFTERMATH
SATURDAY 16 JULY

A fortnight ago I devoted my entire column to discussing the death of my poor little Jack Russell, Gio. I make no apology for returning to the subject. I have been incredibly touched by the letters and emails I have received from readers from all over the country. Indeed, never has my column provoked such a reaction. I guess everyone who has ever owned a pet could relate to the terrible experience I was going through.

It is a cliché, I know, but time is a healer, and it dims the pain. But it will take some time for the grieving process to finish. The house seems to so empty. No pit-patter of tiny paw on the floorboards, warning of an imminent arrival. No barking when dinner is ready. No fur to hoover up from the red carpet every day. No dog bowl by the kitchen sink. No smell of dog in my office. There are so many reminders of the little beast who filled our lives with such joy.

I wanted to bury Gio on my parents' farm in Essex – the place I still call home. It's a property that's never likely to leave my family and Gio used to love going there and playing with his Jack Russell 'cousin' Spike. But my partner insisted that we should have him cremated and keep his ashes in a box. I've never liked the idea of cremation and have always thought there was something vaguely barbaric about it. I've got it written in my own will that I am to be buried, not cremated. Indeed, I do everything I can to avoid going to any funeral that takes place in a crematorium. The sight of the coffin disappearing is one of the most horrific things a human being can experience. Anyway, in the end I agreed to it, and on Thursday Gio came home. Or at least his ashes did. In some ways, there's something vaguely comforting about the fact that he is back in his own domain and that, if I want to, I can go and sit by his little box and have a chat with him. The trouble is, every time I do that, I know that the waterworks will start again.

Many kind people said we were wrong to think that getting a new dog would be betraying Gio's memory. In fact they were very persuasive. No dog can ever replace Gio, but we have now decided that in the autumn we will welcome not one, but two new dogs into our lives. We'll get another rescue Jack Russell and we've already chosen a mini schnauzer. They will be company for each other. But they have a lot to live up to!

NEW PUPPIES
WEDNESDAY 10 AUGUST

As readers may remember, we lost our Jack Russell, Gio, at the beginning of July. His death left a real void in our lives. We hadn't intended to get a new dog for a long time, but the house seems very empty. Indeed, so empty that we decided to get two dogs – a mini schnauzer and another Jack Russell. I wanted to get a pup from Battersea, which is where we got Gio from, but they don't have any. Last week my partner went to the south coast to see a JR pup we had seen advertised on the internet. It wasn't a pleasant experience. It turned out to be a very dirty and disgusting puppy farm on a gypsy encampment. In the tradition of *News of the World* reporters, he made his excuses and left. Then last Saturday we struck gold. We found what looked like a very cute Jack Russell puppy in Bedford, and sure enough he was. In fact he's adorable. We took him home immediately and a week on it feels like he is already a fundamental part of our lives. He's called Dude, and he lives up to his name. Like most puppies he has an on/off switch. He plays manically for an hour, then switches off and goes to sleep. We've been very lucky, even if, ahem, he's not exactly housetrained yet.

Today we're picking up our second puppy, a mini schnauzer called Bubba. I just hope they both get on. Ideally we'd have got them both on the same day so they could bond together in the house without one trying to rule the roost, but that didn't work out. But I suppose we all know that any Jack Russell will be master in his own home. I know my place. I wonder if Bubba the schnauzer will know his?

THIRD TIME LUCKY ON *ANY QUESTIONS*
FRIDAY 9 SEPTEMBER

Last Friday I made my third appearance on *Any Questions*. The old saying that once you have done something once it's easier the second or third time doesn't really apply to *Any Questions*, as there is so much scope to make a complete idiot of yourself. One stupid answer to a question, one remark that you think is clever but which falls flat can ruin an otherwise reasonable performance. So it's one of the few things I get nervous about doing.

However, I am a firm believer that too much preparation for a programme like this can be a very bad thing. If you are overprepared it can make you seem very flat and a little boring. But on the other hand, if you wing it, it's also a rather dangerous thing to do. While it is true that the panel don't know the questions in advance, you'd have to be a bit of a fool if you couldn't guess at least half the subjects that will come up. This time I got them all right, apart from one, so that wasn't a bad strike rate. Indeed, the one which I didn't guess (planning) last night, I felt was one of my stronger answers, so maybe there's a lesson there.

My first mistake yesterday was to drive myself to Somerton. I had been up since 5 a.m., as I had been presenting LBC's breakfast show all week. I was already knackered having only had four hours sleep on Wednesday night. My own stupid fault, as I had forgotten to cancel my regular Wednesday night appearance on the Sky News paper review. So by mid-morning on Friday I wasn't exactly feeling my best, and a business meeting on Friday morning went on far longer than anticipated so my preparation time was cut to the bone. I ended up leaving for Somerton an hour later than intended, and then it was the turn of the A303 to scupper my plans to have tea with some friends in nearby Langport. In the end I arrived at the pub in Somerton (the White Hart) where the panellists (John Kampfner, Norman Lamont and Joan Bakewell were my debating partners) were to meet for dinner at 5.30. So, half an hour to prepare for the fifteen subjects I figured might well come up. Hey ho.

And then it began. First question on banking, second on planning, third on the Dale Farm travellers, followed by defence cuts and then one on school discipline. And then we came to the final question. What stupid things did the panel do in their youth? My mind went completely blank and I prayed Martha [Kearney] wouldn't come to me first. She didn't. I had thought I would talk about driving a combine harvester, unsupervised, at the age of eight, but right at the last second I changed my mind and talked about being in the 'Making Your Mind Up' Bucks Fizz video we made with *Total Politics* last year. It got a good laugh.

Of the three times I've been on the programme I certainly felt more comfortable about how I'd done at the end of this one than the other two. That's all I'll say! There were no real spats and I guess some people felt we all agreed with each other a little too much. Joan and I had a bit of a contretemps over the travellers, but that was really the only bit of controversy. I'm just too consensual!

THE TOILET HABITS OF DOGS
FRIDAY 7 OCTOBER

Many of you have emailed asking how our two new puppies are settling in. Dude and Bubba are now just over three months old and are getting on like a house on fire. They are both very different characters. Dude, the Jack Russell, is super-intelligent, while Bubba is, well, a bit of a thicko. I'm not even sure he knows his name yet. But he is a delightful and very loving little dog. I've never had a mini schnauzer before, but he's a great addition to the family. Their toilet habits still leave a lot to be desired, but that's the only bad thing I can say about them. They seem to have on/off switches. They're either acting like Duracell bunnies and creating havoc or they're asleep. There doesn't seem to be a middle way.

THE GARY SPEED TRAGEDY
FRIDAY 2 DECEMBER

I never met Gary Speed and yet when I heard about his death, I was very affected by it. I think that's a common reaction among many people who are affected by the death of a celebrity. You kind of feel they are your friend, even though you have never met them. I remember walking down a street in London a few years ago and walking past Dame Judi Dench. I found myself saying hello to her. She smiled a little and we both went our separate ways. Afterwards I felt a complete fool, but my instinctive reaction was to say hello to someone I knew. Or thought I knew. I bet you've done the same.

Gary Speed's death illustrates a number of things. It shows that none of us knows what we are capable of. We don't know what others are capable of. How could someone, no matter what pressures they are under, do what Gary Speed has done? How could he do it to his wife. To his two teenage sons? It's too early to analyse. It's too early to even understand. But it's not too early to think. To try to come to terms with something that is so shocking it almost defies logic.

His death also shows we have no idea what goes on behind closed doors. To the outside world Speed had a perfect life, and yet he was clearly suffering beyond belief but putting a very brave face on it.

We don't know exactly what caused Gary to take the ultimate step, but it may well be depression. Some people, to this day, not only think depression is something invented by people of weak minds, I hope they will think again. Think about German goalkeeper Robert Enke. Think about Stan Collymore's ongoing battles. Read Alastair Campbell's diaries. We all need to try to understand more about depression. It's no good just telling someone who feels depressed to 'pull yourself together and just get on with it'. The best thing one can do is sit down, hold someone's hand, and just be there. And then listen.

Gary Speed was a hero to many. While the manner of his passing doesn't befit the career he enjoyed, he leaves with our respect, admiration and sympathy.

•••

Every Wednesday night I do the late-night newspaper review on Sky News (at 11.30 p.m., since you asked) with the lovely Anna Botting.

More often than not my sparring partner is former Labour Home
Secretary Jacqui Smith. This week one of those 'I can't believe she
just said that' moments occurred. Jacqui was regaling us about her
dislike of nature programmes on TV. I sat open-mouthed and asked
her, 'So, Jacqui, what do you actually like watching on TV then?'
But before she could answer, Anna Botting said, 'Oh, we all know
what she likes to watch on TV...' Surely she wasn't making a reference to, well, you know. Do I really need to explain? Remember the
porn video rental saga? I looked at Anna and said, 'Well, I wasn't
going to go there,' and then it suddenly hit Anna as to what she had
said. She was bereft. 'Oh my God, I didn't mean that, I really didn't,'
she flustered. It turned out she was making reference to a piece on
Downton Abbey which was on the front page of the next day's *Daily
Telegraph*. Meanwhile, Jacqui, to her credit, was roaring with laughter. Well, poor woman, what else could she do? When the cameras
stopped rolling Anna couldn't stop apologising. Jacqui has a very
well-developed and earthy sense of humour and didn't seem at all
bothered, but I do wonder if, deep inside, constant reminders of that
semi-scandal wound more than she lets on. Politicians, and indeed
ex-politicians, are only human and have the same feelings as the rest
of us.

2012

On Saturday I went to see the *Iron Lady* film with, it has to be said, a degree of trepidation. The initial publicity suggested it would be a complete hatchet job, but it was far from that. The cinema was completely full and half the audience seemed to be under the age of thirty. I was surprised on both counts.

Meryl Streep was fantastic and worthy of an Oscar, but I can't say the same about her co-star, Jim Broadbent, who played Denis Thatcher. Don't get me wrong, Broadbent is a brilliant actor – one of Britain's best – but his performance meant that a potentially Oscar-winning film doesn't actually deserve to get nominated. Some of the scenes involving him were just unimaginable.

If one good thing can come from this film it will be to widen the understanding of dementia and Alzheimer's. It was dealt with sympathetically, and although it dominated the film far too much, I can see why the director used it in the way she did – as a path back to episodes from Lady Thatcher's life. Yes, you can question the appropriateness of doing it this way, but it never made me squirm in my seat. And I thought it would.

There were lots of little inaccuracies which jarred with a political geek like me. Both Francis Pym and John Nott appeared in 1990 scenes. Nott left Parliament in 1983 and Pym left Parliament in 1987. Margaret Thatcher did not wear a hat while making speeches in the House of Commons as Education Secretary. Margaret Thatcher did not run after Airey Neave's car when it was bombed. She wasn't there. Again, I could go on.

But this is to carp. Overall, I enjoyed it immensely. Any neutral in the audience will have left the cinema thinking better of Margaret

Thatcher than when they entered it. It was a very sympathetic portrait of her, and her aims in life.

At the end of the film, the entire audience stayed sitting and waited till the credits had finished before leaving. That doesn't happen very often. And it spoke volumes.

CRYING
SATURDAY 14 JANUARY

Like Alastair Campbell, I have always been a little lachrymose. I cry really easily, which if you're a radio presenter isn't always a good thing. Last week I nearly lost my composure talking to a lady called Shona Lidgey, a GP from West Norfolk whose doctor husband David left home at the end of June and hasn't been seen since. I read about her story in the EDP and even though my radio show is London-based, I thought her story would really resonate with my listeners. When I read that Mr Lidgey might be in London, I was determined to track her down and talk to her on air. It can't have been an easy thing to do, but Shona was calm, composed and absolutely fascinating. I have written before about missing persons and the subject remains a source of bewilderment for many – especially those affected by a close family member simply disappearing. Anyway, I got to the end of that particular interview with my tear ducts still dry – just – but on Thursday this week, they well and truly opened.

If I tell you it was Caroline Flint's fault, you'll probably think I am making a political point. But you'd be wrong. Caroline gave an interview to the *Evening Standard* in which she spoke movingly of her upbringing. Her mother was an alcoholic. Reading it, and thinking back to my own rather idyllic and perfect childhood, I wondered what on earth it must be like to live with an alcoholic. And of such thoughts are radio phone-ins born.

It didn't get off to a good start. The guest we had booked didn't pick up the phone so I went straight to a caller called Sue in Twickenham. It wasn't her real name. Sue had had an alcoholic step-mother. She had run away from home at the age of fifteen. This was back in 1975. And so started a call that was to last around twenty-five minutes. Sue's story was graphic, moving and inspirational. Eventually, because the news bulletin was dawning, I reluctantly had to let her go. Texts and emails from listeners were piling up.

I rarely read texts before I read them out loud. I'm assuming my production team have vetted them for suitability. This was the next text:

> Today, I came home and saw on our fridge. 'Please don't drink anymore, I'm really worried about your health' written by my seven-year-old daughter. I figured she wouldn't ever find out, so I opened the fridge. But I found another note on a can that said: 'So you're going to drink anyway?'

I can't explain it, but as I read the text I could feel the tears welling in my eyes and my voice cracked. I had to stop after the word 'daughter' to collect myself. I ploughed on, but could feel myself going again. I stopped again. I was now worried about breaking down completely. Not good. But it was a text for God's sake! So I went slightly early to the travel news.

At the time, I felt a bit embarrassed by my reaction, but that feeling has passed. All I did was reflect what many in my audience were feeling. My producer was very keen to reassure me I shouldn't feel I had reacted overemotionally. 'Cracking bit of radio,' she said. I'll take her word for it.

BEHAVING BADLY
SATURDAY 21 JANUARY

Last night I apparently trended worldwide on Twitter. It was quite an experience being at the centre of a Twitter storm. Twitter is a very spontaneous medium. Many have come a cropper by posting something in haste and then repenting at leisure. It's certainly happened to me in the past. And when I think I have got it wrong I usually step forward and immediately apologise. This time I didn't.

Every Friday night when I leave the LBC studios in London's Leicester Square to walk down to Charing Cross station, it's like walking through a warzone. Drunken people tottering around, hurling abuse at each other and passers-by. It's Britain at its worst. It's ugly and repellent.

I don't drink, but it doesn't mean I criticise those who do. However, I will indeed criticise those whose only purpose is to go out on a Friday night with the specific purpose of getting legless. What kind of person does that? Inevitably it means that others get caught in their drunken exploits. Most of the time these antics are fairly harmless and merely cause minor embarrassment and inconvenience to the general public. In some cases, though, things go too far. I find drunks of either sex embarrassing and repellent. In the four minutes it takes to walk from Leicester Square to Charing Cross I was accosted by two people who were obviously the worse for wear, one female and one male. I brushed them aside without comment and walked on.

Just after the train left London Bridge a drunken woman got on my carriage and asked me to move the bag off the seat next to me. I asked her politely to sit in the seat opposite as I had no wish to sit next to a drunk in case she puked on me. An entirely reasonable thing to do in the circumstances. She then continued to act in a drunken manner, albeit not so legless that she wasn't aware what she was doing. I started tweeting about the experience. Again, she tried to sit next to me. I'm afraid I told her in no uncertain terms to go away. She went back to the other seat. Someone on Twitter then said: 'Take a picture of her.' And this is where it started. Perhaps unwisely I did so and posted the picture on Twitter along with the comment that I found her to be a 'disgusting slapper'. Not very nice, and certainly not very chivalrous, but it was what I felt at the time. And then the heavens opened.

I do find people who are drunk in public absolutely disgusting and find it appalling that most people on Twitter seemed to think it was perfectly normal and acceptable. Well, it isn't. It's a classic example of anti-social behaviour.

In short, the politically correct brigade started launching vicious attacks on me. They reckoned I wouldn't have done the same if it had been a man. How would they know? (I would, actually.) It was an attempt to portray me as some sort of misogynist. One even reckoned I was a potential rapist. Another suggested I should stick to cruising for little boys on Clapham Common. Nice.

They also complained that I had taken a picture of someone without their permission. If she was identifiable, they might have had a point. But she wasn't.

I can wholly accept that many people found what I did wrong, and impolite. And I have no problem with them saying so. But the majority then found it necessary to accompany their criticism with the most foul and abusive language. Again, their prerogative, but they didn't seem to see the irony of what they were doing.

And my biggest offence of all, it seems, was to cause offence. As if it was a crime. It isn't. Yet.

But none of them wants to address the real point. Is being blind drunk in public, on public transport an acceptable way to behave? It isn't, and I won't hesitate to keep pointing it out.

SEX TALK WITH AN OAP
SATURDAY 4 FEBRUARY

It's not easy talking to a 69-year-old woman about intimate sexual acts, but that's what I had to do on Thursday night. Her name was Mimi Alford and she was the Monica Lewinsky of her time. She's written a book outlining in graphic detail the affair she had with President Kennedy, while a White House intern, in the early 1960s. She described the night when, at the age of nineteen, she lost her virginity to JFK in his wife's bedroom at the White House. She told me about the time the President offered her 'poppers', a drug designed to enhance a sexual experience. She then proceeded to tell me that the President had asked her to perform a sex act on his close friend while the three of them were swimming together in the White House swimming pool. She complied. I remember saying to her I found it very difficult to talk to a 'woman of a certain age about issues like this', but then again she had written it all in the book. She had kept the secret for forty years but couldn't seem to give me a convincing answer as to why she had now, at the age of sixty-nine, decided to bare all. She reckoned it was so her grandchildren would know the truth. Hmmm. When I told her she could have written it for them and them only, and not published it to the wider world, she didn't really have an answer. Funny that.

RENT, EXTRADITION AND VEGANS
SATURDAY 25 FEBRUARY

I'm looking for a flat to rent in London. I don't want anything very luxurious or spacious, as I will effectively only be there to sleep three or four nights a week. I have to admit I was staggered by the cost of renting in central London. I just cannot work out how anyone in a normal job, paid an average salary, could ever afford to live there. It's virtually impossible to find a two-bedroom flat in Westminster or Pimlico for under £2,000 a month. Even a studio flat will go for £1,300–£1,500. And frankly most of them are places you wouldn't let your dog live. The trouble is that the rental sector in this country is inhibited by laws which act as a disincentive to property owners to rent out rooms, flats or houses. So if there's a lack of supply in a particular area, inevitably prices will rise. The same thing is true in the centre of Norwich, where some rentals have reached London levels. Renting also has a bit of a social stigma in this country. People tend to look down their noses at people who rent. It's not like that in other European countries. Many people in Germany, for example, rent all their lives and think nothing of it. Fifty per cent of people in Germany rent. I wonder what it would take to encourage property owners here to rent out more of their properties.

•••

It is outrageous that Christopher Tappin was extradited to the United States. Yesterday he was flown to America to face charges in an American court under the terms of an extradition treaty agreed to by the last government. There are no reciprocal arrangements under this treaty. We couldn't extradite people from the States in the same way. It is a disgrace that a British government rolled over and agreed to this treaty. But what is even more of a disgrace is that the coalition government hasn't sought to renegotiate it. They promised to in opposition, but haven't lifted a finger. As Mr Tappin said, Abu Qatada has more rights than he does. David Cameron and Theresa May have let down Mr Tappin and let down the entire nation.

•••

Are you a vegetarian or a vegan? Do you feel you're not particularly healthy? Well, a man called John Nicholson answered yes to both those questions. He'd been a vegetarian for twenty years but felt very unhealthy. He constantly felt tired. But then one day he decided to eat meat. Just to see what it would be like. Within forty-eight hours he was a changed man. And now he's written about his fascinating story in a book I published this week called *The Meat Fix*. As soon as it was published he was deluged with hate mail from vegetarians and vegans who, to put it mildly, felt let down and betrayed. Veganism is a pseudo-religion and anyone who strays from the true path is regarded as a pariah, it seems. Nice people. Not.

OLD MAN'S GLASSES
SATURDAY 10 MARCH

People can be very cruel. I had my eyes tested recently and my distance vision has worsened a little so I decided to treat myself to two new pairs of glasses. On Tuesday, I picked them up from the opticians. The main pair has a frame with a mild tortoiseshell effect and has received a lot of compliments. Not bad for £99. However, I wish I could say the same for the second pair. I put them on and showed my assistant, whose reaction was to roar with laughter. 'Oh my God,' he said, 'you can't possibly wear them!' 'Why?' I asked. 'Because they make you look eighty,' he said. They have a gold rim and the frame goes along the bottom of the lens, not the top. 'Norman Tebbit would wear glasses like that,' he continued. 'Well, if they're good enough for Norman Tebbit, they're good enough for me,' I retorted with some indignation. I put them back in their case. And if I am honest, that's where they have stayed.

NEW ON SUNDAY
SATURDAY 24 MARCH

LBC announced yesterday I would be taking over their Sunday morning political show from next Sunday – 1 April. It's a great slot to broadcast in and I'm really looking forward to it. More than ten years ago I was part of the *Sunday Service* team on a Sunday morning on 5 Live. It was a great programme, hosted by the incomparable Fi Glover, who I still regard as the finest female radio broadcaster of her generation. Doing the Sunday show means I get Friday nights back to myself, but it will still be odd having a weekend which consists of a Friday and Saturday rather than the normal Saturday and Sunday. I suppose I had better think of a really good April Fool to play on my listeners. A few years ago I made out I was running for Mayor of London. It was astonishing how many people got in touch to wish me well in my campaign. Nothing, but nothing would persuade me to do that for real.

AND IN A PACKED PROGRAMME THIS MORNING...
SUNDAY 1 APRIL 2012

Starting a new radio show is always a bit daunting, even when you've been doing one for a year and a half. Doubly so when you are taking over a slot previously inhabited by two friends. This morning I broadcast my first show in the 10 a.m. 'til 1 p.m. slot on LBC 97.3, having taken over from Andrew Pierce and Kevin Maguire. When the LBC management asked me to do this show we agreed on one main thing – that it would be different from my weekday evening show. It had to be, or there was little point in me dropping Friday nights to do Sunday mornings. Bang goes the weekend!

Currently there is very little competition in the political field on the radio on Sunday mornings. 5 Live has *Double Take*, but that finishes at 11. After Broadcasting House at 9, there's little for current affairs fanatics on Sunday mornings on Radio 4. So I think there is a good opportunity to make my Sunday morning show a real destination for all the people who may watch Andrew Marr and Andrew Neil but have little to entertain them in between on the radio.

LBC is known for its phone-ins and we certainly want our audience to remain a big part of our show. But we also want to introduce a bit of humour and quirkiness into the format. Older readers may remember that I used to deputise for Andrew Pierce on 5 Live's *Sunday Service* ten or so years ago, presented by Fi Glover. That show managed to make politics accessible and entertaining, something which most radio productions have struggled with ever since. It's too easy to fall for gimmickry and rudery and go for the lowest common denominator. I give you the *10 O'Clock Show* on Channel 4 as evidence. OK, it's TV, but you know what I mean.

We also want to use the LBC website to offer our listeners something extra. Today Julian Fellowes was our first guest. I pre-recorded the interview and we used about half of it on the programme but have made the whole thing available on the net. So we didn't use the stuff about the *Titanic* on air, but for those interested it is available online.

Similarly, our package on Ed Balls was ten minutes long and included an interview with the charity he is running the London

Marathon for. We couldn't use it all on air, so we put it online. Audiences are now getting used to listening to more online, and this enables them to get more value out of the parts of the programme they really like.

Sunday morning radio and TV shows always want to get a bit of a scoop and make the odd headline or two. So when I saw Ed Staite's blog on Friday about the sting operation, I asked him if he'd like to come on to talk about the experience. He agreed to do so and decided to talk exclusively to us and turn down Sky and 5 Live. Bosses very pleased. And the interview provided a fascinating insight for listeners into how the media works. Or shouldn't work.

At 11 we talked to Adam Boulton about the politics of populism, which was really an excuse to look back on the week in politics before we then looked forward to the week ahead with LBC's political correspondent, Tom Cheal, and Olly Mann, who will be playing a big role in the show in forthcoming weeks, I hope.

At 11.30 we introduced a feature which could have gone rather awry, but it seems to have gone very well. I'm a big fan of David Letterman-style Top Ten Lists and wanted to think of a way of introducing them into the programme, so I hit on a format of offering advice to someone in the news. So this week's victim was George Galloway. I'll reproduce it here, but you have to imagine it being played out over the song 'Respect Yourself'.

Top ten pieces of advice from LBC 97.3 to George Galloway
- Get the name of your constituency right. Not all northern towns begin with B.
- Watch your Twitter account for 'hackers'.
- Stay away from foreign dictators. Especially ones with big moustaches.
- Don't get a cat. But if you do, be sure to call it Rula.
- Don't wear red lycra at PMQs.
- Avoid words like 'indefatigable'.
- Don't walk out of interviews. It ain't clever and it ain't funny.
- Ditch the Scottish accent. Learn to speak West Yorkshire.
- Sit with the Lib Dems in the House of Commons. It will confuse them.
- Repeat after yourself: Respect is a two-way thing.

• • •

We then had a quick chat with David Cameron's personal trainer,

Matt Roberts, who almost succeeded in persuading me that I really need to get more exercise or I'm going to die.

And at 11.45 we launched our bid to find Britain's cleverest politician. Tom Harris came into the studio and did reasonably well to get twenty-six points out of a possible fifty. We'll be putting up a league table on the website in future weeks, not that we're copying Jeremy Clarkson's 'Star in a Reasonably Priced Car'. Oh no. Never let it be said. I'm now thinking about who to get on next week. Ideas?

Our final piece, it has to be said, was very atypical of what we'll be doing in subsequent weeks. We decided to do an hour on the Falklands. We had Sukey Cameron from the Falkland Islands Government Office in London in the studio, along with Michael Nicholson, one of the two TV reporters who sailed with the Task Force. We also talked to Major-General Julian Thompson, Rick Jolly and Alan West, captain of HMS *Ardent*, and then went live to Port Stanley to talk to four Falkland Islanders. The hour flew by. In all honesty we had too many guests, but they were all very informative and entertaining.

And so ended a very full three hours. Reaction so far has been overwhelmingly positive, but whenever there's change there will be people who hanker after what they were used to.

And so the planning for next week begins!

MY WONDERFUL DAY AT WEMBLEY
SATURDAY 19 MAY

Back where they belong...

Oh West Ham, we love you. Despite you making us tear our hair out, despite you being the most wonderful but frustrating team, we still come back for more. And today showed both sides of West Ham, but who cares? We are Premier League, I say we are Premier League! And there were many times today when I thought that wasn't going to happen. And, if we're honest, we could so easily have lost today. You could say that class showed in the end, and you might have a point, but at times in this game, Blackpool were all over us, especially the middle period of the second half. At times they cut through our defence like butter, but we survived. Indeed, shortly after Carlton Cole's opener, Vaz Te had a good chance to put us two up. His shot went slightly wide of the post. If that had gone in, I suspect we'd have chalked up another hatful. But credit to Blackpool, they fought and fought and they nearly did us over.

My day started at my parents' home at Ashdon, near Saffron Walden. I got up and instantly felt nervous. Four of us were going – my Blackpool-supporting dad and a friend of his, Dennis Peach, who's also a Blackpool supporter – and a Hammers-supporting school friend of mine, John Bidwell. We'd booked a car to pick us up at 10. It turned out to be a Skoda. Great. Just what I always wanted to travel to Wembley in. And the driver decided to go the scenic route. Even greater. We had arranged to meet some other friends under the Bobby Moore statue at 11.45. It soon became clear that would be an ambitious target. Not only had we got a driver whose familiarity with satnav proved illusory, but he hadn't got a clue where to go when we actually had the Wembley Arc in our sights. My dad is eighty-two so I needed to get as close to the stadium as possible as he's not so sharp on his pins. Eventually we got there, and my blood pressure was sky-high. I managed not to tell the driver quite what I thought, sorely tempted though I was. Manners won out in the end.

We slowly made our way up to the statue, my dad having to climb countless steps to do so. We then continued up to the Club Wembley area – thankfully via escalators. My dad hadn't been to Wembley since 1948 and his eyes were on stalks. I had only been to a concert in the new Wembley. Before we went into the Arc restaurant to eat, we took a peek at the pitch. It looked perfect. I have to say, the food wasn't worth the price, but it was nice to be able to relax before going to our seats. We decided to forgo the half-time drinks and stay in our seats. We were about the only ones to do so! Most of the people near us weren't even back for the Blackpool goal. But I am getting ahead of myself.

The first twenty minutes didn't see a single free kick given. Blackpool probably had the better of that period, mainly because we weren't getting stuck in. Indeed, I don't recall a single West Ham shot, while Blackpool had a couple of good chances. I began to get nervous, mainly because we normally start so strongly. Nothing was happening in midfield and we just couldn't get our passing game together. But we started to improve and had a succession of corners. Cole started to impose himself on the game and it was he who scored the opener after a wonderfully flighted ball into the box, which Cole chested down and volleyed into the net. It reminded me a little of David Platt's goal against Belgium in the 1990 World Cup. A few minutes later Vaz Te slid the ball wide when it looked easier to score. Half time. We were feeling slightly lucky to be ahead.

By this time West Ham fans were in full voice. Even in the Blackpool end, where I was, there were loads of West Ham fans. What a shame (and a scandal) it was that there were so many empty seats in the Blackpool end. That should never happen again.

Only three minutes into the second half and Cole gave the ball on the halfway line and Thomas Ince (son of Paul) ran into the penalty area and slotted the ball home diagonally past Rob Green. Terrible defending. Ince got loads of boos, which I thought was a bit off. It's not justified to visit the sins of the father on his son, but there you go. This started a purple patch for Blackpool and they could easily have had a couple more goals. But they didn't and that's the main thing. We weathered a prolonged storm and it was only when we reached the seventieth minute that we gradually got back into it. I looked at the clock. Eighty-one minutes. 'If we get one now, we'll win this,' I thought to myself, having previously been convinced that Blackpool were going to win through. Julien Faubert hit a screamer of a volley which hit the bar. Come on, You Irons. And then he did it. Ricardo Vaz Te hit a rebound high into the net and that was it. Apart from a very marginal penalty appeal, Blackpool never looked like scoring. We did the professional thing and kept the ball well. Eventually, after a totally unjustified four minutes of injury time, the whistle went, and the party started.

Winning promotion via the play-offs probably means more than automatic promotion. Neither Reading nor Southampton had a party like ours in full view of a national TV audience, let alone in front of 78,000 people. It really did feel like winning the cup. Carlton Cole reacted as if he'd won the lottery – and perhaps he has. It clearly meant a lot to him. After the presentations, he led the jollifications on the pitch. One slightly jarring note was the way Ricardo Vaz Te didn't join in, and headed straight down the tunnel on his own. I'm not quite sure what to read into that. The other players stayed on the pitch for a good twenty minutes after he disappeared.

By this stage I had shouted myself hoarse, which is not a good thing when you have to present a three-hour radio show in the morning. Anyway, we went back to the restaurant for a few drinks and a bit more food before I managed to have a very loud disagreement with a jobsworth Wembley steward who wouldn't let us leave the stadium on the same level as the Bobby Moore statue. I explained that I couldn't expect my 82-year-old dad to walk up two lots of very long stairs again. He still wouldn't open the door and let us out, so I am afraid the Dale temper was on full display. An unpleasant end to a fantastic Wembley experience. We eventually got to the waiting car and I waved off my dad and his friends back to Essex, while I queued for the tube to get into central London.

And of course there are now so many questions. What effect will our promotion have on our planned Olympic stadium move? Which players will leave? Who will Sam want to sign? How much are season tickets going to rise to? All those questions are for the next few weeks. For now, let's bask in the glory of today and revel in the victory. But let's also empathise with Blackpool. They have the makings of a really good team. They play great football and they gave us a real game today.

NORTH NORFOLK HOLIDAY DIARY: DAY 1
BRANCASTER STAITHE
THURSDAY 12 JULY

I don't take many holidays, and seeing as this one is to mark my fiftieth birthday, I thought I would record the events here. Yesterday we arrived at our holiday home in north Norfolk, although even the arrival was more by luck than judgement. We set out from Kent at around 12.30, having watched PMQs and settled the house sitter in. As we have the dogs with us, we stopped for a break in our journey at my parents' near Saffron Walden. It's the first time I have been back since my mother's funeral a fortnight ago. I took the dogs for a walk down to the cemetery to visit her grave and had a little tear. Although I am a very lachrymose person, I still don't feel I have cried enough. Very unlike me.

'It's only fifty-nine miles to Brancaster,' said John. 'It'll take an hour and a quarter.' I was somewhat dubious. 'It's got to be longer than that,' I protested. 'Well, that's what the satnav says,' he rejoined. Oh well, it must be right, then. My suspicions further mounted when we turned off the A14 to Ely, but knowing what

Simmo thinks about passenger-seat drivers, I kept my thoughts to myself. It was only when we were ten miles south of King's Lynn that I dared say something. 'You've typed the wrong Brancaster into the satnav,' I ventured. Never having knowingly admitted wrongness, Simmo looked like a goldfish. Who knew that there were two Brancasters in Norfolk? In fact, if you include Brancaster Staithe, there are three.

Anyway, as we drove into Brancaster I got my usual holiday feeling, which goes something like this: 'What if we hate the house/hotel?' But I needn't have worried. The weather had improved. There was blue sky all around. I had a good feeling about this. And so we arrived. What a house! The pictures on the website looked good, but the reality was far better. Admittedly we had really pushed the boat out when we chose this house, but it really does take your breath away. It was used as a hospital in the First World War. There are eight bedrooms, two fabulous living rooms and a massive kitchen.

The dogs raced around investigating, having endured the longest car journey of their one-year-old lives. Bubba was prancing around as if to say, 'Daddy, this is great, isn't it?' And it was.

A short time later our friend Jenny arrived. She had had her own journey dramas. Having driven up the M3 from Dorchester she somehow contrived to miss the M25 and knew something was wrong when she saw a sign to Kew Gardens. She ended up driving right through central London. It was a miracle she arrived at all.

On Saturday I'm having a party to 'celebrate' my half-century. Simmo has enlisted the assistance of our very good friend Pepi Simpson (wife of MP Keith) to help with the catering. She arrived at 8 p.m. and we decided to go to Sainsbury's in Hunstanton (or 'Hunston' in the local lingo – remember, we are in North Norfolk Digital country) to buy the booze. We were told that it was a 'superstore'. We got there to find possibly the smallest Sainsbury's in Christendom. And sure enough, they only had three bottles of the wine we had chosen. I sense a trip to King's Lynn coming on.

At home the dogs usually go to sleep around 8 p.m., so they were, to coin a phrase, dog-tired when we finally put them down at 1 a.m. Needless to say they were up and about by 5 a.m. wanting to be taken out. Tough luck.

NORTH NORFOLK HOLIDAY DIARY: DAY 3
SATURDAY 14 JULY

Getting older has never really bothered me. Being thirty or forty meant nothing. There was no mental anguish, no depression at the passing of my youth. So why is it that reaching the age of fifty this weekend feels something of a milestone?

Last week I tweeted about how I was feeling and ended the tweet with the hashtag #midlifecrisis. It was gently pointed out to me that the age of fifty was a little way past 'midlife'. Thanks for that.

The thing is, it's got nothing to do with my own mortality, which, by the way, I don't measure in years left. I count the number of World Cups I'll still live to witness. At least six or seven, I hope. No, even though my own mother's death last month made me think a little more about lifespan, reaching fifty doesn't make me think I'm on the way out. But it is salutary to think that I may only have a decade of my working life left. Indeed, there aren't many radio presenters left who are over sixty, although come to think of it, there aren't that many over fifty either. Luckily publishing is somewhat less discriminating, age-wise.

Landmark birthdays inevitably make one rather reflective, and lately I have been doing a hell of a lot of reflecting, thinking about what I have achieved in my life and what I have failed in. And then thinking about what I want to do in the next decade of my life. Charles Clarke said to me recently that every decade in his life had been better than the previous one and that he has really enjoyed his sixth decade. I hope he's right, as I fully intend to follow his lead.

I read somewhere a few days ago about a woman who has written a list of fifty things her husband should do in his fifties. And there's even a book that tells me fifty things I should do in the next twelve months. So far I have resisted temptation, and haven't bought it. But knowing me I will soon relent but then ignore its advice.

People seem to be very willing to offer me their own 'helpful' tips. 'You can't wear jeans after you're fifty,' said one friend, with an evil glint in her eye. 'I expect you'll be buying a flash car,' said another. Well, sorry to disappoint, but I went out yesterday and deliberately bought three new pairs of jeans, and I already have a car that's quite flash enough!

Quite frankly, despite the fact I have been reflecting on reaching fifty, I don't expect an awful lot to change in my life, apart from wanting to have a little more downtime. With two full-time jobs this is not an easy thing to achieve, but I am giving up the London flat and will now travel home each night. And I will work a little more from home. Well, that's the intention.

• • •

I am now halfway through a fortnight's holiday. Well, when I say holiday, I use the word in its loosest term. For the first two days, despite having an 'out of office' message on my email, everyone at my publishing company kept bombarding me with queries, most of which could easily have been answered when I was actually at work the previous week. I really am now trying only to look at email once a day. It's like coming off crack cocaine. Well, not that I know how that feels, but I genuinely have email pangs. Sad, really. Perhaps that should be something else to change in my fifties – stop thinking the world ends if I can't access my Blackberry every five minutes.

• • •

Rather than have a big party in London, to which I would have to invite scores of people I didn't really want to, we decided to be very low key and have family to stay, along with assorted friends. I would have given anything for my mother to have been alive to be with us, but I'm sure she will be watching over us as we all go paddling in the sea. She loved the Norfolk coast, and whenever I walked along a Norfolk beach I would phone her so she could hear the waves. There's nothing quite like the Norfolk coastline. I remember when I was at university in the mid-1980s and was going through a tough time emotionally, I would often drive up to Mundesley at midnight and walk along the beach alone with my thoughts. Somehow the crashing of the waves helped. One night at 1 a.m., I encountered a university friend on the beach doing exactly the same thing.

Yesterday was a bit of a washout holiday-wise. It started raining mid-afternoon so a trip down to the beach with the dogs didn't seem a very good idea. John went into Norwich for what seemed like hours to buy some stuff for tonight. Somehow he and Pepi Simpson managed to contrive to spend two hours in the Macro cash and carry. While they were out my family start to arrive. They seemed rather impressed with the house. Nobody could be bothered to cook so we ordered fish and chips from the Ship pub just down the road. And our minds now turn to the events of tonight.

I am told I am going to get a lot of surprises. I have spied a PA system. Do you think John has booked Bjorn Again?[†]

THE GREATEST SPORTING NIGHT OF MY LIFE
SUNDAY 5 AUGUST

I never thought I could attend a sporting occasion which surpassed the 2006 FA Cup Final. And then along came this year's Championship Playoff Final. Last night I attended the evening session of the athletics at the Olympic stadium. Well, we all know what happened. It proved to be the greatest night in the history of British athletics. And I was there. I still find it difficult to believe that the lottery of Olympic ticket applications gave me one of the most wonderful sporting experiences of my life, and one I doubt will ever be surpassed. Even if West Ham won the Champions League, I am not sure it would rank alongside. OK, I lie.

Like everyone else, I applied for tickets many months ago. I went through all the sports and decided that it was really only the athletics I was interested in. Knowing what I know now, I'd happily have had tickets for the gymnastics or cycling, but in the event I only applied for tickets on two nights – last night and tonight. I went for Category A tickets rather than AA, as I thought the AA ones would be hugely popular. I waited, and waited. And waited. I heard nothing, so assumed that like hundreds of thousands of others, I had been unlucky. C'est la vie.

But then, three months later, I opened a credit card statement for a card I hardly ever use (Visa!) and saw that £590 had been debited. WTF! And then I saw www.London2012.com. My joy was unconfined. Scroll forward to yesterday.

I decided to take my thirteen-year-old niece, Philly, with me, as I knew it would be an experience she would never forget. We set off from Tonbridge around 2 p.m., arriving at London Bridge forty minutes later to change to the Jubilee Line. We decided to get off at West Ham and walk for twenty-five minutes along the so-called Greenway to Stratford. It proved to be quite an experience with street performers and the Gamesmakers entertaining us along the way. The Olympic Park itself had the feeling of a county show.

---

† He hadn't. It was Thatcher impersonator Steve Nallon.

There was plenty to see and plenty to do as we waited for the gates to the stadium to open at 5 p.m. We gave up on the queue for the Olympic shop and instead sampled some of the food on offer. I did think £16.60 for two hot dogs, a Coke and a Fanta was a bit much, but you expect that at big events like this, I suppose.

The great thing about the day thus far was the fact that you could smile at and talk to complete strangers without them thinking you were weird or a pervert.

And so the moment came when we finally got to look inside the Olympic stadium, the place I hope will be the future home of West Ham United FC. The place I will go every other Saturday afternoon. Would I be disappointed? Would I look in horror at the distance from the seats to the pitch? What would the acoustics be like? All these questions were about to be answered.

Climbing the steps into the stadium and looking in for the first time takes your breath away. Yes, it really is that impressive. But it is much smaller than you think. TV pictures make any football ground and pitch look bigger than they really are. I was sitting at the end opposite the Olympic flame towards the back of the lower tier. The view was fantastic (unless I wanted to see the long jump, which was off to one side). I could also see that the grass in the middle was only about half the size of a football pitch, and once it was enlarged the view would be even better. But what about if you're in the upper tier, row Z? Well, I went and had a look again, fully prepared to be horrified. I wasn't. The view was far better than the view I had from high up in the Blackpool end at Wembley in the play-off final. I'd even go so far as to say that I'd be quite happy for my season ticket to be there. Unless you have been inside the stadium, you just cannot comment on it. But that doesn't stop people from making reference to binoculars and the like. Karren Brady was right. The views from every seat in the stadium are not just acceptable, they are outstanding. I could also see how they could put in retractable seating to make the pitch closer to the crowd. No doubt I will get crucified by West Ham traditionalists for saying this, but anyone who doesn't think this move ought to be crucial to West Ham's future is the football equivalent of a Luddite. My heart says 'stay with what we know', but my head tells me something very different. Trust me, when you have seen it for yourself you will know what I mean.

Towards the end of the evening, just before Jessica Ennis's medal ceremony, the crowd starting singing along with 'All You Need is Love'. It was spine-tingling. For a moment I imagined 60,000 Hammers fans belting out 'I'm Forever Blowing Bubbles'. I got quite emotional at the thought.

Would West Ham fill 60,000 seats for each home game? No. But as long as we are in the Premier League I'd be very surprised if the attendance ever fell below 40,000. And for games against Man U, Man C, Arsenal, Liverpool, Spurs and Chelsea we'd be full. That's one third of home league games, just for the record.

There's little I can add to the athletics that hasn't already been said. It was a privilege to watch it. Not just Jessica Ennis and Mo Farah, but also Greg Rutherford winning the long jump. In fact the whole evening was a delight. I had never been to an athletics event before but I do think I will go to one again after this. It's a shame that events like the long jump and discus seem to play second fiddle to the track, and I felt very sorry for Greg Rutherford in a way. He was about to do his final jump when Jessica Ennis appeared alongside him on the track, doing her lap of honour. He fluffed his jump, but in the end it didn't matter.

Mo Farah's run was astonishing. Twenty-five times he ran straight in front of us, and it was right in front of us that he made his move. I have never heard such a cacophony of noise as that which accompanied him down the home straight. We were all shrieking our heads off. No one can tell me that that kind of support doesn't spur an athlete on to even faster times. I guess our medal haul is proof of that.

We all felt rather cheated that we didn't get to witness the medal ceremonies for Farah and Rutherford, but the evening closed with Jessica Ennis receiving her gold. Hearing the national anthem belted out by such a crowd was something all of us there are never likely to forget. It was a great night to be British.

The amazing thing about the whole day was that everything worked. And it's not often you can say that in this country. Even getting home on the Javelin train proved to be fairly easy. The Gamesmakers and stewards were fabulous – pleasant, smiling and approachable. And they even tried to entertain queuing crowds. I hope the government does two things to reward them – create a British Olympic Medal, and then do what Sydney did in 1996 and organise a parade through the centre of London. The volunteers have made these Games memorable in a way no one could have predicted. Yes, it has been all about athletic achievement, but for those in the crowd they made the Olympic experience a very different one, and one which those of us who have witnessed it will not forget for a very long while.

EPILOGUE

It seems fitting to close this book with a tribute to the woman who has had more influence on my life than any other: my darling mother. I guess I am not alone in having this thought, but through my entire life, the day I have dreaded was the day I would lose one of my parents. I have always known that my life would never be the same again. Sadly that day arrived on Saturday 9 June 2012 when my dear mother, Jane, departed this earth. The bond between a mother and son is like no other, and several months on I still feel that part of me has been ripped away.

I knew it was coming, as she had been very ill. Two weeks before she died, my two sisters and I brought her home from Addenbrooke's Hospital in Cambridge – and the least said about that particular hospital the better – because we knew she would want to die at home, among her family, in the house that she had called home for nigh-on fifty-three years. She spent the final days of her life looking out onto the garden she had so lovingly cherished, watching birds feeding and pheasants walking across the lawn.

My two sisters became her angels, her carers, and their devotion was a sight to behold. The three of us spent three weeks at home, the longest we have been together in thirty years. To be honest, I felt a bit of a spare part at times, rather helpless while my sisters cared so lovingly for their darling mum. But I was there. That was the important thing.

Mum loved Norfolk. Indeed, she and her father, Geoff Orbell, farmed in Stibbard, near Fakenham in the late 1940s and early 1950s. Her mother is buried at Stibbard and I remember spending a morning locating the grave a few years ago. She liked nothing better than to visit the north Norfolk coast and many happy days were spent at Hunstanton, Brancaster and Wells as a child. A bit of her will always belong to Norfolk, and she was so proud when I was selected to fight the North Norfolk constituency back in 2003. She never did quite understand my political ambitions, and when I told her last year I would never fight another election she was both delighted and relieved. Although she loved seeing her son on television, and listening to my radio programme, she hated the public scrutiny that came with it. And, do you know what, I now think she was right.

The funeral took place a fortnight after her death, in Ashdon Parish Church. We asked the vicar who confirmed us all back in 1978, Michael Yorke, to return to conduct the service. I had the task of writing and delivering a eulogy to the woman who has given me so much unconditional love through the years. It's probably the most difficult thing I will ever have to write, and I was desperate to do her justice. Like my mum, I give in to tears all too easily. And, like her, it doesn't really embarrass me. Crying is a sign of emotional strength, not weakness. It's a natural thing to do. Yes, we grieved, but any tears were in celebration of a wonderful life. Funerals are never easy, but this service was perfect. Her grandchildren sang and read, reducing most of the church to tears. We made sure the church was full of flowers, and in my eulogy I did my best to reflect the wonderful start in life my mum and dad gave the three of us. As you can imagine, I was worried about breaking down completely, but I needn't have. We all got through our various tributes and readings intact, although there was the odd quavering of the voice. I loved my mother with all my heart, as did my sisters. We know our lives will never be the same, but we continue in the knowledge that somehow, somewhere she is watching over us, looking out for us in the way that she always did.

Anyway, I leave you with the words of my eulogy. Reading them again now, I'm shedding more tears than I did when I delivered it. She was a very special mother.

'What survives of us is love', said the poet Philip Larkin. And over the last fortnight my family has discovered just how true those words are. Throughout any child's life, the day they most dread is the day they lose a parent – the day any husband dreads is the day he loses his wife, because they know life can never be the same. There are no words of comfort anyone can give because grief is indeed the price we pay for love.

The only comfort we have is each other.

There are very few women who can live a life eighty-one years long and leave this mortal earth devoid of enemies, but Jane

Elizabeth Dale was one such woman. Can there ever have existed a sweeter, more innocent, kinder woman? Many of you have very kindly sent condolence cards, recognising the outstanding qualities our mother possessed.

She was devoted to her husband, our father. Her life revolved around her children and grandchildren. In short, her family was, and is, her life.

Jane Elizabeth Orbell was born on 27 March 1931 near Bury St Edmunds, to her parents, Geoff and Edith. Her early years were spent at Hanchett Hall, near Haverhill, only five or six miles away from the boy she would go on to marry. Now from the Jane you've all come to know and love, you might think she was a demure, well-behaved, perfect child. Not a bit of it. She was a tomboy, and could at times be a very naughty child. Her neighbour was a little girl called Eleanor Daniels, who would go on to be her lifelong best friend – and godmother to the three of us. They became to each other the sisters neither had. But it was Jane who would lead her best friend into trouble.

It has to be said that Jane – two years older than Eleanor – sometimes led her astray. Indeed, if ASBOs had existed in those days Eleanor and Jane would have worn them as a badge of honour. One day they stood on the railway bridge over the Haverhill road, throwing stones down on passing cars. Eleanor would be the watch-out as Jane went bird-nesting. Despite Jane moving to Norfolk, their friendship endured.

Jane and her mum and dad spent the war years farming in Stibbard, near Fakenham and she attended boarding school at Felixstowe. Norfolk is somewhere Jane always loved to return to. I remember we went on a childhood 'This is Your Life' trip and visited all her old haunts. Eleanor used to take us for day trips to the Norfolk coast in her blue Morris Minor. Mum loved nothing more than to paddle in the sea. Whenever she knew any of us were at the seaside she'd ask us to have a paddle for her. We'd phone her so she could listen to the waves.

But in 1951 her life changed, just as ours has now. Her mother died, a grandmother none of us would ever get to know. She and her dad decided to sell up and buy Emson's Farm in Linton. And it was there that they took in a lodger, Molly Dale, who would eventually introduce Mum to her two brothers, Garry and John. John met Jane first and went back to tell Garry about her. 'What's she like?'

inquired Garry. John's reply consisted of one word: 'Phwoar.' Garry wasted little time in asking her out.

Dad and Mum got married in the autumn of 1958, taking a honeymoon in their Ford Prefect around the coast of England and Wales, reflecting again Mum's love of the sea. When they got back home they had travelled 1,995 miles – so Dad immediately drove to Saffron Walden and back, to make it 2,000.

They soon bought Hall Farm from Mum's aunt, Hope Chivers, and eight years later bought another seventy acres from Ivy Todd Farm. After setting up their farming business, their family started when I came along in 1962, followed two years later by Tracey, and another eighteen months later by Sheena.

We had the most idyllic childhood anyone could wish for. Growing up on a farm, plenty of fresh air, the freedom to roam, to play on our own, a close village community and a good local school. But above all we had such loving parents.

As we grew up, Mum's only wish was that we would all be happy in whatever paths our lives took us on. We were never harangued about homework, we were encouraged. We never had career paths designated for us, we were free to go our own way and make our own successes and mistakes.

I know Mum missed Tracey and I terribly when we went off to university. I remember to this day leaving for my gap year in Germany in September 1980, going up the escalator at Harwich to catch the ferry, with Mum in floods of tears at the bottom. She told me later she truly thought she would never see me again.

Jane's grandchildren were the lights of her life. Issy, Philly and Zoe have been extremely brave in the church here today. Their grannie means the world to them and they know that she loves them with all her heart. They always brought such a beautiful smile to her face, and she relished her role as grandparent, teacher and playmate.

Yes, in recent times Mum had a constant battle with her health. Five hip replacements and a broken femur brought their own challenges, but right up until a couple of months ago, she was mobile and could get around. She had more pain that we probably know. But she was stoic. She got on with it. She never complained.

Sheena, Tracey and I tried to ensure she always had something to look forward to by taking her on trips away. Tracey took her to Corsica and Venice, I took her to Zurich and the Swiss mountains and Sheena took her to Malta and on an unforgettable trip to

Edinburgh with Zoe – one they had hoped to repeat this Easter, but it was sadly not to be.

Several times she came to visit me in Germany when I lived there, and her impish humour was on display, especially when we were driving on the autobahns. She was tickled pink that the motorway exits were signed 'Ausfahrt'. I taught her to swear like a trooper in German, but she always combined it with that trademark giggle. Indeed, it's a good job we did take Mum on holidays, because Dad considered going on holiday unnecessary when he had everything he ever wanted right here at home. He was happy, however, to take Mum to Shadwell Wood, where she used to wander among the trees looking at the bluebells. On the one family holiday we did go on – in 1969 to Westgate-on-Sea – Mum couldn't even persuade him to take his socks and shoes off on the beach.

Village life was incredibly important to Mum, and no more so than the church, where for many years she would arrange the flowers.

I'm so pleased to see Michael Yorke back here today – for those who don't know, he was vicar here between 1974 and 1978 – and our family is grateful to him for agreeing to conduct this service.

We are going to miss Mum so much. Those fantastic Sunday roasts. Those wonderful harvest picnics sitting on the straw beside the combine. Watching her tend to the garden she loved so much and made so beautiful. Hearing her shriek at Dad when he appeared in the garden with his knapsack sprayer or strimmer. On Christmas morning being woken to the sound of Mum preparing breakfast, singing very loudly the words to 'It's Christmas Day in the Workhouse'. Watching her disappear into the orchard with Zoe aboard her scooter. I'll miss ringing her at midnight every Wednesday night after I do the Sky News paper reviews. I'll miss her telling me how brilliantly I had performed, even when I knew I had been rubbish. Well, that's what mums do, don't they?

At heart, Mum was a farmer. Farming was her life. She loved her animals. It broke her heart when the Common Market forced us to give up the cows and pigs. She was never happier than when out in the fields. Mum never learnt to drive a car, but she happily drove a tractor. Well, apart from when reversing a corn trailer to unload, which she always found a challenge. She remains the only person in the history of this country who has crashed into a police car while driving a tractor. But it wasn't her fault. Honest.

Mum welcomed new members to the family with open arms. Joining a new family is never easy, but Alan, Richard, John and Peter will testify to the fact that she couldn't have been more welcoming.

Dad, you were Mum's inspiration. She loved you like no other. She was devoted to you in a way few of us can imagine. It was unconditional love, and you reciprocated it. Even when you went and bought yet another piece of farming memorabilia at a farm sale, which she couldn't understand, she'd shake her head and say 'silly old fool', and we'd all laugh knowingly.

Dad, however difficult this time is for the rest of us, we cannot possibly imagine what you're going through. We will always be there for you and we love you with all our hearts.

Issy, Philly and Zoe, her beloved grandchildren. Your grannie may not be here to tell you how proud she is of the three of you, but her spirit lives on and will guide you through your lives. Her love for you will be a constant in your life, and whatever you end up doing, she will be there watching over you.

To Mary Norden and Jean Start: you already know what you did for Mum, not just in recent months, but throughout the last fifty years. You have been true friends to her. Mabel Smith, who can't be here today, has been far more than a cousin. She was a confidante, and the mother of one of Mum's favourite people in the world, Norman Smith. So many of you here today have been true friends to her.

When someone close to you dies, there are usually huge regrets. You regret unkind things that were said. You regret those things you never said. The things you never had the chance to say, the things you were too embarrassed to say. We British leave a lot of things unsaid, trusting that unsaid things really don't need to be said. Well, we didn't leave anything unsaid. We didn't need to tell Mum we loved her, she knew. But we did, nonetheless. She left this earth in no doubt about the love we all had for her.

Let me finish by saying this: Mum hated the mention of death. She particularly hated talking about funerals. She hated going to them even more. But I suspect she's watching over us from above, thinking to herself, 'Well, if I had to go to my own funeral, I'm glad it was here, in Ashdon, only a few hundred yards from my beloved Hall Farm, here, among all of you, the people who made my life so happy and contented.'

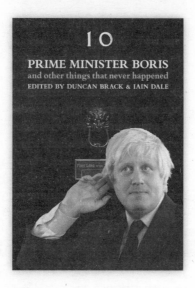